Photo courtesy of the Democrat and Chronicle - Rochester, New York

Fred W. Sarkis

Born in Rochester, NY in 1926 he is the second of ten brothers and sisters. From age 8 to 14, after school, he became the "Prisoner of the Truck". At age 16, he graduated from a business high school, first in his class. He purchased a home for his family before he entered the US Navy in WWII, at age 18. At age 20, he worked full time while attending the University of Rochester at night. He started a business at age 24. He merged his national award-winning company with a major national firm and became a multi-millionaire at age 34. He became the financial father of a ski area and founder of a major resort community. He received many awards for community service. He is a proud husband, father of 5 children and grand-father to 11. At age 77, he has given 152 talks to over 25,000 kids and educators. His energetic volunteer goal is to reach 100,000 and to make his website a non-profit and on-going national motivational center to help children, teachers and parents. All royalites from this book go to the Prisoner of the Truck Foundation. Visit YesPa.org for the character education mission of the Foundation and a free download of the textbook "Yes Pa."

Prisoner of the Truck

Fred W. Sarkis

ISBN: 1-4107-2491-3 (e-book)
ISBN: 1-4107-2492-1 (Paperback)

Library of Congress Control Number: 2003093275

This book is printed on acid free paper.

Printed in the United States of America
Bloomington, IN

Cover designed by Jane Alden
Book Layout by Tom Jacoby
Editing Assistance John Joe & Deanna O'Connell\
Editing Changes Phil Vitale
Website Development Cathy Vitale

1stBooks – rev. 06/23/03

PREFACE

*"Messages of Character have to be delivered by a person of character. Fred Sarkis is such a person, and the story of his remarkable life will help anyone, young or old, to be a better person and lead a better life. 'Prisoner of the Truck' and 'Yes Pa' * have the power to touch hearts and bring out the best in us all."*

Dr. Thomas Lickona
Author of "Education for Character" and "Raising Good Children"
Received a 1992 Christopher Award "for affirming the highest values of human spirit"

Dr. Thomas Lickona, a developmental psychologist and educator, is an internationally respected authority on moral development and education values. He is Professor of Education at the State University of New York at Cortland, where he has done award-winning work in teacher education and currently chairs the Teachers for the 21st Century project. A past president of the Association for Moral Education, he has also held teaching appointments at Boston University and Harvard University and is a frequent speaker at conferences and workshops for teachers, parents, religious educators and other groups concerned about the values and character of young people. He has lectured in the United States, Canada, Japan, Ireland, Switzerland and Latin America. He has been a guest on numerous radio and television talk shows including Good Morning America, Larry King Live and Latenight America.

* ***"YesPa" is a digest of "Prisoner of the Truck". It is freely available for students, parents and teachers on:***

www.yespa.org

Review by J. R. Smith

What gives meaning to a man's life? Is it an unquenchable determination to succeed, the pursuit of honesty in relationships with others, an abiding faith that goodness will prevail, a belief that a spiritual resource is ever present, an attitude of enthusiasm that meets the challenge of each day, the ability to recover from personal crises, the development of one's introspective nature, or is it the inner motivation that urges a person to continue to create new goals to achieve?

In his autobiography, Prisoner of the Truck, the author, an American of Lebanese ancestry and a self-described "skinny, bow-legged, knock-kneed, pigeon-toed, dark-skinned boy who was mocked by his classmates" reflects on those shaping forces in his life which have carried him from his youth to his current aspirations at age 75. Deeply grounded in Roman Catholicism as a young boy, his faith supports him through the many trials which confront him on his way through school, military service, business, parenting, and retirement. Much of his success as well as his personal turmoil derives from his relationship with his father, his "incarceration" as a prisoner of his father's vegetable truck, and the lessons he learned from this experience.

A successful businessman several times over, the author details his struggles to achieve self esteem in his boyhood, to attain financial success as a young man, to recover from his devastating losses in business, to understand the complexities of human afflictions, and his desire to share his wisdom with all who may be captivated by his spirit. Each episode in his life journey is crafted with insight and humor, reflecting the author's perceptions of how human relationships guided him in positive ways.

Throughout the book the reader will find innumerable life lessons to be applied, and all conveyed with an openness and frankness revealing compassion and conviction of a man tested by the depths and heights of human emotions. The author shows that hard work and inventiveness, the persistent pursuit of a dream, the reliance on moral integrity, and the expression of caring can be fulfilling and a way of finding meaning in one's life.

This is a book that will inspire you with its message as it reveals the inner strength of a man who loves life, who confronts adversity, and who demonstrates how to be of service to mankind.

J. R. Smith is a Professor Emeritus, Earlham College, Richmond, Indiana. He was an educator for 38 years – a secondary school English teacher, a Coordinator of Humanities, a Director of Demonstration School and then a College Professor. He taught at Abington High School in Abington, Pennsylvania for 10 years, and at Earlham College for 24 years. He majored in English and French at Wabash College in Crawfordsville, Indiana, and followed that with graduate studies at Harvard University, the University of Pennsylvania, a fellowship at Yale University, and the University of Massachusetts.

Dedication

I dedicate this book to my deceased mother whom I loved so dearly. She was goodness throughout her 95 year life. Her example and her counsel helped me to strive for goodness in whatever endeavor I pursued.

I also dedicate this book to my father. In two short lessons, he planted the seeds that led me to a search for excellence in school, in business and in family. Although he died 50 years ago, through recent events in my life, he has given me a new *mission in life - to help to motivate young and old alike to be the best they can be and to find peace and happiness in that pursuit.*

Acknowledgements

My Family

I thank my wife, Helen, who in the writing of this book, allowed me to spend more time on my word processor than I did with her and who looked after me with such unselfish and loving care.

I also thank:

My daughter Gina and my son-in-law Grant Cushing, who helped me to improve my story telling to children both in my book and in my talks to students.

My sons Greg, Wade, Fritz and their spouses Mary, Joscelyne and Kelley, who loved the initial chapters and who encouraged me to finish the book before the end of the year 2000.

My son Josh, for his experienced input and his support of my writing style.

My good spirited and fun loving sisters Betty, Ann, Vicky, Deanna and their families who lovingly kept saying, "Fred, please finish the book."

My grandchildren, Leigh Frances, 12, Hannah, 8, Skylar, 11, and Zachary, 11, who in reading the first chapters, could not wait for their grandfather to escape the Prison of the Truck. To Zachary for posing for the front cover. To Skylar for saying, "Grandpa you should dedicate this book to your mother and father. You couldn't have written it without them." My future readers, Sierra, Sage, Remi, Peter, Frederick III, Chloe and Sydney Sarkis, for whom this book is a legacy.

I thank my brother Joe and his family. In 1999, Joe shared my deceased father's secret addiction that eventually led to a greater love, understanding and compassion for my father – one that resulted in a new and happy mission in my life.

I also wish to remember my brother Jim. Jim was a Roman Catholic priest. His request for an orderly dispensation from his priesthood sat in many similar cubicles in Rome beyond a reasonable time period. Jim left the priesthood to further his education in a new career. He has earned the trust of many investors as a stockbroker. His wife, Jeannie, in addition to being a registered nurse, has a degree in library science. Her work, in organizing data for greater efficiency and usefulness in hospital care, became one of the models for the nation.

A special thanks to my English, drama, music, motivator, teacher-brother Ken, who guided me in my path to completion.

Special Assistance with the Book

Jim Smith and his wife Natalie for initial editorial assistance.

Mary Lou and Tom Jacoby, Kenn and Liz (Sarkis) Jacoby for editorial and photographic assistance.

Jane Alden for cover artwork and a unique sensitivity for the Prisoner.

John Joe and Deanna O'Connell for 2nd edition editorial assistance.

Phil and Cathy Vitale for editorial corrections and ***prisonerofthe truck.com*** website development.

Volunteer Motivational Talks to Kids

I thank Rick Born for his faith and belief in my potential as a motivational speaker for all age groups. One talk to his class led to talks to thousands of kids and adults in Western NY and Florida.

In 1999, in attending a clown school in Niagara Falls, Canada, Ron "Papa Clown" Cormier, received three of seven awards from "Clowns Canada". The Clowns Canada News read, "Although he is supposedly 'retired', Papa is well-known in Toronto and Barrie clowning circles for the vast amount of time he spends clowning". Papa Clown, a big loving man, with a professional clown costume and make up, does a mini-tight rope act. I use a five-minute version of Papa Clown's tight rope act to launch my 45-minute motivational talks to kids and I thank him for his inspiration in the development of my act.

To many Relatives and Friends

To my many relatives and friends who read portions of the book and who encouraged me to finish it:

Alan and Sally Garraway from England, my cousin Dr. Richard and Lynne Sarkis, Bernice and Chet Caprini, Phil & Marilyn Salit, John O'Donnell, Jean and Simond Taylor, Vic Muncy and Joan Kullman, Harvey and Marilynne Anderson, Sugi and Mary Suguitan, Jean and Price Blackwell, Dr. Dennis Boike, Jack Jones, Richard P. Miller, Faith Miller, Bill & Muriel Coleman, Dan and Stency Wegman, Robert and Peggy Wegman, Jack and Janice Adams, Sue and Larry Dickens, Denise & Alan Lupton, Sam Halaby, Ken and Linda Halaby, Sue & Larry Dickens, Mike Fowler, Donnie Leigh, Mary Buscemi, Patrick and Rita O'Hara, Richard & Mary Beth O'Hara, Jerry and Ange O'Hara, Eileen and Bud Stellwagen, Dale and Brenda Stoker, Dan Fuller, Joe Kohler, Ted Spall, Ann Hewitt, Pat and Ron Engebrecht, Warren Halliday, Dick and Patricia Johnson, Andy and Anne Marie Hagler, Jonathan Holstein, David Bouchard, Officer Daniel Ball, Chief of Police Patrick W. McCarthy and his wife Patty, Mike & Barb Hanna, Sue and David Reh, Jim

Roman, Deacon Mike Piehler, Ed and Nancy Snyder, Jerry & Joanne Veiner, Mary Jane and John Bartemus, Jim Adamson, Dave & Vicki Breneman, Bob & Joyce Crawford, David and Linda Clarke, Al and Bonnie Frost, Larry & Michelle Klepper, Carolyn and Jim McDonald, Ellie and Eddie Holtzman, Wayne Moore and Betty Ryan, Tim Mattle, Jeannine Fraser, Joseph P. Holleran, Jeff Kime, Mark Knickerbocker, Charlie Richardson, Lew Williams, Joy Bennett, David Renner, Clara and Perry Matz and to Jim Ryan, who encouraged and arranged my first Rochester, New York talks given to kids in WIN schools, (Wegman's Inner City).

My Healers

I thank Dr. Abe Cockett for a complicated but successful 1976 prostate surgery. I thank retired Dr. Joseph Guattery, who monitored my PSA test for the early detection of Prostate Cancer in 1991. I thank Dr. Philip Rubin, a nationally renowned authority in cancer research. Shortly after the detection of cancer, Dr. Phil visited my home to advise me, Helen and Gina on a treatment program. He orchestrated 32 radiation treatments at Strong Memorial Hospital in Rochester, NY. He monitored my PSA for nine years and I finally got him to say in September of 2000, "Fred, I can definitely say, you are cured."

Live each day to the fullest

Live each day to the fullest.
Get the most from each hour,
each day, and each age of your life.
Then you can look forward with confidence,
and back without regret.

Be yourself. But be your best self.
Dare to be different and to follow your star.

And don't be afraid to be happy.
Enjoy what is beautiful.
Love with all your heart and soul.
Believe that those you love, love you.

Forget what you have done for your friends,
and remember what they have done for you.
Disregard what the world owes you, and
concentrate on what you owe the world.

When you are faced with a decision,
make that decision as wisely as possible,
then forget it.
The moment of absolute certainty never arrives.

And above all, remember that God helps those
who help themselves.

Act as if everything depended upon you,
and pray as if everything depends upon God.

Author - Unknown

Introduction

A Prison does not have to have bars to be a Prison. In the World Book Dictionary, one of the definitions for "Prisoner" is "A person who is kept shut up against his (or her) will or is not free to move." Under this definition a Prisoner can be a person:

- Who has a poor self-image about his or her race, creed, color, religion, weight, lifestyle or appearance.
- Who lives with a single parent, wishing for both parents in the home.
- Who must cope with a loved one who is addicted to drugs, alcohol, gambling, etc.
- Who has endured some form of heart breaking child abuse.
- Who takes care of a sick or dying mother, father or relative.
- Who feels trapped in a job, marriage or profession that is not fulfilling.
- Who is addicted to electronic games and bad computer behavior that steals time from study, self-improvement or helping others.

- Who fails to accept responsibility for bad behavior, placing the blame on others.
- Who fails to set goals.
- Who lacks the drive, determination and *enthusiasm* needed to develop good habits that can lead to success and happiness.
- Who is inflexible to the situation or to the times.
- Who fails to recognize and use the hidden power within us and with God's help, to become the best he or she can be.
- Who never attempts to achieve for fear of failure instead of regarding failure as a learning experience and an opportunity to do better the next time.
- Who hasn't learned how to love and forgive himself, herself or others.
- Who allows the pursuit of material things to completely replace spiritual values that can make life more fulfilling and happy.
- Who trades moral values for self-gratification.
- Who suffers from a serious disease or illness

In my boyhood prison, self-pity crippled my attitude and motivation until I turned 12. This was when my father gave me a five-minute demonstration in selling strawberries and the five-minute lesson that changed my attitude, *enthusiasm* and my search for a key to freedom.

In terms of prejudice as well as technology, times have changed dramatically since I was a child. As we launch the new millennium, I believe that any human being in America from age twelve on, regardless of heritage, is the captain of his or her own destiny. For anyone with desire, drive, determination, conviction and faith in God, there is the opportunity to take hardship, adversity and failure and turn it into success in school, at work or at home. How we fuel and energize ourselves in these enlightened times is up to each individual.

Nothing comes easy — study, hard work, practice and facing reality are an essential part of success. When these characteristics are combined with sincerity, honesty, goodness and an *enthusiasm* that reflects in whatever we say or do, there is nothing too difficult to achieve. Above all be patient and calm. To quote Tiger Woods on June 19, 2000 when he broke all kinds of records in the U.S. Open. "All week I had a sense of calmness that I haven't had in quite awhile. I was able to keep my composure and focus on the shot I needed to make."

If you feel you are in some form of prison, "shut up against your will and not free to move"; whether this prison has been imposed on you by others or by your own self-imposed attitude or behavior, I pray that this book will help you to take command of your own life, to find your own key to freedom, success, happiness and peace of mind.

CHAPTER 1

My Boyhood Prison

It was 1937. Her gentle hand touched my 11-year-old shoulder. "Get up, its 4 o'clock," my mother whispered. I had to be quiet. There were six brothers and sisters still sleeping in two of the three small bedrooms on an upper flat in the inner city of Rochester, New York. Betty was 13, brother Joe was 8, Ann 6, Jim 4, Vicky 2 and my mother was pregnant, as it seemed she was throughout most of my boyhood memory.

These were sad times for my mother. My father had lost his confectionery store on Main Street in Rochester, NY in 1929, the start of the great depression. He became a "huckster," starting with a horse and wagon in 1929 when I was three years old. He would rise at 4 AM, arrive at the public market at 5 AM, buy fruits and vegetables from farmers and sell them to regular customers in middle class neighborhoods that he established on the east and west side of Rochester. He would call on his regular customers every other day — the east side on Tuesdays, Thursdays and Saturdays and the west side on Mondays, Wednesdays and Fridays. If he lost a customer, he would knock on doors until he found a replacement.

His eight-year financial struggle as a huckster from 1929 to 1937 failed to save the home on 470 Driving Park Avenue in Rochester. Like so many others in the depression years, he was forced to surrender a spacious four-bedroom home in this attractive middle class neighborhood. The house furniture, purchased on an installment plan, was taken away for non-payment. A cousin, also named Fred Sarkis, helped us to move the remaining furniture to Ormond Street.

Our new home was cramped — about half the size of Driving Park Avenue. The furnished flat included three beds and mattresses. The flat was dirty and roach-infested. Bed bugs occupied the bedroom mattresses. My mother declared war on dirt, roaches and bed bugs. A powder was used for the roaches. The bed bugs were removed with a sticky mixture of flour and water. Several hand pads were made of this mixture. Under my mother's direction, the older children would surround the mattress, front, back and sides. We would apply the sticky mixture to visible pockets of the bed bugs. They would be trapped and would wiggle themselves to death. This was done periodically, and with the regular washing of bed sheets, bed bug bites became infrequent, if at all. A fresh coat of paint on the walls and woodwork made our flat into a comfortable small home. My mother kept the flat spotlessly clean. She would have it no other way.

During the cold season, it was my daily job to keep the flat warm. The furnace for the inner city flat was in the basement. The basement was extremely dark. There were no light bulbs - - only a red gleam of light coming from cracks in the furnace door. I shook the furnace grill with a grill wrench, sifted the ashes through a screen to catch partially burned coal, recycled the unburned coal fragments back into the furnace, shoveled in new black coal from the bins and adjusted the exhaust pipes as required. I shoveled the ashes into fireproof metal bushel baskets and lugged these heavy containers outdoors for collection by city trash collectors. Monthly, the coal deliveryman replenished the supply of coal by inserting a metal chute through an open cellar window and emptying the contents of his truck into the coal bin.

I hurried through my task as best I could. The basement was cold and damp. I heard noises in the dark corners — my presence disturbed the rats. On occasions, the coal in the bin would shift minutes after shoveling, making a frightening noise. I imagined that there was someone lurking in the dark shadows. Each winter morning, it seemed that I had to muster my boyhood courage to finish my task and rush to the warmth, light and safety of the second floor flat.

That was my first task at 4:00 AM on this winter Saturday morning in 1937. This was my third year on my father's truck. I started when I was eight years old. I dreaded another 17 hour Saturday workday that would end around 10 or 11 PM. The only person who seemed to get up earlier was the milkman. There was an outdoor milk box where he would place two quarts of milk daily. In those days, milk was not homogenized. The cream portion rose to the top of the glass quart bottle. To make the milk whole, we had to shake the bottle. On this morning, frigid weather had frozen the two quarts of milk; the cream portion pushed the round cardboard cover upward, one or more inches outside the top of the bottle. We had no thermometer, or newspaper, or radio. Television had not yet been invented. The milk bottle told the weather story. I knew I was in for a long and cold miserable day.

My mother wrapped a scarf around my neck and pulled my woolen cap down over my ears. I returned her hug. She knew how much I hated to face the long frigid day. She compassionately said, "Shouldn't you let him stay home today?" My father, taking a quick glance at me, turned to her and said, "No, I need him." As always, my father's word was final.

It took fifteen minutes to drive to the public market, which opened at 5 AM. Ford had invented the Ford truck as well as the Model T automobile. My father had sold his horse and wagon and bought a used Ford truck. There was an enclosed cab section that held two adults and a small open back section not much larger than a wagon pulled by a horse. In the cold season, this back section was enclosed. It was about five feet high. My father had to stoop when he entered it. A kerosene lamp was used to prevent the fruits and vegetables from freezing. The cab section had no heater. There were cracks in the wooden floorboards. From the light of the street lamps, I could see the ice and snow on the plowed and bumpy roads through the cracks in the boards. Shivers went through my cold skinny body. I wiggled my toes to keep them from freezing. I glanced at my father, big and strong, oblivious to the cold that enveloped me. He broke the cold silence with, "Did you wear your long underwear?" I wanted to say that I forgot, hoping that he would turn back, feeling some sorrow for my thin and tiny body and let me return to the warmth and security of my bed and home. I said, "Yes, ma made sure."

When we arrived at the public market, I went to the enclosed back of the truck. I huddled next to the kerosene lantern to get warm. I took off my shoes and pressed my socks to the warm glass of the lantern. My fingers and toes were numb, frostbitten from the frigid drive to the market. As I sat in the cold isolation of the truck waiting for my father to complete his task, I thought about earlier times, when being with my father was an adventure.

(On a few occasions when I was five years old, he would take me on his horse and wagon for one or two days a summer. We would start at 5 AM and would return around 5 PM. My father appeared proud when the farmers and his customers would say, "Mike, what a handsome young man." My dad must have thought that in America, "Mike" was a better name than his real name, "Wady". These infrequent summer outings, as a very young boy, were an adventure to me. I could feed and brush the horse as they did in the silent cowboy movies. Children along the way would look at me with envy as I sat beside my father on the wagon. We were moving from place to place. I was traveling. I was meeting people. I was riding high on a horse and wagon just like the cowboy movies of the times.)

But this earlier childhood memory of a summer adventure had turned into a frigid winter nightmare. I wanted to be free to play with my neighborhood friends. I wanted to be like the kids I saw on my father's route. As much as I dreaded these winter Saturdays during the school year, eventually it became a summer nightmare as well. I feared the summer school vacation when I would have to be on the truck from 5 AM to 9 PM, Monday through Friday and on Saturdays as late as 11:00 PM, close to 100 hours a week. This was my third year on the truck. I was a very unhappy child.

On this bitter-cold Saturday, as well as every Saturday during the school season, I was confined to this small-enclosed truck. I began to identify myself with schoolbook photographs of young boys who were prisoners of the coal mines. I was aware of child labor laws that stopped this practice. I wondered why my father was exempt from such laws.

At 5:00 AM the public market was already busy. The farmers were the first to arrive to present their produce to the hucksters and restaurant operators who were arriving about the same time. Around 7 AM, the general public would arrive for direct purchases from the farmers. Outdoor covered sheds provided shelter for trucks to back into stalls on each side of a mid-section. The mid-section was used by the farmers to display produce for sale. Buyers would walk in this mid-section to inspect and buy their produce. Farmers were under sheds in one section of the public market and hucksters were in another separated section. Stall numbers identified the location of the farmers and hucksters. Each huckster wore a large purse with a strap that hung over his shoulder. One compartment was for bills and the other for coins. Hucksters used the purse to pay cash to the farmers as well as to collect cash from customers.

Our market stall number was 103B. There were about 40 other hucksters in this section of the market. In the summer months, when I worked six days a week, my father was the last huckster to leave the market. He took more time to buy the best quality he could find. He also was able to negotiate lower prices from farmers who would otherwise return the fresh produce to their farms.

In warm weather, when the back section was uncovered, unlike many hucksters, my father spent a considerable amount of time arranging his truck for the best presentation of his fruits and vegetables that were freshly purchased. By using empty orange crates and boxes of different sizes for support, he would create an attractive, colorful and angled display of his produce that faced the homemaker when he brought them from their front doors to the curb site in front of their homes.

When the truck was enclosed in the winter, many of the customers put on their winter clothing and entered the back of the truck. An aisle was left in the middle of the truck. In a cramped setting, customers could select their fruits and vegetables on either side of the aisle. Year round, a scale hung from the truck's interior.

My father's customers were primarily of German, Scottish and Irish heritage. They liked the quality of produce presented to them. More than that, they liked him. They were willing to pay a higher price for the quality and his personal door-to-door service.

Year round, most of the hucksters worked alone. A few had adult helpers that assisted them in the summer months. If a huckster worked alone, he would either deliver the produce to his own stall or have the farmer's helper deliver them. Most hucksters were ready for business and left the public market at 8:00 AM. My father was an exception. The entire process of buying, trimming, displaying and selling started at 5:00 AM when we arrived at the market until 8:30 AM when the truck was prepared for calling on customers.

Before we called on the first customer, my father would spend about an hour in the public market restaurant "having coffee" while I waited in the truck. Often, we would not get to our first customer until 9:30 AM.

When he called on customers directly in front of their homes, I would wait for him to prepare and price the order. Then I made the delivery, something he could have easily done himself. On Saturday nights, he called on his last customer, Hedges Bar & Grill on the corner of Joseph Avenue and Leo Streets. We would arrive about 6 PM. We would depart as late as 10:30 PM.

On the winter Saturdays, when we arrived at Hedges Bar & Grill around 7 PM, I was locked in the back of the truck. I had two empty glass quart bottles — one to drink out of and one to urinate in. My dinner consisted of whatever fruits and vegetables I wanted to eat. My father's pattern for Saturday evenings consisted of filling an order for the Norocki's, the owner of the bar and grill. The rest of the evening was spent selling the remaining fruits & vegetables to the men in the bar to take home to their wives. My father said, "They feel guilty for being in a bar and would take home fruits and vegetables as a peace offering to their wives — like flowers or candy." He said that the remaining fruits and vegetables were his profit and if he did not sell them in the bar on Saturday night, they would spoil and we would lose that profit.

I was never allowed in Hedges Bar & Grill. As the four evening hours at Hedge's passed, my father would occasionally come back to the truck, unlock it, and without a word, without my help, fill a peck basket with fruits and vegetables. When he returned to the truck to fill a peck basket, he was in a trance - wearied and troubled. He did not notice me. He did not speak to me. On this cold Saturday evening, this eleven-year-old boy felt a deep compassion for his father and the long hours he was working to provide for his family.

Since my father returned to the truck only three or four times in four to five hours, I reasoned that it was a difficult job to sell fruits and vegetables to wayward husbands, even by a well liked salesman as good as my father. My 11-year-old heart went out to him. I wished I could hug him and more than that I wished he would acknowledge my presence and hug me. But he never did. I sat chilled with need. But he never did.

My compassion for my father was mixed with a search for understanding. I wondered about my usefulness to him on the truck in the winter as well as the summer. From the time we arrived at the public market until the time we returned home, I was not needed 95% of the time. He performed all of the market functions. In the winter, farmer's helpers delivered the produce to the inside of his truck as they did for other hucksters who had no helpers. When my father was finished with buying produce, he would remove the delivered produce to the outside of the truck and organize the interior for the best possible showing to customers. All I did on these winter Saturdays from 5 AM to 8:30 AM, was sit next to a kerosene lamp to keep from freezing or, when he was organizing the truck, pass him fruits and vegetables – a task that I knew other hucksters did alone. I often wondered why my strong 39 year old father "needed" me.

When he entered the public market restaurant for a hot breakfast, I wondered why he did not take me with him. At night, he spoke of bad behavior by men and women in Hedges Bar & Grill in the evening hours. I wondered if this was why he did not take me into Hedges Bar & Grill for a hot dinner. I wondered why it took him as long as 4 hours to sell the remaining fruits and vegetables to husbands in the bar while I waited in the back of the locked truck. I wondered if he would have kept me from school if there were no U.S. laws that made him send me. I thanked God for those laws. I wondered why he did not allow me to spend a nickel for a trolley ride home instead of locking me in the back of the truck for all those hours.

I began to think of myself as a timid prisoner, afraid to speak up. The truck was my traveling prison. My father was my dominant warden.

At age 11, at 10:30 PM on this particular Saturday night, in the solitary confinement of the back of the locked truck, sitting on an empty orange crate, huddled next to the kerosene lamp, I came to the realization that I was indeed, a "Prisoner of the Truck." I had to develop a plan to escape. The plan had to include my mother, confined in the crowded upper story flat in the inner city with my brothers and sisters, all of whom I loved so dearly.

We arrived home around 11:00 PM. The children were sleeping. My patient and loving mother served us a hot meal. I welcomed the warmth of my bed, the time for Church and family on Sunday and the school week that kept me off the truck. I prayed that God would help me to find a way to escape.

CHAPTER 2

My Heritage

Wady Sarkis was born in 1893, in Ain Kafa Zabid, a small village near Zahleh in Lebanon. His Lebanese name was "Wadiah". He was the youngest of seven brothers and sisters. The children all worked on their father's farm and tended to sheep as well. Unlike his older brothers and sisters, my father completed grammar school and learned to read and write Arabic. In 1910, at age 17, he immigrated to find a new way of life in America. He stayed with his relatives in Rochester who preceded him. He became the communicator to relatives in the "old country." He was a bright, ambitious and industrious young man. In 1918, at age 25, he opened a confectionery store on Main Street in Rochester, New York, not far from the Eastman Theatre, named after George Eastman, the founder of Eastman Kodak Company. In 1922, at age 29, his business was thriving and he obtained a large bank loan to expand his store. He imported Italian marble to enhance its attractiveness. The future in his new country looked bright. It was time, he thought, to raise a family and he began his search for a bride.

In Olean, New York, Frances Dwaileebe was born the first child of Richard Dwaileebe and Jennie Ash. Richard and Jennie were born, raised and married in Zahleh. Jennie was 16. Richard was 20. Shortly after their wedding, they immigrated to America. During their marriage, they had 14 children, two of whom died.

The first seven born were girls. All of the children were born in Olean. The Dwaileebe family lived on 488 Higgins Avenue. They farmed several acres of land adjacent to their home and fished the Allegheny River.

The population of Olean, adjacent to the Pennsylvania border, was about 4,000. Unlike, Rochester with its industrial might and its then population of 250,000, Olean had few enterprises. People were dependent on Mother Earth for crops, chickens, eggs and milk from cows. There were few jobs in the service trades. The railroad passed in front of Higgins Avenue where the Dwaileebes raised their family. Their farm was behind their home. A large lumberyard, adjacent to the railroad trucks, was also a neighboring business. One silent movie theater, a confectionery store, a grocery store, a department store, a dozen restaurants, a bank and the Olean Hotel served the community. There were many Lebanese families in Olean. They represented about five percent of the total community.

Frances attended high school for two years. After school, she worked at Jim Nahara's confectionery store on Union and Wayne Streets in Olean. After work, she helped her mother with family chores. She also worked on her father's farm when needed on weekends and summer vacations. When she was 17, her father opened a confectionery store, called the Sugar Bowl. A 17-year-old boy frequently stopped in the Sugar Bowl and by his mannerism, Frances knew that he was attracted to her. Richard and Jennie knew nothing of this innocent Sugar Bowl romance. They were very strict with their eldest daughter and they simply did not trust the intentions of young men if they did not know their parents or if they were not of the Lebanese heritage. Frances knew that she could never have a date with her Sugar Bowl suitor. Further, she had to help her mother care for the children; assist with cooking, laundry and house work; and work on the farm when required.

A friend of Wady took him to Olean to meet a woman by the name of Alice Ash. Alice was a first cousin to Frances Dwaileebe. This would be Wady's first trip to Olean. The train ride took four hours. Wady spent a few days courting Alice. Her parents were impressed with him but Alice was not. Wady returned to Rochester with a deep sense of rejection.

In Rochester, my father's Uncle Deeb and sister-in-law Cecelia Sarkis began to take matters into their own hands. As was common for parents in Lebanon, they wanted to play the role of Wady's deceased parents. They were aware of the Dwaileebe family and their many daughters. In Lebanon, they knew of the Dwaileebe and Ash families before they immigrated to America. The Sarkis families lived in Ain Kafa Zabid. The Dwaileebe families originated from Zahleh. Uncle Deeb and Aunt Cecilia accompanied Wady on his second visit to Olean. They would vouch for him; his devotion to St. Nicholas Church; his involvement as a sub-deacon and founder; and his success in the confectionery store business.

My father was a handsome man. He had fair skin and hazel eyes, self-confidence, and a winning way with store customers. He was a leader in the Rochester Lebanese community. People looked up to him and relatives sought his opinion and advice. Because he was one of the few emigrants to read and write Arabic, he was the communication link between relatives in America and relatives in Lebanon.

With this heritage and background, my father looked forward to his second visit to Olean to meet Richard and Jennie Dwaileebe and their seven unmarried eligible daughters.

There were then 10 living Dwaileebe children ranging in age from one to 21. In later years, three more children were born to Richard & Jenny.

At the time of Wady's visit, Frances, the eldest, was now 21. Frances was shy. As a baby, she fell from a high chair onto a broken baby bottle. This left a severe scar on the right side of her forehead. She combed her hair so that it lay over the scar. Frances perceived herself as unattractive, but to others, she was petite and pretty, with dark complexion and a loving sparkle in her eyes and her smile. She was a loving, caring and sensitive woman.

In preparation for the arrival of the Sarkis family, Richard Dwaileebe slaughtered a lamb and gathered vegetables from the Dwaileebe farm for freshly made salads. Jennie and her daughters were well organized for the two-day visit. Jenny's sisters and their husbands were also guests. They prepared a wide variety of Lebanese foods. Kusa is a small green squash stuffed with rice, lamb, and spices and cooked in tomato sauce. Kibbee is ground lamb meat mixed with wheat grains, onions and spices. It is served raw or baked. When raw, the plate is decorated with a touch of oil, onions and parsley. Kibbee, when baked, is layered with pine nuts and onions in the center. Lubbin is a form of yogurt used to compliment the grape leaves, which were rolled and stuffed with lamb meat, spices and rice and simmered in lemon juice.

Frances was excited about the preparations. She knew that these grand preparations were expressions of hospitality well known in the Lebanese community, that it had something to do with a potential suitor. She was aware of the tradition. Her parents would want to see the eldest daughter chosen by the suitor. But Frances was uncertain about marriage. The Dwaileebe family was a large, happy and close family, with great love for one another. She knew that friends her age were either courting or married and that her parents had to approve of Wady. If they did, she hoped that her feelings for Wady would be the same.

The Sarkis family arrived around noon on Saturday. A great deal of time was spent reminiscing about parents, relatives and friends in the old country. The Dwaileebe's recalled how members of the Sarkis and Dwaileebe families would visit each other's village in Lebanon. In addition to farming fruits, vegetables and olives, the Sarkis family raised sheep for slaughter. They would trade Dwaileebe cheese for Sarkis lamb. For those who emigrated, lamb remained the meat dish served in America.

Wady was a great storyteller. One Saturday evening, in the Dwaileebe living room, he held every one's attention telling a story. He was 13. It was his night to guard the sheep from wolves that would occasionally come out of the hills. He tried to remain awake and alert to the animal noises of the night. In the bright moonlight, he saw the wolf slowly approach the sheep. He knew he had to be patient. There was only one shot in his rifle. He lined up his sights. His heart was pounding. The wolf drew near the restless sheep that sensed danger. He held his breath as he pulled the trigger. The wolf howled and began to flee. A few yards later, it fell to the ground dead from a clean shot through the heart.

Other memories and events were shared around a Turkish smoking pipe, pronounced "Ugeelee", in Arabic. This was a water pipe using Turkish tobacco. It stood two feet high and came in two parts. One part was a twelve-inch decorated water bowl with a narrow neck and the other part was a straight eighteen-inch decorated metal pipe. The metal pipe was designed to fit snugly in the water bowl. The pipe had two openings, one at the lower part of the pipe and one at the top. A long and narrow, patterned hose was attached to the lower part of the pipe. At the top of the pipe, there was an opening covered by a metal screen. Dampened Turkish tobacco was placed on the screen. A red-hot charcoal was placed on top of the tobacco. The hose had a pearl tip used to draw air through the pipe. A strong draw of breath was needed to bring air down through the upper pipe. Air was passed through the charcoal-tobacco, down to the water, bringing the tobacco smoke with it. This caused the water to bubble. The bubble contained the smoke that was filtered by the water. The smoke rose from the water to fill a space between the pipe and the water bowl. It was this filtered smoke that entered deeply into the lungs of the user. After six or seven puffs, the pearl tipped hose was passed from user to user, cleaned by a linen cloth in between uses. The pipe would be passed around until it was necessary to replenish the tobacco and charcoal.

The Dwaileebe and Sarkis men would smoke the pipe while they were being served raw liver from a freshly slaughtered lamb. Chunks of white onions were used to scoop up the sliced pieces of liver and used as chasers for the shot glass of rye or the transparent liquor that turned milk white when added to water. The men gave a toast of good health and happiness to each other and their families. Young Lebanese boys looked forward to turning 18 when they were allowed to participate totally in this tradition, and be acknowledged as men. When a young man was "initiated," he would gulp the whiskey and with watery eyes, quickly reach for the raw liver. Drawing on the pipe took practice. Coughing for first time users was common.

After the meals were served, and the kitchen was cleaned, the women would gather in the living room to smoke the Turkish pipe while they talked about their children, old-times, match making and old friendships. None of the Lebanese women were permitted to smoke cigarettes but the use of the pipe was an accepted tradition.

During this Saturday evening, Richard and Jenny Dwaileebe had ample time to size up this young man from Rochester whose purpose and intent were clear. Frances was the first daughter whose hand would be sought in marriage. The fact that Uncle Deeb and Aunt Cecilia accompanied Wady made the event a serious one. Having put in a full day of hospitality, the Dwaileebes went to bed.

That Saturday night, in spite of the fact that Wady had little time to spend with Richard's three eligible daughters, he advised Uncle Deeb and Aunt Cecelia to express his interest in Victoria, the 18-year-old third born daughter who he found most beautiful.

An old Dwaileebe photograph of Victoria would make one guess that she was a silent film star of the 1920's.

On Sunday morning, the families went to St. Joseph's Church in Olean. This was followed by a breakfast of zlabee and eggs. Zlabee is specially prepared dough that puffs up when fried. With butter and syrup, it was a special treat. After breakfast, the elders went into the living room to visit. Deeb and Aunt Cecelia, in a somewhat nervous state, advised Richard and Jennie Dwaileebe that Wady was interested in Victoria and recognized her as more beautiful. However, Richard and Jennie made it clear that it was to be Frances that they would permit to be Wady's fiancée and no other daughter. Frances was 21. She was the eldest. That was final.

That Sunday afternoon, encouraged by "the arrangers," Wady and Frances talked in the parlor alone. Later they went for a walk on Main Street, within a few houses of Higgins Avenue. Wady wasted little time. He asked Frances if she would consider marriage. After all, he reasoned, it was traditional for the parents to select a suitable mate and it was generally accepted among those so chosen to cooperate with the wisdom of the parents. Frances said she needed time to think. She promised an answer at the train station on Monday. Her answer shocked Wady. It was no, she was not sure that she wanted to marry him, especially since she was aware that she was his second choice. Uncle Deeb and Aunt Cecelia were broken hearted.

Wady retreated to Rochester undaunted. He told Uncle Deeb and Aunt Cecelia that the trip would not be in vain. He admired Frances's spirit and he wrote a poetic letter to Frances in Arabic. This was good strategy. Since Frances could not read it, Richard would read it at the dinner table to the entire Dwaileebe family. Frances was embarrassed. Her younger sisters did not pass up the opportunity to lovingly tease her. She was still unsure. Nevertheless, the letter opened the door to three more weekend trips to Olean. Most of the time was spent visiting the Dwaileebe family. Richard allowed them to go to the silent movies and to the confectionery store. Frances told her parents that she would accept Wady's proposal. Richard and Jenny Dwaileebe advised Wady that Frances would accept his offer of marriage with their blessings.

Frances looked forward to her move to Rochester, NY. In contrast to the small town simplicity of Olean, Rochester was a large, thriving metropolitan area of 250,000 people, the home of Eastman Kodak, Bausch & Lomb Optical Company, Ritter Dental Equipment, Taylor Instrument, Gleason Works and many other thriving industrial firms. In addition to excellent employment opportunities and good paying jobs, George Eastman's generosity enriched the cultural, theatrical, educational, medical and recreational aspects of the total community. It was a city of beautiful parks and worldwide recognition, a city of great pride. "A city," Frances thought, "that would offer greater opportunity to her husband and future children."

The wedding took place in Olean in 1923. Wady's brothers, George and Charlie, Uncle Deeb and Aunt Cecelia, the wife of George, Peter Michaels and George Saikley (good Lebanese friends) accompanied Wady for the trip to Olean. Lebanese food, music and dancing prevailed. Jennie and Richard were proud. Their first daughter was married to a fine young businessman from Rochester, the home of Eastman Kodak. To Frances, marriage seemed the right choice. She was the eldest daughter. Her chores were significant. At age 21, this was her chance to escape into a life of her own and to have her own family. Little did she realize that she was leaping from the frying pan into the fire.

After their marriage, Wady and Frances agreed to temporarily share the inner city home of George and Cecelia, Deeb & Regina and their young children. There were now three Sarkis families living in one household. After two months the married couple moved out and rented a nearby apartment.

My sister Betty was born in 1924. She was a beautiful baby. In later years, I would hear relatives say that Betty should have been entered in the Eastman Kodak baby photo contest.

I was born in 1926. I do not recall similar comments about me as a baby.

In 1928, Jenny Dwaileebe came to visit and to help her daughter Frances with the complications of her third child, Shirley who was born premature. Wady took Frances and Jenny on a trolley to Driving Park Avenue. This was a lovely middle-class neighborhood on the west side of the Genesee River. There were Catholic schools nearby. Wady was planning his family's needs. The broker met them and opened the door. It was the finest home Frances had ever seen and it had four bedrooms. Her hope became a reality. My father's confectionery store on Main Street in Rochester was flourishing. The American dream for both of them had come to fruition.

CHAPTER 3

470 Driving Park Avenue

Shirley, the third child was a premature baby born in 1928. The Doctor's said she would die within a few days of birth. Shirley was so tiny my mother kept her in an empty cigar box filled with cotton and lined with linen. Neighbors marveled at my mother's determination to keep the baby alive. My childhood friends didn't believe that I had a baby sister in a cigar box, so I brought them into the house to show them. For 24 hours a day, the cigar box was placed near a coal stove in the kitchen to keep her as warm as possible. The coal stove was watched carefully to maintain an even, warm temperature. In spite of my mother's heroic attempts to keep her alive, Shirley, in her eighteenth month, died of pneumonia.

My brother Joe was born in 1930. Betty was now six. I was four. After losing his confectionery store on Main Street in the Great Depression, my father bought a horse and wagon. His brother George and Uncle Deeb were already in the huckster business and were supporting their families in the inner city. They encouraged my father to enter this business and to begin to develop a route of regular customers by knocking on doors in Rochester's east and west side middle class neighborhoods.

I had no comprehension of how huckstering would change the rest of my life. At four years old, I was a happy boy. Driving Park Avenue was in a middle class neighborhood. School kids either went to Holy Rosary or to the Public School. Life was an adventure. I had many playmates. At five, I was mother's helper. I ran secret errands for her. Newspaper ads were promoting a new cigarette, "Old Gold." A coupon was attached to the pack of cigarettes. This entitled you to enter a contest. You had to write three or four sentences about why you liked Old Gold cigarettes. The year was 1931, two years after the market crash of 1929, which led to the ten-year depression. Cigarettes were inexpensive; taxes on cigarettes were minor. My mother was worried about mortgage payments on the Driving Park Avenue home. My father's major remodeling of his confectionery store in 1928 was ill timed. He lost the store to a mortgage foreclosure in the crash of 1929. Winning the Old Gold contest would save our home. I would go to the small corner grocery store with mother's written list. The last item on the list was a pack of Old Gold cigarettes. My mother, who entered these contests for two years, never won.

At the start of the contest, mother didn't smoke; my father's eldest brother, Uncle Charlie did. Unmarried, he would visit our family frequently. He loved Frances and the children. He knew something of my father's habits and temper. Even after Charlie married, he remained concerned for her happiness and at times spoke to my father about his temper. Charlie spoke to my mother in Arabic which mother had learned at home and in her marriage. He always brought something to eat or a toy for the children. Mother would secretly give the unopened cigarettes to Charlie in appreciation for his gifts. Charlie, unlike my father, did not have a problem with women smoking. After a few months, mother began smoking during Charlie's visits. It wasn't long before mother was smoking the entire pack. Old Gold won the contest; my mother was addicted.

The secret of mother's cigarette smoking was kept from my father throughout her life. Uncle Charlie and all nine children shared the secret. When my father's fruit and vegetable truck pulled into the driveway, the family went on alert. The children would quickly open the windows and wave towels to be sure that he did not smell cigarette smoke.

At five, I came home one day with a very small toy truck that I found on the sidewalk. My mother asked me to knock on the door in front of the home where I found it to see if it belonged to someone. There was a saying in those days, "Finders keepers, losers weepers." My mother didn't buy this slogan. I refused to do what she said. She walked me to the place where I found it, knocked on the door and asked the lady of the house if it belonged to one of her children. It did. She took me home, reached for a needle from her sewing kit and pricked the back of my hand six or seven times and made me promise that I would never take anything that did not belong to me.

I turned six in May of 1932. In addition to the pack of Old Gold, my mother permitted me to spend a penny on a package of flat bubble gum. There was an assortment of photographs of famous baseball players on a stiff card in each pack. I became addicted. Kids would pitch baseball cards against a wall. Whoever got the closest would win the card. All the kids were doing it. I would win and lose - most of the time breaking even. One day, I played pitching cards with Bobby York who was my age. He had about 25 cards. I won them all. Mrs. York came over to the house demanding the return of the cards. My mother said she would talk to me about it. It was a short discussion. I said, "I won them fair and square." In my mind, this was not the same as "finders keepers, losers weepers." I lost the argument. My mother went to get her sewing kit. I ran up the stairs to the front bedroom facing the street. My mother pursued me. It was summertime. I opened the window, leaped out onto the porch roof and went to the edge. I said, "If you come after me, I'll jump." Her tone of voice changed. She begged me to return. I made her promise me that she would not use the needle. She kept her promise. Instead of the needle, she spoke of good and bad losers; she agreed that I won fairly and squarely; the decision was mine to make. I returned the cards. When I came home she told me how proud she was of my decision.

The glow that I felt has never left my memory. Never again did my mother ever have to use the needle. Reasoning, not needles, prevailed.

I learned to play baseball that summer. Gloria Porcelli, at age ten was four years older than I was. She was a tomboy and leader, who attended the neighborhood public school. A gang of kids would go to the public school playground. To choose sides, Gloria would pitch a bat to a ten-year-old boy. He had to catch it somewhere in the middle with one hand. The catching hand had to remain in place. Gloria would put her right hand over his catching hand. They would alternate hands until they got to the top of the grip on the bat. The last full handgrip would be the winner. A flat rock was used to pound on the top hand if the hand was slightly above the grip. If it didn't hurt, the hand on top could pick the first team member from the group standing by. Gloria would choose me over older kids. She made me feel important. I lived up to her expectations. I was a good batter and left fielder.

Also at age six, my father taught me the "Our Father" in Arabic as well as the Arabic alphabet. There were many Sarkis families in Rochester, most of them living in the inner city. They visited often. During these Sunday visits, my father would take great pride in calling me into the living room for the "Our Father" recital in his native tongue. I liked Sundays. My father seemed more loving and peaceful. He would wear his only suit with a white shirt and tie and shiny shoes. We never missed Mass on Sundays. My father played an active role in the church services.

At funerals, like a priest, he would bring tears to the eyes of those present as he vocally praised the life of the deceased in the Arabic language. This would trigger the "wailing of women." In Arabic, women chanted something personal about the life of the deceased. For example, "He was a good provider to his family and he would always put their needs first." Another voice would chant, "He was a good father and he was kind and gentle to his wife." Yet another voice could be heard to say, "He was a religious man and never failed to attend Church on Sundays and Holy Days." If the deceased was a woman, a chanter would say, "She was a devoted wife and mother. She found time for both her family and her relatives. She was generous with her time and would share Sunday meals with family, relatives and friends." The wake and chanting would last for two full evenings bringing tears and moans of sorrow from most in attendance. This ritual would be broken with periods of silence.

I did not understand Arabic. On occasion, boyhood friends or their parents, who were not members of our church, would attend this funeral ritual. I knew that their wakes were different; a few prayers by a priest or minister and silence were more common. At first, I felt embarrassment when my friends attended our wakes. The wailing sounded so primitive. My mother spoke and understood Arabic and her interpretations would bring sensitive tears to my eyes as well as my friends.

Our many relatives attended the same church. Almost every Sunday, after church, we would go to the inner city to visit them. I felt more at home with my aunts, uncles, cousins and their friends in the inner city than I did on Driving Park Avenue.

I had few problems in the first semester of my first grade at Holy Rosary School, about a 15-minute walk from home. The classes were large, about 40 children per class. The children were of German and Irish heritage. But the second semester was different. It began on Valentine's Day. The first grade Sister gave all 40 children the names of all class members. My mother helped me to write 40 envelopes — with a valentine for each member of the class. They were inexpensive little valentines that were purchased in a bulk package. On the day of distribution, I noticed that most kids got 30 to 40 cards while I received two.

A few months later, on a warm day in May, I was devastated by another school event. I was wearing short pants. As we lined up for the walk from school to church, I overheard two girls snickering, "He's not only skinny, pigeon toed, bow legged and knock kneed, but he's black as a nigger." Crushed, I went home that afternoon and stood in front of a mirror. Indeed, I discovered I was all five combined with pitch-black hair and brown eyes. There was no doubt about it. I was different from the other kids at

Holy Rosary. I began to develop strong feelings of inferiority. I found some solace at the public school playground, playing baseball and football with kids who organized their own games. It seemed that, in baseball, my athletic abilities concealed the misfit that I thought I was, but the seeds for my life-long bitter hatred of any kind or form of prejudice were planted in my mind on this day.

I began to think that I should talk to my mother about my feelings. But she was on her feet from 5 AM until 11 PM. She always seemed to be taking care of a baby, or cleaning the house or preparing a meal, or washing clothing. She did not get the chance that I did to escape into a baseball or football games or to explore the year round wonders of nature. Moreover, she was preoccupied with my father's financial problems but too fearful of his temper to mention them. He insisted that she be up at 5 AM to make his breakfast and to see him off to work. I began to perceive my mother as a living saint and my father as the man who gave her the opportunity to become one. How could I possibly burden this mother of mine, this Prisoner of Love with my feelings of inferiority?

I could not share my frustration with my sister Betty. I didn't think that she would understand. Betty was a beautiful fair-skinned girl. Her Valentine ratios were fairly equal. I did not believe she could help me.

My sense of inferiority continued in the second grade. The two girls who crushed my boyish spirit were still in my class. With 40 kids in the class, the second grade Sister was too busy to know that the skinny looking, dark skinned boy of seven was having problems with his identity. On one occasion, I asked my mother if I could live with the family next door for a while. They had children with blond hair and blue eyes. In my seven-year-old mind, I was aware that you caught measles, chicken pox and colds from other kids. I thought that if you lived with a family long enough, you would catch the color of their skin, hair and eyes. There was another reason why I couldn't explain my feelings to my mother. She was also dark skinned. I thought it would hurt her if she knew that I did not like my body or the color of my skin. When I asked if I could live next door, she seemed puzzled and said, "No honey, your place is at home."

A second grade experience made matters even worse. Three boys in my class, pinned me to the ground and "pantsed" me, running off with my pants and underwear. A husky redheaded boy in the 6th or 7th grade came to my rescue. He retrieved my clothes, took me by the hand and walked me to the safety of my home. He was my hero. In the silent movies, the hero was constantly in danger of losing his life. For weeks, I would imagine my hero in trouble. If necessary, like the silent cowboy movies, I would have jumped in front of a bullet to save his life.

On another occasion in the second grade, I was excused to go to the bathroom. I returned to the classroom. A short time later, the Sister left the room. When she returned, she asked me if I had spit gum into the drinking fountain. Since I did not, I found it easy to say "no." In spite of my denial, in front of the entire class of 40, she struck me over the head with her knuckles and lectured me on the importance of telling the truth. A few weeks later, the same Sister asked the class, "What city in New York State was once famous for the discovery and drilling of oil?" When I saw no other hands going up, I shyly raised my hand and in a soft voice said, "Olean." (In visits to my grandparents in Olean, I was shown the site of an abandoned oil rig.) The good Sister said, "Very good Freddie." Wow, I thought, even though I have this inferior body; even though I was accused of lying about the gum, I could still receive praise from a teacher for having a right answer to a question. I noticed that several classmates turned around somewhat amazed. Was it possible that the silent, dark skinned, skinny boy with the pigeon toes, bowed legs and knock-knees had a brain inside that freaky body? They didn't know that I was just lucky.

CHAPTER 4

Onward Christian Soldiers

When I started the first grade at Holy Rosary, there were no lay teachers. The Sisters of St. Joseph staffed the entire grammar school. Religious education was taught in each of the eight grades. By age six, I had received three of the Seven Sacraments of the Roman Catholic Church: Baptism, Holy Communion and Penance. I knew that Jesus loved me, probably more than the other kids. After all, I thought, I was the lowliest of the low.

My mother would help me with my Catechism. In the first grade it was "Who made the world? God made the world. Who is God? God is the Creator of Heaven and earth and of all things. Why did God make me? God made me to know Him, to love Him and to serve Him in this world and to be happy with Him in the next world." There were many other questions and answers committed to memory and still remembered.

Penance was weekly. The first graders were lined up single file. Father sat in the middle of the confessional booth; the children would enter each side. Father would hear a confession on one side, open a sliding wooden window and hear the confession on the other side. I entered the door that had just been closed by the previous penitent. I knelt down in the darkness. I could faintly hear voices in the confessional box. I heard the other sliding wooden door close as mine was opened. There was an inner maroon curtain that concealed me by inches from Father's face and voice. I began, "Bless me Father, for I have sinned, my last Confession was one week ago. Since my last confession, I did not love certain classmates twice and I disobeyed my mother once." Because there was always a line of children, Father responded quickly. I knew he would go easy on me because these were "venial" or small sins. He asked, "Is there anything else?" "No," I said. He replied, "For your penance, say three Our Fathers and three Hail Mary's and now make a good Act of Contrition." While he was absolving me of my sins in Latin, I would recite, "Oh my God, I am heartily sorry for having offended thee and I detest all my sins because I dread the loss of Heaven and the pains of Hell. But most of all, because I have offended Thee my God, Who art all Good and deserving of all my love. I firmly resolve with the help of Thy Grace to confess my sins, to do penance and to amend my life, Amen." He would then say, "Go in Peace". I would return to the church pew, kneel and quickly say my penance.

I wondered if the two girls who mocked my bowed legs, pigeon toes and knock-knees would confess their sin against the second commandment, "Thou shalt love thy neighbor as thyself." It had to be a venial sin. I wondered if Father would treat their sin as a mortal sin. If so, I hoped that their Penance would be at least twice that of mine.

When I was eight, I had to deal with the sixth commandment, "Thou shalt not commit adultery." There was a confessional guidebook on the sixth commandment. You sinned against this commandment if you had impure thoughts and desires whether you were married or not. A bunch of kids went down to Maplewood Park in the summer of 1934. With our clothes on, hiding in the bushes, we played doctor. We took turns lifting shirts and skirts the way the Doctor did when he examined us. Since we did not have a stethoscope, we would use our ears.

I was grateful for the penance guidebook. I merely said, "Since my last confession, I have had impure thoughts and desires once." I waited for the confessional booth to explode. I was shocked. There were no questions. I didn't have to be specific about playing Doctor. It only meant two more Our Fathers and two more Hail Mary's.

My preparation, at the age of 12, for the Sacrament of Confirmation was the most meaningful spiritual experience of my life. I had spent two years as Prisoner of the Truck. As I studied and prepared for this Sacrament, I felt that Confirmation would somehow help me with my feelings of inferiority as well as my prison sentence.

We were required to memorize the Seven Gifts of the Holy Spirit as well as their meaning. We were to become soldiers in Christ's army, living and preaching the Message of Christ, just as the Apostles did when the Holy Spirit descended upon them. Again, my mother would ask the questions and from memory, I would recite the answers. I was well prepared for Confirmation.

My cousin Charlie and his wife Lena were my sponsors. They drove me in their "coupe" to church. It was my first ride in an automobile. The coupe had a front seat only. I sat in the middle. Lena was a very large woman. I was sandwiched in between both of them. I felt warm and protected. It was a special day for my family and me. Like the other boys in the Confirmation class, I was dressed in black pants, a white shirt, black tie, black socks and shoes. The girls were dressed in white. A celebration at home awaited me following the Confirmation service.

I wanted desperately to feel the power of the Holy Spirit descending on me as it did his Apostles during that night when they cowered in fear and confusion after the Crucifixion. I wanted the Gift of "Counsel" so that I could truly speak and listen to others. I wanted the Gifts of "Understanding" and "Knowledge" so that I could know and understand more about family, my relatives, friends and myself. I reasoned that these gifts were the keys to the Gift of "Wisdom". But most of all, I wanted the Gift of "Fortitude". It was "Fortitude", which inspired the apostles to go forth and preach to all nations. "Fortitude" gave me the courage that I would need to cope with the problems I experienced in school and in my father's business. I knew from my lessons that these five Gifts had to be combined with the Gifts of "Piety" and "Fear of the Lord". The good Sisters explained that these last two Gifts meant a strong belief in the message of Jesus Christ. Like a recipe for love, they had to be blended with the other five.

The Bishop stood majestically over me. He anointed me with oil and ashes. But there was no great transformation. I did not receive any magical power. None of my fellow classmates seemed to be any different. None of them spoke in tongues of different countries. I began to think that, like baseball, one had to do a lot of practicing before the Gifts could be truly received. Although I felt no miraculous change within me, I knew that the seeds were planted and maybe when I grew older, the Gifts would grow within me. In that kind of simplicity, I felt that the Holy Spirit was indeed with me and that I was better prepared for any of life's battles including my battle to escape from being a Prisoner of the Truck.

CHAPTER 5

The Age of Reasoning

The seven Gifts began to work within me. I began to "reason" that I had no friends in a class of 40 at Holy Rosary because I had been too timid —- very much like the Apostles, who cowered in fear before the descent of the Holy Spirit. Timid folks don't make friends easily. I was learning that the Irish and German kids in my class were all individuals, uniquely different. I became aware that I had amplified the incidents that happened in school; that indeed, mean spirited and insensitive kids were in a very small minority. Other boys and girls at Holy Rosary were ridiculed; other boys were stripped of their pants; other kids were humiliated at one time or another; other kids were embarrassed by the good Sister. Maybe other kids had feelings of inferiority and rejection. I reasoned that I wasn't the only one. But, from what I observed, none of them were Prisoners of a Truck and none of them had all five of the big physical defects: homely, pigeon-toed, knock-kneed, bow-legged and dark-skinned.

There was a boy my age named Stanley, who lived a few doors behind our house. He was also timid. I wondered if it had anything to do with his hands, which were webbed by skin that stretched slightly beyond the knuckles of his fingers. I took the initiative to become friends. He was a public school student and an only child. His family treated me as if I were another son. They had a large recreation room with a billiard table and table tennis. In inclement weather, I spent many recreational hours with Stan. His father had a compact coupe with a rumble seat — an open seat for two behind the enclosed front seat. Stan and I rode in this rumble seat on many occasions while his father treated us to movies, or trips to the zoo or to the Sea Breeze Amusement Park. Sharing in this experience, which my family could not afford, made this a memorable boyhood adventure. I was grateful for Confirmation. It helped me to overcome my timidity that led to this friendship.

Gloria Porcelli, the tomboy who wanted me on her team, had moved. After I was confirmed at age 12, I became one of the regulars who gathered at the public school to play baseball and football. In baseball, I could play any position and my batting was good. I even got to fling the bat for the choosing of sides. In football, I was fast enough to outrun most kids as a receiver or in defense in blocking or intercepting passes.

I was in the lower half of the class at Holy Rosary. My mother was satisifed with my school marks. There were a few gold stars on certain subjects, including my behavior. My father, who showed great interest in the report cards of his children, constantly asked why I wasn't getting gold stars in all subjects and suggested that I study harder.

My 12th birthday was on May 16, 1938, a week after my Confirmation. Every year in the spring, the public high school band would practice-parade down the streets in the neighborhood while proud parents and neighbors watched. It was a perfect sunny day with a refreshing cool breeze. The band was marching to America the Beautiful, the Star-Spangled Banner and other marching band music. I pretended that this day and this event were a celebration of my 12th birthday. Like the words of an old song, "Thrills ran up and down my spine, Aladdin's lamp was mine", I was healing from my first and second grade hurts. All seemed to be going well at school, and at home with my mother, father, brothers and sisters. I was feeling good about the "inner me" — the "me" who was now Confirmed. I believed that the Holy Spirit loved me and that this love was reflected in the warmth of God's creation, the sun. You had to open your heart to feel the power of the Holy Spirit. You had to step out into the sun to feel the warmth of its rays. On that day, the sun, the music of the band and the Holy Spirit filled me with a great sense of joy and peace. For one day, I forgot that summer was coming and with it, my long summer prison term.

Confirmation brought back memories of two events when I was ten. My brother Jim was suffering from a severe earache. Medication was not working. He was in excruciating pain for a full week requiring day and night treatment with medications provided by the family doctor. An ear specialist diagnosed the illness as mastoiditis (an infection of the mastoid bone behind the ear), which required surgery. Two-year-old Jim came home with bandages wrapped around his head. My heart went out to him. When my mother changed his bandages, I saw that the gap in the back of his ear was the size of a chestnut. I spent many hours in church that week reciting litanies for the relief of Jim's pain and suffering and the agony reflected by my parents.

Shortly after Jim's recovery, there was a heated argument between my mother and father. Before the children knew what was happening, my father lost complete control of his emotions. He was in a violent rage. He pulled my mother to the floor, grabbed her by the hair and dragged her across the kitchen floor. In an instant, I was wrapped around one of his legs trying to stop him, while pounding him in the back. My sister Betty, 12, was trying to release his hands from my mother's hair. My brother Joe, 6, was punching at my father from the side. My sister Anne, 4, and brother Jim, 2 were screaming with fear. My sister Vicky was an infant. The violence stopped as suddenly as it started. My father went into a state of shock. He seemed to freeze in his tracks with all of us surrounding him. He looked down at me wrapped around his leg, at Joe's tiny fists still pounding him and Betty's hands trying to release his grip. He was overwhelmed with grief at what he had done. He retreated to the bedroom, humiliated by his behavior for he had once more, by his behavior, given my mother the opportunity to become a saint.

She defended his behavior. When he retreated to his bedroom in great anguish, she told the family that he was under tremendous stress; that the mortgage payments on the house were in significant arrears; a foreclosure was pending; the bank was going to wait until school was finished. He was devastated that he could not keep his family in the middle class neighborhood of Driving Park Avenue; his pride was crushed. She said that he wasn't himself and that we should forgive him as she did.

I could not forgive him on that particular day. The memory of his violence was branded in my mind. However, after confirmation, I began to think about my father's humanity. He suffered the loss of his business; he was forced into the huckster business; he lost his daughter Shirley; he was distressed over Jim's week of agony; he was about to lose the dream home that he bought for my mother and the family that he wanted to raise. I "reasoned" that I had been so wrapped up in my own feelings, that I was totally insensitive to his. I felt sorrow for his suffering. The Seven Gifts of the Holy Spirit began to come alive within me. There was "Piety" (Devotion), "Fear of the Lord" (Respect for the Teachings of Jesus Christ). I had "Counseled" with my mother. This led to a "Knowledge" of the pressures in my father's life, which led to an "Understanding" of his struggle and the "Wisdom" to forgive him as my mother did and the "Fortitude" or courage to accept whatever God placed in my path for whatever known or unknown reason.

However, the beginning of this 12 year old "age of reasoning" had no effect on my dread of the summer of 1938, my fifth summer sentence of close to 100 hours a week in the prison on wheels.

CHAPTER 6

Ormond Street — The Inner City of Joy

When I was 12, in the summer of 1938, a truck pulled up to the front door of Driving Park Avenue. A cousin, also named Fred Sarkis, volunteered to help us move to Ormond Street, the inner city of Rochester. I did not fully comprehend my mother's sadness. The flat we were moving into was half of the size of Driving Park Avenue, but outside of that flat, I thought, there was a new world of warmth and friendliness for my mother as well as my brothers and sisters. I was elated. I knew Ormond Street well. After church on Sundays, we visited relatives often. It was a mixed neighborhood — a heritage of Blacks, Italians, Lebanese, Jews, Greeks, and Polish, many whose parents were immigrants. The Irish and Germans were a small minority. All of these kids played together both day and night — all brought closer together by poverty. Very few mothers worked; it was common that they didn't. Fathers worked hard to find jobs. Many families had to seek relief from Roosevelt's welfare programs.

I did not escape the summer prison of 1938. With the help of my prayer book, that I carried on the truck and a bit of "Fortitude", I managed to survive my third year sentence. The hours had not changed. It was still a 100-hour workweek, but I had the promise of September. My parole on summer Sundays gave me the opportunity to make friends with many of the inner city kids that I would be going to school with. I loved these new inner city friendships. This, I thought, was where I belonged, where I was comfortable with myself. With great expectations, I looked forward to September and the sixth grade at the inner city St. Joseph's grammar school.

After school, we played inventive street games in the daylight and at night under the streetlights. "Kick the Can" was one of them. Boys and girls of all ages played, joined by an active parent on occasions. It only took a gathering of six or more to begin the game. It would grow to as many as 20 kids. The playing field was on Lundy's Lane, an alley that ran behind Ormond Street homes. Street lighting was enhanced by security lights from adjacent business buildings; there were ample dark corners to make the game more interesting. Boys and girls would take turns as a "tagger." The tagger guarded the can to prevent players from kicking it. If the tagger touched a player, that player became (ironically) a prisoner. Prisoners had to sit on the curbstone and could only be released if another player kicked the can. It required speed, agility and team strategy to get by the tagger in order to free the prisoners. There was a lot of coaching and yelling from the prisoners on the curb hoping that non-prisoners would free them. It was a vigorous and continuous exercise that would last from one to two hours. The best and fastest athlete would win by tagging all players before any one of them could kick the can. When the can was kicked and the prisoners were freed, a new tagger would start a new game. I would go home dripping with sweat giving little thought to the athletic and social benefits of the game. The financial costs of Kick the Can were shoes and sneakers that wore out sooner and one empty soup can. The inventor should have received a civic award.

Television did not exist in 1938. Although the radio was invented in 1926, they were not affordable in most inner city homes. On Ormond Street, a corner grocery store had a radio. For major and minor sports events, kids would socialize around the radio while drinking Cokes in bottles or eating Fudgicles. In addition to a good chocolate flavor, Fudgicles were popular because the word "free" was burned into one of twenty Fudgicle sticks. Turn in the stick and get one free. Young and older kids were constantly gathering in front of this small store. It was a hangout, a place to meet for other fun and games.

Also on Lundy's Lane, there was a business building with a solid cement wall facing Lundy's Lane. On nights and weekends, the business was closed. The lighted parking area was converted to a makeshift handball court with one wall. Chalk was used to mark of the boundaries of the court. During the school year, I practiced alone and played opponents on this court as often as I could in the evening and on Sunday. I beat kids who were much older than I. I loved the exhilaration of winning. I became the uncrowned Champion of the Lundy Lane Inner City Improvised Handball Court, frustrating even adults who challenged me. I was learning, "Practice makes perfect."

When the chestnuts fell from the trees that lined Ormond Street, children would collect them. It was chestnut competition season. Behind the alley, adjacent to the railroad tracks, there was a field of hard earth. A large circle would be drawn in the soil. A slate of marble from the junkyard could be broken up into pieces about the size of the palm of a hand. Four or more kids would put an equal number of chestnuts in the circle. From an established distance, each competitor would fling the marble slate so that it would land flat and slide into the circle filled with chestnuts in the center. The thrower won all the chestnuts that were knocked outside of the circle. When the chestnut season ended, I would end up with a basket full of chestnuts. It didn't matter that you threw them away weeks later. What mattered was winning.

In addition to these inventive games, the good guys would gather on each other's porches during evening hours chatting about classmates, teachers, families, friends, sports, world events and the opposite sex. No one was ever excluded. Race, creed or color did not matter.

In the inner city, there was a difference between gangs — good guys and bad guys. The bad guys broke streetlights and windows in abandoned buildings. Bad guys smoked cigarettes behind their parent's backs. In those days, I never heard about the bad guys getting into trouble with drugs. In fact, the word "drugs" did not exist. It was not uncommon to see a police officer entering the home of an inner city bad guy. Ormond Street was about 70% white and 30% black. Most of the police visits were to the homes of white parents and never related to drugs. Bad guys were in the minority, probably one in twenty kids. The good guys, influenced by their parents or by peer behavior and example, knew wrong from right and behaved accordingly. You had the freedom to pick the gang you wanted to be with. The bad guys had a certain respect for the good guys. You were welcomed to join them or not. There was no pressure. The choice was yours.

Hospitality in the inner city was common. On many occasions, my mother would allow me to have dinner in a friend's home. I had spaghetti in an Italian home, polish sausage in a Polish home, cream cheese, bagels and lox in a Jewish home, and grits in the home of "Shoey," a black boy who got this nickname because he always had holes in his shoes. Shoey was very shy. I was extremely sensitive to his loneliness. I made sure that he joined us in our fun and games. My mother would reciprocate the hospitality of my friends. They would join our family for Lebanese food in our home.

As described in Chapter 1, my mother made the adjustment, cleaned out the roaches and bed bugs and settled down to raising her family in this wonderful and unique environment of the poor — one where relatives and neighbors of all faiths, nationality and color were also good friends — one where help was instantly around the corner for an illness, a misfortune, an accident or the death of a loved one — one where children could instantly gather for fun and games — one where there was little time for boredom. My mother saw the quick and happy adjustment of her children to the new environment; whatever made her children happy, made her happy. With mother, it was always as simple as that.

Just across the alley from the improvised handball court on Lundy's Lane, there was a major junk dealer who bought scraps of metal, clothing, used tires, etc. It was common for kids to bring "junk" to the dealer to earn 10 cents or more to go to the World Theater on North Street or the Strand Theater on Clinton Avenue to see a talking movie. At age 12, shortly after we moved to Ormond Street, my older cousin Ray, my eight-year-old brother Joe and I had collected rags in a burlap bag while my four-year-old brother Jim tagged along. From past rag sales, we knew that Mr. Harrison or his son Les, the proprietors of the junkyard, would weigh them on the scale and pay us a certain sum per pound.

Later in life, Les Harrison became nationally known and honored as a pioneer of the National Basketball Association. He served as the coach of the then Rochester Royals. The senior Mr. Harrison was a good man. He had a soft spot in his heart for inner-city kids and he seemed to know the difference between bad and good kids. One day we took advantage of his goodness. It seemed as if the Holy Spirit had taken a temporary leave of absence in my life.

The rags that we gathered did not weigh enough to collect the 40 cents that the four of us needed to go to the movies. Little Jim understood our plan. He promised to be quiet as we put him in the large burlap bag. We stuffed rags around him and on top of his head and tied the bag. We told Jim that when Mr. Harrison put the ragbag aside on the outside dock, as we watched him do on many occasions, we would sneak up while Mr. Harrison was inside the building, untie the rope and free him. Ray, who was big and strong, threw the bag over his shoulder. We placed it on Mr. Harrison's scale as directed. He said, "This seems awfully heavy for rags, are you sure you haven't put bricks into it?" We innocently said, "No, Mr. Harrison." He said, "Well, I have to be sure that you didn't." He reached for a round, sharply pointed metal stick, which he had used in the past to check for bricks and said, "We'll see." We yelled, "Please, don't Mr. Harrison." We instantly untied the rope. Jim leaped out and we fled. We expected Mr. Harrison to pursue us. Instead, he was frozen in his tracks, pale as a ghost. As we looked back, while running away, he seemed to be holding his chest. I didn't sleep well that night. We never told our parents. Mr. Harrison, who could see the house we lived in from his place of business, did not report us. I rated my behavior as a mortal sin and told it in Confession the following Saturday. The Penance was severe — ten Our Fathers, Ten Hail Mary's and Five Rosaries.

A stone's throw from Harrison's Junkyard was a series of connected garages, each large enough to accommodate a single automobile. Instead of autos, each garage was rented and used for the storage of junk. The junk collector used a hand pulled wagon. At the end of the day, his wagon would be heavy with loaded junk salvaged from businesses and residences.

One particular junk man did not trust kids. If you were walking anywhere near his wagon, he would bark at you. We knew that he couldn't run very fast so we would bark back at him. One day, he chanted repeatedly in broken English, "If I be your mother, if I be your father, I give you whipping, I give you beating." A gang of us, supposedly good kids, invented a response as well as a musical tune to mimic and taunt the poor old junk man in broken English, "If I be your mother, if I be your father, I give you nickel, I give you penny." We would repeat the song over and over again as we followed him down the alley to his garage. He would turn on us to chase us away. We would run a short distance and begin the chant again. We would continue until he locked the garage and left in disgust. The confrontation was almost weekly. We would invent a new chant every week like, "If I be your mother, if I be your father, I give you candy, I give you ice cream." At Confession one day, in my examination of conscience, I finally determined that this was a venial sin that had to be confessed. It turned out to be a serious mortal sin — a violation of the 2nd Commandment, "Thou Shalt Love Thy Neighbor as Thyself." The penance — ten Our Fathers, ten Hail Mary and Ten Litany's of the Holy Virgin Mary. Since confession involves a "firm purpose of amendment," I had to refrain from participating in this weekly ritual. Eventually, other members of the gang got tired of it and stopped as well. The old junk man was happy to be left alone and never barked at us again.

Ormond Street ran into Cumberland Street, the location of Rochester's main US Post Office. There was a long strip of grass adjacent to the Post Office. After school, all you needed was two kids to knock on doors. We would gather about 14 kids to play touch football. We'd chose sides with a flick of our fingers — odds or evens. The game of touch football would begin within thirty minutes of the knock on the first door. Americans of every race, creed and color, good guys and bad guys, blended into two competitive teams and followed the rules of the game. The games were frequent. No organizers, no parents, no automobiles, no TV, no video games — just a bunch of inner city kids, self organized and having good, clean fun.

This is not to say that every day was perfect. There were occasional disagreements and fights. Many kids did use bad language. There was ethnic name-calling but it included every group and was often used to tease rather than hurt — "Jew", "Arab" , "Polock" , "Dago" , "Nigger" , "Mick" , and "Kraut".

To me it was a fun neighborhood for kids. I loved Ormond Street and the Inner City of Joy. As a 12-year-old boy, this was the neighborhood where I wanted to spend all of my parole time.

CHAPTER 7

The Mobilizer at St. Joseph's Grammar School

In September of 1938, at age 12, I entered the sixth grade at St. Joseph's Grammar School on Franklin Street in Rochester, a block from Sibley, Lindsay & Curr's Main Street Department store.

St. Joe's was a 20-minute walk from Ormond Street. I would soon learn that there is a difference between the Sisters of Notre Dame, who taught at St. Joseph's and the Sisters of St. Joseph, who taught at Holy Rosary. The Sisters of Notre Dame simply demonstrated more passion for their work. Maybe, it was because it was an inner city parish, or because it was a tougher assignment involving kids of all races and colors, or because 6th graders needed more attention and discipline. Whatever, I was in for the most dramatic school year of my life.

Sister Amabilis was the sixth grade teacher. In Latin, amabilis meant "of love." Her nickname, chosen by previous classes and adopted by our own class, was Sister the Mobilizer, which means, "Preparation for war." Indeed, we were enrolled in the armed forces and Sister Amabilis was the drill Sergeant.

And like the drill Sergeant, there was no doubt about her objectives. You were there to learn at any cost. If force had to be used, she would use it. I especially feared Civics, the study of U.S. government. Civics was a contest between two teams of kids, each team on opposite sides of the classroom. If a team member failed to answer a question correctly, that member had to extend the palm of his or her hand so that the Mobilizer could strike it with her round stick with as much force as possible. After the first strike on the palm of my hand, the first book I opened at night was the Civics book. The incentive was clear — you had to study or get hit.

The classes at St. Joseph's were smaller than Holy Rosary — about 30 per class. Unfortunately, this meant that the Mobilizer had more time to devote to each student. In the study of mathematics, the Mobilizer would put a student at the blackboard to show the math calculations while other students attempted to solve the same math problem at their desks. One school day, I was the draftee working on the math problem. It required several calculations that would take about ten minutes to solve. In the middle of the calculations, I felt the strong urge to urinate. I raised my hand and asked to be "excused." That clearly meant, "I have to go to the bathroom." The Mobilizer said, "Not until you finish the calculations." I lost my concentration. The pressure was building. I asked to be excused again and was denied. I was panic stricken. I crossed my legs tightly, aware that the entire class was watching me. I felt a warm trickle pouring down my leg, into my socks and shoes forming a puddle of urine on the floor beneath me. I knew my classmates saw the puddle. There was only one choice. I rushed to the door, opened it, slammed it shut and hid in a closet in the boy's room. I stood on the toilet seat so that my feet could not be seen. About 15 minutes later, I heard a classmate calling my name. I was told that the Mobilizer wanted me to return to the class. I did. No one ever said a word, including the Mobilizer. I survived the day but did not tell my mother.

I loved my classmates. Not one of them teased me about the incident. Every nationality was represented in our class including two black students. At St. Joe's, I had no feelings of inferiority. The Mobilizer did not care what nationality you were. When it was time to dish it out, it didn't matter what you looked like or how you were physically built. Her discipline showed no favoritism, except for one student.

His name was Nunzio Venzueala. He sat directly behind me. The Mobilizer was upset with Nunzio. In spite of his inability to keep up with the class, she had never struck him, as she felt free to strike others. There was a defiant presence about Nunzio. No classmate wanted to cross him. One autumn day, the Mobilizer approached Nunzio with her round stick. Nunzio grabbed his ruler and leaped out of his desk. The Mobilizer swung her stick. Nunzio raised his ruler, blocked the stick and said, "On guard." The entire class had seen the movie Captain Zorro and for that one glorious day, Zorro came to life in our classroom. The class forgot their fear of the Mobilizer and the room exploded with laughter as they dueled up and down the aisle between the desks of students. The Mobilizer never caught Nunzio. He defended himself right out of the classroom and showed up the next day without a word from the Mobilizer.

Months later, in the spring of 1937, with Nunzio's encouragement, the devil took hold of my spirit. The Gifts of the Holy Spirit flew out of the classroom window. Or maybe, I thought, it wasn't the devil. It could be the gift of Fortitude flying into the window and into my heart. Nunzio was sitting directly behind me. There was a piece of paper on the classroom floor. The Mobilizer said, "Pick it up, Fred." Nunzio whispered, "Tell her you did not drop it." I summoned my courage and said, "Sister, I did not drop it." The Mobilizer left her desk with her poised pointer. Nunzio, who had witnessed me receiving at least a dozen whacks in previous months whispered, "Don't take it, run." I got up and ran around the room as the Mobilizer chased me up and down the aisles. My classmates were in awe. I could not believe it was me. It was my first act of defiance either at home, on the truck or in school. Finally, breathing heavily, she stopped. She summoned my sister Betty from the 8th grade class and told her to advise my parents that I had humiliated her in front of the entire class and should be punished accordingly.

That night, when my mother confronted me, I told her about the urinating episode, the number of times I was struck by the Mobilizer and the reason why I ran with Nunzio's coaching. On my behalf, my sister Betty spoke of the Mobilizer's reputation for striking students. Mother was shocked. She told my father. I often wondered whether my father's temper was brought to bear on the Mobilizer. I only knew that the Mobilizer seemed to have more respect for me and she never struck me again. I wondered if the Mobilizer had, indeed, forced the Gift of Fortitude out of my timid nature. I wondered if the Holy Spirit had spoken to me through Nunzio.

Like the Army drill sergeant, the Mobilizer knew the importance of exercise and recreation. There was a small schoolyard adjacent to the school. Every day, weather permitting, the Mobilizer supervised a game called dodge ball. The class would form a circle. Each student would take a turn in the middle, attempting to dodge a large beach ball thrown by circle members. This small, skinny, knock-kneed, pigeon toed, dark skinned boy was the most difficult kid to hit with the ball. I dodged it, leaped over it and enjoyed every minute of it.

Later in my life, my teacher-brother Ken said that the sixth grade is a turning point in the life of a student. This is the time when habits (good or bad), are formed, changed, motivated, encouraged or hampered. Sister Amabilis was faced with a most difficult class of inner city students. Nunzio was the only member of the class to escape her wrath. I sensed that she had a special affection for Nunzio because Nunzio was being the best he could be. Years after he left the sixth grade, Nunzio visited Sister Amabilis because he knew she cared about him. If Sister Amabilis felt that a student had potential, she was determined to nurture it, even if it required a shock treatment. One may question her methods, but for me, that was the beginning of my awareness that I could do much better in school if I tried harder.

In addition to the motivation of Sister Amabilis, *and far more importantly*, there was a five-minute highly emotional conversation with my warden on the prison-truck that dramatically changed my motivation, attitude and study habits. (This is recorded in a later chapter.)

I went from an average student to third from the top of our class. Although Sister Amabilis used fear as a weapon in teaching, her motive was to get you to strive to reach the limits of your potential. When I entered the seventh grade, I thought her nickname should have been The Motivator. I remember her with love and respect, in spite of the fact that she caused me to wet my pants in front of an entire class.

CHAPTER 8

Sister Marietta—The Pacifier

St. Joseph's Parish consisted of a grammar school, a commercial high school, an orphanage and a majestic house of worship serving both the inner city and the business community that surrounded it. The parish was served by Redemptorist Fathers. The Sisters of Notre Dame directed the orphanage and both the grammar and the commercial schools.

Sister Marietta was the first grade teacher. In addition, she was responsible for the training of the altar boys who served the Redemptorist Fathers during Mass, Funerals, Weddings and Novenas to Our Lady of Perpetual Help, the mother of Christ. She was gentle, sensitive, and saintly — a marked contrast to the teaching style of Sister Amabilis. She recommended Clarence Pecoraro and me for the honor of becoming altar boys. We joined six older altar boys who were also trained by Sister Marietta.

Training was after school. Serving several Redemptorist Fathers was daily. Masses started at 5:30 AM and continued every half-hour until 8 AM, not counting Sunday Masses that extended beyond 8 AM. Sister Marietta taught us the Latin responses and duties required for daily Mass, Funerals, Weddings, Benedictions and Novenas. For early Masses, with few parishioners in attendance, one altar boy was assigned to one Redemptorist Father. For the children's 8 AM Mass and Sunday Masses, when Clarence and I were assigned to serve, we executed every movement and every step, erect and in perfect unison — every genuflection, every flip and return of the altar cloth for the communion rail. We were taken for twins — the pride and joy of Sister Marieta who was proud of us and let us know it.

At Communion, we would hold a gold plate under the chin of every recipient to catch the Host in the event it fell from the fingers of the Priest. I had a chance to look closely at many faces and many mouths. I often wondered how many of them, like myself, went to the Eastman Dental Dispensary for tooth cavities or to their own dentists. I would feel a sense of guilt that I was distracted from the pomp and circumstance of assisting with the Sacrament of Holy Communion. I would also feel a sense of sorrow for people with bad teeth because I knew how much pain they would suffer from the drilling and pulling of their teeth. In those days, there were no methods of pain prevention. My visits to the Eastman Dental Dispensary were frequent. I had several teeth drilled and filled and several teeth pulled. I could not help this distraction at communion because I had truly suffered the anguish of the large drills and pliers in the hands of dental students practicing on those who could not afford to go to a Dentist.

A major benefit of being an altar boy was to be excused from the class of Sister Amabilis to serve Funeral Masses — which averaged one a week. At funeral masses, I would try to guess the relationship of those in attendance to the deceased by the amount of tears shed. The Redemptorist Fathers were gifted speakers. They would bring tears to the eyes of the relatives of the deceased that would affect me emotionally. I was moved to tears and had to reach through the buttons on my altar boy black cassock and white frock for my handkerchief. Families of the deceased would notice me crying. They knew I was not related and they would cry even harder. This was especially true of Italian Funerals that represented more than half of the Funeral Masses at St. Joseph's.

Every Wednesday afternoon at 12:15 PM, at St. Joseph's there was a Novena to the Mother of Perpetual Help, followed by a Benediction. The church overflowed with people who worked in the downtown Rochester area. I was in awe of these services — spiritually and emotionally touched by the beauty of the Latin ritual and Latin songs as well as the English songs in praise to the Mother of God. This weekly demonstration of love and faith, enriched by the singing of hundreds of worshipers, filled my heart and soul with love and peace.

One rainy morning, in preparation for the 5:30 AM weekday Mass, I woke up at 4:30 AM. It was usually a 20-minute walk to St. Joseph's. Lundy's Lane was wet and dark. My playground had turned into a frightening alley. I ran as fast as I could past the buildings with narrow separations between them. I feared that someone might leap out and grab me. As I approached the end of the alley, I witnessed a man bashing another man's head against the wall of a brick building that housed a restaurant, which was open for breakfast. Blood was pouring down the head and face of the victim. Panic stricken, I ran into the restaurant and screamed, "A man is having his head bashed in on your outside wall." I then ran the rest of the way to serve Mass and in the warmth and peace of this environment, I offered my Mass for the victim. I never knew if the victim survived or if there was an arrest. For every early morning Mass that followed, I became the fastest 11-year-old who ever ran up Lundy's Lane.

In addition to the honor of being an altar boy, which provided me opportunities to skip the class of Sister Amabilis, the entire sixth grade class was excused for an hour a week to be with the music teacher, also a Sister of Notre Dame. Spiritual music became an important part of my childhood. Singing praises to the Lord, to the Mother of God and to St. Joseph at Mass, Benediction and Novenas illuminated the Seven Gifts that I carried in my heart and soul.

Sister Marietta was not only an altar boy teacher; she was a friend who stayed in contact with me for the next ten years of my life, often getting me to pinch hit, even as an adult, on Sundays as an Altar Boy at St. Joseph's Church.

CHAPTER 9

Compelling Lessons from the Warden

Continuing from the first chapter, the bitter winter of 1937-1938 finally came to an end. The 1938 summer recess signaled the return to my 100-hour weekly sentence. I was now twelve years old. The summer routine was the same — get up at 4 AM, go to the public market, buy the produce and call on the regular customers. The rolling prison would return home around 9 PM Monday through Friday. On Saturdays, we would again arrive around 7 PM and my warden would be in the Hedges Bar & Grill on Leo & Remington Streets, as late as 11 PM trying to sell the remaining fruits & vegetables.

My warden was generally the last huckster to leave the public market. Hucksters paid rent for their stalls for the hours that began at 5 AM and ended at 12 noon. Hucksters would trim their produce, leaving the refuse in the gutter for the clean up crews. The clean up crews would generally start at 9 AM because most hucksters had departed for their day of business by 8 AM. On this day in 1937, my warden was late one morning. I thought he was in the public market restaurant "having coffee." It was about 9:30 AM. He was trimming his produce when the Market Master approached him and said, "Mike, you are holding up my cleaning crew. Why can't you get out of here on time like the other hucksters?" My warden angrily replied, "I rent this stall until 12 noon so don't bother me." The Market Master said, "You foreigners are all alike. You come to America and act like you own the country." In an instant, my strong and husky 39-year-old warden wrestled the Market Master down into the gutter face down. As my father rubbed his face into the rotted refuse along the curbstone, he said, in his Arabic inflection in broken English, "Don't you ever call me a foreigner again, I am a citizen of the United States of America and don't you ever forget It.". The Market Master, pale as a ghost, fled from the scene. I thought he had left to summon help from the police. The police did not arrive but the Market Master never bothered my father again. Although I was frightened by the possible physical harm that my warden could have caused, I felt a tinge of pride for his strength and his spirit.

His strength was demonstrated on another occasion at the public market restaurant. After the truck was attractively prepared for the warden's first customer, my warden would move his truck to the market restaurant. One summer day in 1938, I realized why. I was waiting for my warden in the truck. Unlike the winter, when the truck could be locked, my summer prison confinement included security work — to prevent anyone from stealing produce when the warden was away from the open truck. My attention was attracted to the front door of the restaurant. I heard the restaurant proprietor screaming, "Mike, what the hell do you think you're doing?" My warden was carrying a coin-operated pinball machine through the front door of the restaurant. He was loading it onto the truck in spite of the heated objections coming from the mouth of the proprietor, who said, "You just can't do that, Mike, are you out of your mind?" My warden, whose face was red with anger said, "I put enough nickels in this machine to own it, so I'm taking it." The police arrived. He calmed my father down while the proprietor and his helper returned the heavy pinball machine to the restaurant. This was my first awareness that my father was putting coins in a machine with the hope of a pay off. I reasoned that this was why he spent up to an hour a day in the public market before we called on our first customer. I wondered if he did not want me to see this behavior as a bad example. I wondered if this was why he did not let me join him for a hot breakfast.

My prisoner allowance, which I frugally saved to give to my mother, was the value of empty peck baskets made of thin layers of woven wood, which I would stack in fours and sell back to the willing farmers for five cents each. At the end of the summer my basket transactions totaled about 1200. This amounted to $60 for about 1000 hours of summer work or about 6 cents per hour.

How Not to Sell Strawberries

When I turned 12, in the summer of 1938, during the Strawberry Season, in an effort to increase the family's income, my warden would buy several crates of strawberries at the Public Market. That meant getting home later so I was not happy with the strawberry season. One day, my warden decided that he would take my eight-year-old brother Joe along to assist with strawberry sales after finishing with the regular customers. At around 7 PM, he would start with a narrow street in Rochester. He gave Joe and me two peck baskets. In each basket, there were three quarts of strawberries. He positioned Joe on one side of the street and me on the other side. As we rang doorbells or knocked on doors, he would drive his truck ever so slowly slightly ahead of us, repeatedly yelling at the top of his voice, "Berries, Berries, Home Grown Strawberries." His strong voice seeped through the open front screen doors on this warm summer evening. After covering the second street, I came back to the truck to replace the six quarts that I had sold. My warden said, "Fred, what are you doing wrong?" I said, "What do you mean Pa?" He said, "Your brother is eight years old. You are twelve. Yet he comes back to the truck for more strawberries four times to your one. What are you doing wrong?" In a mildly angry tone, I said, "Maybe he has the better side of the street." He said, "No, you are doing something wrong. I am going to watch you." My world was about to collapse. My warden, who has ordered me around for four years, who gets me up at 4 AM every summer day for six days a week, who makes me a prisoner for 100 hours a week, who locks me in the truck while calling on Hedges Bar & Grill in the winter, who has a broken English accent is going to humiliate and embarrass me in front of other people by watching me selling strawberries. I was trapped. There was no other choice. I went to the next house while he stood by me. I knocked on the door. The lady of the house appeared. I held the two peck baskets in my hand loaded with three quarts of strawberries in each peck. While holding the two peck baskets, I stood at her looking through her screen door and with my head shaking no, I said, "You do not want to buy any strawberries, do you?" The shaking "no" of my head succeeded in getting a "no" from the lady of the house. After all, I thought, she can see the strawberries in the peck baskets. If she wants any she will say so. If she likes them, she'll ask the price. If she likes the berries and the price, she would buy some.

My father spared me any public humiliation in front of the lady who said "no." He walked me back to the truck and said, "Do you want to get home earlier tonight." I said, "Yes." He said, "We go home early when we sell all the strawberries. There is a dumb way to sell strawberries. There is a smart way to sell strawberries. I will show you the smart way. Are you ready to learn?" I said, "Yes, Pa." He took the two peck baskets out of my hand. He walked up to the next house. He laid the two peck baskets on the porch. He picked up one of the quarts in readiness for the lady of the house. He rang the doorbell. The lady appeared. He said, "Good evening m'am, these strawberries were picked early this morning on a farm in Webster New York. As he held the quart of strawberries in his hand, he said, "Look how fresh they are." Then he immediately shifted his body to allow the contents of the entire quart to roll up his arm to expose every berry and with excitement said, "See, there is not a bad berry in the quart. No mold. No bad ones. They are 10 cents a quart. Three for a quarter. Do you want one or three?" The lady said, "I'll take three." When we left the porch, he said, "You think I was lucky, huh?" I thought maybe he was. I said, "I don't know." "OK, he said, we'll try the next house." He repeated his sales approach. The lady took one. I was convinced. I practiced the lesson. It was a remarkable experience.

It helped to build my self-confidence. By changing my attitude, I caught up to the sales of my eight-year-old brother, Joe who, by his very outgoing nature had quickly learned the art of selling strawberries smart, not dumb. This five-minute lesson from my warden was a tremendous confidence booster.

(My brother Joe and I successfully used this selling technique with other high quality products for the rest of our lives. At age 24, when I was involved with a franchise for a coffee vending machine, I built a very successful business by serving the best cup of coffee from a vending machine. After convincing the customer of the quality in side-by-side taste comparisons with competitive machines, I would ask, "Do you want one on every floor or every other floor?" Or, "Do you want one in the center of your factory or on either side?" I never again gave a business prospect a choice between yes or no.)

My Warden's Five-Minute Lesson That Changed My Life

That same year, 1938, at age 12, shortly after the Strawberry Lesson, there was a dramatic event that had a major impact on my attitude on the prison-truck.

I had just completed a delivery to a customer on a third floor of an apartment without elevators.

When I returned to the truck, my warden asked if I had returned the two empty peck baskets from the third floor customer. Knowing that we called on this customer every other day, I politely said, "I forgot, I'll pick them up day after tomorrow." In a mild voice, he said, "No, you get them now, they are worth five cents each." I don't know what possessed me. In an instant I thought of the gift of "Fortitude". I wondered if and when I would ever use that gift in talking to my warden. I quickly thought, "I'm twelve years old. Do I speak up, or as always, do I just obey? In a soft tone of voice, I replied, "Pa, they are my baskets. I sell 120 a week back to the farmers to earn $6.00. That is how you pay me for my work. I give $5.80 to mom to buy whatever she needs for the house. I keep 20 cents a week for penny candy. Since they are mine, why can't I make the decision to pick them up day after tomorrow?"

He never expected this response. His face turned red with anger. He pounded on the steering wheel of the truck and screamed, "No, get them now. They are worth 5 cents. Day after tomorrow you may forget to pick them up. Do you hear me? Get them now?"

I ran to the third floor, politely asked the customer for the empty baskets. I rushed down to the truck prison without walls. I cannot say my face was "red with anger". I was too dark for any red to show but I was burning up inside. I slammed the basket in the back of the truck, opened the truck door, swallowed hard and with all the might I could muster slammed the truck door shut. I sat in rigid silence, fearing a display of temper from my warden for the first anger I had ever shown in the past five years on the Truck-Prison.

He started the truck without saying a word. My fists were clenched; I felt the blood rushing to my head. By slamming the truck door shut, I had dared to use one of the gifts against my warden — the gift of Fortitude. As my warden drove a distance to his next customer, he remained silent for several minutes. Did he sense my anger? Did he choose to ignore it? Was he aware that I had not shown anger before?

With a calm and quiet voice, he broke the silence and said, "You hate this work, don't you?" This was my opening; this was my opportunity; this was my chance to "Counsel" with him, to let him know how I felt from the depth of my heart. I could not lie. He never missed church on Sunday. He always wanted his son to be truthful. I gritted my teeth and shouted, "Yes, I hate this work." He then calmly asked, "How would you like to be a huckster for the rest of your life." At age twelve, in our five years together on this prison-truck, he never heard a tone of anger in my voice. This was my chance to let him know how much I hated being a Prisoner of the Truck. My voice, choking with emotion, loudly screamed, "I would rather die."

Again in an unexpected calm voice, he said, "Why do you think I do it?" I did not expect this response. I expected a long and stern lecture. I wondered where this "Counseling" was going. Fortified by the previous rage in my voice that he seemed to accept, and gritting my teeth in anger I said, "I don't know why you do it."

As he gripped the wheel of the prison truck to make a turn onto a street to call on the next customer, again in a calm voice, he said, "Well let me tell you. I am a huckster because I do not have an education and if you don't want to be a huckster for the rest of your life, you have to get a good education. I watch you on this truck. You always have a long face when you are waiting in the truck. I am sick and tired of looking at you. Instead of a long face, when I am busy taking an order or at Hedges on Saturday night, you should have your books and your bible on the truck. You should study your books. You have lots of time. You are not that busy. In the summer, you can study in the daylight when you are waiting for me to come from a customer; you can study under the streetlights while I am calling on Hedges. In the winter, while you are inside the truck, you can study under the kerosene lamp the way Abraham Lincoln studied under a candle." He pulled up to the next customer. This ended our "counseling" session.

From that day forward, I carried my schoolbooks, my prayer book and my bible on the truck. My warden had spoken. He wanted me to find my own key to the lock of the prison, and I was determined that I would. I would no longer sulk or feel sorry for myself. I would study - it was the way to freedom – it was the way to use my idle time to be free of this 100 hour a week prison and the terrible, lonely long four hour Saturday nights when the prison was parked outside of Hedges Bar & Grill.

Shooting Dice

My warden gave me another heart rendering lesson that summer. The workday had ended. He stopped into a mechanic's garage seeking repairs needed for his truck. The mechanic advised him that it would take about two hours to perform the repair. In the corner of the garage, four men were shooting dice. My father watched them for about 15 minutes. He began to put money down on the concrete floor, sometimes winning and sometimes losing. The game was in progress around 7 PM that weekday evening; it did not end until 9 PM. My father's purse was empty. He traded fruits and vegetables for the mechanical service performed, much to the objection of the mechanic who had no other choice. I was in a state of shock. I could not believe that all the income collected on that particular day had been wiped out.

As we drove home, my warden broke the first five minutes of silence as if he was suddenly aware that I had witnessed this tragic event. He said, "Do you see what I did? I lost every cent we earned by working all day. I made a big mistake. You see how much I suffer now. You see that I have to work harder to pay our bills. It was a foolish thing for me to do. It is not good for me to take the bread out of the mouth of another family no more than he should take the bread from our family. Gambling is a bad thing. Let this be a lesson to you. If you are ever tempted to gamble in your life, remember this day."

My warden was so full of sadness that I felt compassion for him. I tried to conceal the tears that were rolling down my cheek as we finally drove home. As the summer of 1938 ended, I was becoming sensitive to the humanity of my warden and the life struggles he was facing.

Again, I related this experience to the seven gifts of the Holy Spirit. My warden had "counseled" with me about the "art" of selling strawberries. He "counseled" with me about my negative attitude on the truck and how I could turn the prison into a study center and he warned me about losing my hard earned money or taking the hard earned money of someone else.

As a result of the "counseling," I became more "knowledgeable." I "understood" he was a huckster because he did not have an American education. He did not want that life for me. This new awareness made me a bit wiser – "wisdom." I would have the "fortitude" to focus on my studies on the truck-prison, and with God's help, I would see the day when I was no longer a Prisoner of the Truck.

In spite of this new feeling, I dreaded the upcoming winter Saturdays when I would be locked in the back of the truck, sitting on an orange crate next to a kerosene lamp, feeling non-productive for 95% of that day, while I waited for my warden to end his Saturday call at the Hedges Bar and Grill on the corner of Joseph Avenue and Leo Streets.

When we arrived home, my mother would serve our late dinner. There was a dreadful silence between them. My father was not very talkative. I wondered if she suspected something by his mood. As I left the room, I heard them speaking in Arabic. I did not like the tone of my father's voice. I wondered if it had something to do with money she needed to buy groceries.

I hastened to my bed, making room on my pillow for my Guardian Angel, as I did since the first grade Sacrament of Holy Communion — ever mindful of the painting of the Guardian Angel who watched over the young boy standing at the edge of a steep cliff.

CHAPTER 10

Age 12 to 14 Activities In and Out of Prison

Stein's Bakery

We moved to Ormond Street when I turned 12. My mother gave me a pleasant assignment. During the school mornings when I was not in prison, I would go to Stein's Bakery about a half-mile down the street. My job was to buy a dozen of "yesterdays" doughnuts. "Yesterday" was a better word than "stale." During my visit at 6 AM, I found the front store of the bakery closed. I went around to a side door and entered. Baking operations were in full swing. The sweet smell of baked goods permeated the production space. The heat of the ovens felt good to my cold body, especially on winter mornings. A heavy man approached me. He was dressed in white with a large baker's hat. His black shoes were white with flour. His uniform had spots of colors from the fillings inside the doughnuts, dusted with traces of flour and powdered sugar. In broken English he said, "What can I do for you young man?" I held out a ten-cent piece and said, "My mother wanted me to buy a dozen of yesterday's doughnuts." He walked over to a bin while I followed him. He said, "Do you want them mixed?" I said, "Yes". To avoid crushing the doughnuts, he gently put 12 of assorted yesterday's doughnuts into a brown paper bag and said, "I'm giving you an extra one". I said, "Gee, thanks" and rushed home with my family's first taste of doughnuts for breakfast.

After a few more visits, he must have noticed my big brown eyes popping out of my skinny 11 year old, pigeon-toed, knock-kneed, bowlegged, dark-skinned body, peering at the fresh doughnuts coming out of the ovens. After filling my bag with 13 of yesterday's doughnuts, he went to the container of hot fresh doughnuts, dipped two of them with liberal amounts of powdered sugar and gave them to me in a separate smaller bag and said, "These are for you." My eyes opened even wider as I said, "thank you Mister". My enthusiastic appreciation was rewarded each day thereafter with two warm fresh doughnuts of my choice — glazed, assorted jelly flavors, cream filled, etc. I took this bag to Church with me every morning. After receiving Holy Communion, I ate those doughnuts with fiendish delight.

I used to ponder on my failure to share these oven-fresh doughnuts with my brothers and sisters. The baker said, "These are for you." Yet, I wondered whether I was selfish by not sharing the fresh doughnuts with my brothers and sisters. I decided that this was not greed. It was not a venial sin and did not deserve mentioning in my weekly confession. After all, I thought, the Prisoner of the Truck deserved this special parole treat and since I didn't eat any of yesterday's doughnuts, family members could have more than one each. A few years later, buying the doughnuts fell to my brother Joe who was four years younger.

(One of these days, I must ask Joe if the generous baker treated him as well as he did me. If I know Joe, he probably talked the baker into three fresh ones.)

The George Eastman Dental Dispensary

Whether it was the penny candy store or Stein's Bakery or the fudge that my sister Betty made, I found myself facing the agony of visiting the George Eastman Dental Dispensary on Main Street for on-going cavity treatment and pulling of teeth by young men being trained to become dentists. Thanks to the founder of Kodak, this facility was available for anyone who could not afford a dentist. This was a terrifying experience. Whenever I had a toothache, my mother would make an appointment for me. I entered the waiting area, a massive room with high ceilings, where patients checked in. There were rows and rows of dental chairs in one large room with high ceilings. After my first visit, they seemed to resemble the electric chairs I had seen in newspaper photographs that were used to kill convicts, with two people in white near each chair prepared to conduct the execution.

As one of the wounded victims left a dental chair, those waiting in turn would be called. After listening to the moans and screams of the patients, it was a long and frightening walk to the chair. I prayed that I would get a dental trainee with a kind looking face. The white cloth was placed over my shirt. A nurse stood by to assist. The drilling device was not the high tech version of today. It was slow moving, requiring considerably more time and excruciating pain in the dental chair. There was no Novocain then. I gripped the arm of the dental chair praying to Jesus to minimize my agony. By age 14, I had over twenty cavities filled and six teeth pulled. If I had believed then that it had something to do with penny candy, fudge and fresh doughnuts, I would have given all of them up after my first visit to George Eastman's Dental Dispensary, my benefactor of Kodak fame.

Spiritual Bouquets

In St. Joseph's Church, there were containers that held many leaflets. One of these containers held "Spiritual Bouquet Cards." Artistic renderings of Jesus and his Blessed Mother decorated the cover and interior of the card. A plain white envelope was included. The good sisters of Notre Dame encouraged their students to give Spiritual Bouquets as gifts to our loved ones. On the card itself, you could list the number of Masses, Rosaries, Stations of the Cross, and special prayers to the Mother of God and to the Heart of Jesus.

As an altar boy, I served many Masses. In addition, I began to make special daily visits to St. Joseph's Church when it was inactive. The inner Church would be very silent and awesome in its dimension and beauty. The air was cool. There were so many objects of beauty to behold on the ceiling, walls and altars. It was a place to pray and to meditate. Jesus was present in the form of a breaded host on a special locked gold chamber on the main altar. Often, there were a dozen people lost in the immensity of the Church benches, kneeling in prayer and meditation. Half of them were Italian women dressed in black mourning clothes, their lips moving in silent prayer.

As in every Catholic Church, St. Joseph's had the Fourteen Stations of the Cross. There were seven stations on either side of the Church. Each station showed the various stages of the persecution and death of Jesus. With my prayer book I would walk from Station to Station, just as the good Fathers did in public prayer. I would genuflect and say, "We adore Thee, Oh Christ and we Praise Thee." I would rise and say, "By thy Holy Cross, Thou hast redeemed the world." There was a meditation recital and a prayer at each station of the 14 steps leading to the crucifixion. In each step, I would imagine that I was there walking with the crowd alongside Jesus. I imagined the sorrow I would feel for his suffering. I wondered if I would have hidden in fear if I were one of his disciples.

In the prayer book, there were "Litanies" or Prayers to the Blessed Virgin Mary to the Sacred Heart of Jesus. I would recite these prayers. After a 50-year absence from these Litanies, I still remember portions of the magnificent Litany to the Blessed Virgin Mary. Each Litany is followed by, "Pray for us." In praise to the Mother of God She was referred to as, "Mirror of Justice, Seat of Wisdom, Cause of our Joy, Mystical Rose, Arch of the Covenant, Gate of Heaven, Morning Star, Help of the Sick, Refuge of Sinners, Queen of Angels, Queen of Saints, etc".

Before Mothers or Fathers day, I would fill in the blanks of the Spiritual Bouquet card. 100 Masses. 100 Holy Communions. (This was difficult since I could not have anything to eat or drink before Mass. I consumed the bag of fresh doughnuts after each Mass). 24 Stations of the Cross. 50 Litanies to the Blessed Virgin. 50 Litanies to the Sacred Heart. Twenty Rosaries. 10 Wednesday Novenas to the Blessed Virgin Mary.

In the years that followed, there has never been a gift of any material value that I have ever given to my mother or father that seemed to generate more emotion and tears of love, joy and gratitude than the annual "Spiritual Bouquets" of my childhood.

(At this moment in my writing, I am motivated to say that the Prisoner of the Truck did not consider his father his Warden on the following days: Father's Day, Christmas, New Year's, January 6, the Feast of the Epiphany, his birthday of July 4, (chosen by him upon immigration), and on Sundays when he drove his family to church or picnics in the converted "fun vehicle on wheels". On these specific days, he was not my Warden and I was not his Prisoner. Rather, I was his loving son and he was my loving father.)

Easter Sunday and Welfare

At age 12, I became more keenly aware of the lingering impact the depression of 1929 continued to have on the lives of so many people. Just before Easter, I learned about the U.S. Government Program called "Welfare". On Easter Sunday, it was traditional in the Roman Catholic Eastern Rite church for children of the parish to march around the church several times in the Easter procession. Parents, who remained in their pews, would beam with pride as they watched their children parade.

Some parents would carry a baby, dressed in white, in their arms. Girls would be dressed in lovely white or light colored dresses and hats decorated with lace, all of different styles. Boys would wear navy blue short pants, white shirts and navy blue socks and ties. Shoes were black, either of paten leather or polished to a mirror shine.

Many, who paraded around the church, carried large one to two-inch diameter candles they had purchased. These candles were impressively decorated with religious symbols. Other parishioners carried small one-quarter inch diameter candles provided by the parish. The differences in candle sizes and candle decorations seemed to distinguish between those who had money to spare and those who didn't. My sister Betty, fourteen, myself, twelve, brother Joe, eight, sister Anne, six, brother Jim, four, sister Vicky, two, were dressed in simple but new clothing carrying small candles. Joe and I would guard our brothers and sisters, watching the flames on the church-provided candles to prevent any accidental burning of hair or clothing. I knew we must be poor by the size of our candles but I knew we were rich in love and togetherness.

Betty, who gave so unselfishly of her time, love and devotion as a second mother to all of us, carried my baby sister, Deanna who stared at the candle in Betty's hand. The honor of naming Deanna had been given to Betty because she was held in such high esteem by our parents. My father sat in the front seat of the church, serving as a Deacon, assisting the Pastor in the Mass, then spoken in both Arabic & Greek rather than Latin. Few Roman Catholics realize that there are two divisions in the Roman Catholic Church. In the Western Rite, Mass was said in Latin. In the Eastern Rite, Mass was said in the Native Language of a particular country. Both Catholic rites are under the Roman Catholic Pope of Rome.

In preparation for Easter, on Palm Sunday afternoon, my mother and father would pile the children up in his truck and head for the many competitive clothing stores on Joseph Avenue to fit the children with new clothes. As the various clothing merchants tallied their bills, my father spent considerable time negotiating the final volume discount and whatever he could trade in fruits and vegetables. My father had given in to Welfare. Our shoes were obtained from a shoe annex, which catered to Welfare persons. Welfare included coal for winter heat, milk, bread and shoes. In the shoe annex, as all of us were being fitted, I noted that my father's face was flushed with humiliation and embarrassment. I knew from his conversations with my mother that both of them considered this a deep shame on the family name. I prayed that someday, I could help to eliminate this shame, especially since I knew how much it disturbed my mother.

Prison on Wheels – A Sunday Fun Vehicle

The Prison on Wheels became our family's only means of transportation on Sundays. On summer Sundays, my mother would sit in the small cab section with my father and the youngest baby on her lap. The enclosure for the back of the "winter" truck was removed. Left over fruits and vegetables were stored in a garage, covered with quilts and blankets to minimize spoiling. The children would sit on empty orange crates nestled against each side of the truck. The metal side of each side of the truck served as a backrest for its passengers. We would sit on either side, facing each other.

(In the winter, when the truck was enclosed, we sat on orange crates in the middle of the truck, surrounded by fresh fruits and vegetables. Betty had to constantly remind us that we could not break our fast until after Communion. This made the half-hour ride to St. Nicholas on Remington Street seem that much longer. The ride home was easier. Bananas, apples, oranges and grapes were a break-the-fast-treat.)

Each of these summer Sundays were special times for all of us. They were filled with joy, love, happiness, songs and sharing. Almost every Sunday, one of the brothers or sisters had a friend who joined us for church or picnics. It was rare that a Sunday would go by when we did not sing in the back of the truck on our way to and from Church or to and from a summer picnic. To avoid any possibility of an accident, my father drove slowly. In the summer months, occupants of passing cars would smile as they drove past. As a passenger vehicle, we were an uncommon sight. Children in automobiles would stare at us, it seemed with envy, as we happily sang in a spirit of family togetherness. I never wished for a family automobile. On these occasions, my prison-truck became a carrier of love and joy on wheels, if only for one day a week, and my warden became my Sunday father who made it possible.

I entered the seventh grade at St. Joseph's with a new attitude and purpose. I would study at home and on the truck. Higher marks became my new goal. Sister Frieda, the seventh grade teacher was calm and patient. Nunzio, who left his mark of Zorro in the sixth grade, did not return. I missed him and regretted that I never thanked him for teaching me to be somewhat courageous under the fire of Sister Amabilis. I do not recall any traumatic events in the seventh grade. The seeds of motivation for studying, planted by my Warden, began to bear fruit. My mother and warden were pleased with the added gold stars that began to appear on my report card. I was learning that recognition and honor could make up for the sense of inferiority I continued to feel in school and on my warden's truck.

Inner City Fun & Games

In the fall, when the leaves were dry, kids would stuff them loosely into empty cans punched with holes. A long single piece of wire or rope was attached to two opposite sides of the can. The length depended on the height of the user. The dry leaves were lit with a match and the can was swung around in many different circular paths. This emitted a large stream of smoke, kept alive by the speed of the swing. To the kids of the neighborhood, the smell of the burning leaves, as they paraded up and down the street, was the wonderful autumn perfume of the inner city.

In the winter, we attached cheap dual-blade ice skates to our shoes and skated on patches of ice that formed on deserted plots of land in the neighborhood. Pieces of cardboard were cut from cartons found in the trash of a nearby ice cream plant. They were used as toboggans on the nearby slopes of the New York Central Railroad. Lundy's Lane, a downhill alley, infrequently traveled, pitched downward for about a quarter mile making it ideal for sledding.

During winter thaws, as the snow melted on Lundy's Lane, a mini-river of water would flow from Cumberland Street where it began to the end of the Alley. The water took different paths down the quarter mile stretch, rushing over and under the transparent ice. This was ideal for matchstick races. Kids would paint their matchsticks different colors and the races would begin. There were usually four to eight contestants. Each would keep pace with his matchstick, cheering it ever forward in its 20-minute journey to the end of the alley. If an obstacle in its path stopped the match, contestants were allowed to assist with a slight nudge of their finger. At the end of each race, a new race would begin. Whoever won two races was the acknowledged winner of the Annual Lundy Lane Alley Race. Melting snow weather conditions had to be ideal and we were ever watchful for the right time. Occasionally a vehicle would drive down the alley, crushing our water racecourse with its massive wheels but the rushing water found new paths and new directions in its persistence and determination to keep moving forward. In reflection, this example and use of the melting snow of Lundy's lane is very much like life itself — we find new obstacles— we find new ways around them.

In the summers, on Sundays after church, inner city kids chose sides and played baseball on the street, stopping often to permit traffic flow. Others roller-skated with inexpensive skates attached to their shoes. Sidewalks were marked with chalk for skipping games. Jumping rope, card games, jacks and other inventive games rounded out spontaneous and unorganized recreational activity. Kids continued to gather at the small candy store, where a penny would buy candy and a nickel, a popsicle or a coke.

(It should be noted that in the summer of 1939, postage stamps were three cents, a pound loaf of bread was eight cents, milk was 14 cents a quart, gasoline was 19 cents a gallon, an average house cost $6,900, a movie 10 cents, a trolley ride 10 cents round trip. The minimum wage was 30 cents per hour. This should help the reader to understand that the 120 baskets that I sold for five cents each represented good buying power for my mother's needs. However, if $6.00 a week for 120 baskets involved 100 hours of work, my wages were six cents per hour in prison wages compared to the minimum wage of 30 cents per hour.)

Two More Years of *Summer* Prison

My prison work continued through 1939 and 1940, ages 13 and 14. My books became my constant companions. In the *summer* on Saturday nights from about 7 PM to 10 or 11 PM, my Warden continued to stop at Hedges Bar & Restaurant at the corner of Leo and Remington Streets in Rochester to sell remaining fruits and vegetables. He would park under a streetlight so that I could study. On occasions, I would sneak a look through a narrow crack in the window of the bar. I would see my warden playing a dice game with other men with a cigar in his mouth. I could not see the top of the bar. I could not see any exchange of money. In other sections of the smoke-filled bar, I observed men with their arms around women. My warden would occasionally come back to the truck, load up a peck or two of fruits and vegetables and return to the bar. I began to think that husbands, who were out late drinking, took home fruits and vegetables as peace offerings to their wives. I never asked my warden questions and he never volunteered any information. Trucks were not refrigerated in those days and certain produce had to be sold before spoiling. They would not be fresh by the following Monday. On these "summer Saturdays", I felt like I was the prison-guard of the fruits and vegetables while my father tried to sell them.

Two More Years of *Winter* Prison

In the *winter*, on Saturday nights when I was padlocked in the back of the truck, I wondered why I was needed. The fruits and vegetables were secure. I was not allowed in the bar, not even for a hot meal. I wondered if my father was trying to protect me from patron behavior in the bar that he did not want me to see. I made no deliveries. In spite of my books, the time from 7 PM to 11 PM seemed to go so slowly. My mind would drift to thoughts of my warm home and loving mother. I wanted to be with my brothers and sisters or playing outdoors with friends.

The pattern was the same. I would sit on an empty orange crate with my back up against a sack of potatoes, remove my shoes and put my stocking feet on the kerosene lamp to keep them warm. My dinner consisted of fruits and vegetables. In addition to tomatoes, cucumbers, lettuce, radishes, celery, onions, green onions and carrots, I ate raw potatoes, turnips and parsnips. I ate the green stems of the green onions and chewed on the green stems of the carrots. I would read under the light of the kerosene lamp. I drank water from one quart glass of water and urinated in another.

Grammar School Achievement

Seventh Grade

At the end of the seventh grade, in a class of 35 students, my marks were the third highest. Angelo Costanza, the son of a grocery merchant in the inner city neighborhood, was first. Margaret, a lovely freckled-faced girl with red hair, who lived outside the inner city, was second. My effort had been rewarded. I went from an average student to an excellent student and developed a new sense of scholastic competitiveness sparked by the five-minute conversation with my Warden the previous summer.

As the number one boy in scholastic achievement, in the spring of that year, Angelo Costanza earned a free six-dollar year round membership to the YMCA (the equivalent of 120 empty baskets or my week's wages). He turned it down. I found myself entering the lobby of the YMCA with great enthusiasm and excitement. Awestruck, I toured the active basketball court and the running track on the upper level. Since I did not know anyone, I thought I would first use the swimming pool. I was assigned a locker and given a towel. I saw a sign that said you must shower before entering the pool. I showered, put on my bathing suit and headed for the pool. An attendant yelled, "Hey kid, did you take a shower?" I said, "Yes." He then said, "Where are you going with that bathing suit?" I said, "To swim." He said, "We don't wear bathing suits in the pool." Trying to conceal my shock, I replied "Oh!" I went back to the locker room to contemplate what I heard. I could not believe that the Young Men's Christian Association would have a swimming pool where people would swim naked. I took off my swimsuit, wrapped a towel around my bow-legged, pigeon-toed, knock-kneed skinny frame and walked quietly by the attendant. He did not utter a word. He did not ask me to remove the towel. I entered the pool area. I could not believe my eyes. There were two men in the pool, stark naked. Never in my childhood had I seen a naked grown man - maybe a statute or a painting, but not a live naked man. I knew the story of Adam and Eve. I knew the word Christian was in the YMCA. Therefore, I reasoned, it must be OK. I wondered if women would come into the pool naked. I avoided any eye contact with the men, waited until they turned away, hung my towel on a hook and quickly stepped into the shallow end of the pool, breathing a sigh of relief. They couldn't see my private parts, and I couldn't see theirs. Then one of the men lifted his weight from the edge of the pool, and I saw the whiteness of his bottom. He reached for his towel. While he dried his head with the towel, I gazed at the front of his lower body. This altar boy saw this man's private parts so much larger and hairier than his. I dipped my full body into the pool and pretended that I was swimming in the shallow water. In the following school months, I made the big adjustment. Naked boys and men in the swimming pool became routine. I enjoyed many of the activities and experiences of the YMCA, thanks to Angelo Costanza. The summer of 1939 finally ended.

At 13, I entered the eighth grade. Sister Philinilla was kind and patient. It was a peaceful school year. I continued to serve the Fathers at St. Joseph's — regular masses, weddings, funerals and Wednesday devotions to Our Blessed Mother. I learned that there were men's day and ladies' day for the YMCA swimming pool. In thinking about swimming naked, I reasoned that Adam and Eve, because of their sin against God, were ashamed to be seen naked by each other. I thought if Adam had a brother, it would be OK if Adam saw his brother naked and if Eve had a sister, he could see her naked. I wondered if a man and woman, who were married, could see each other naked, and as I write this, I must admit that I still don't know if the ladies of 1939 really swam naked on ladies' day. No matter, in 1939, I thought the Young Men's Christian Association had to know right from wrong. I was not ashamed of my nakedness among the boys and men of the YMCA. I was dreadfully afraid of sinning by being seen naked by a girl or seeing a girl who was naked, especially a girl who suddenly seemed to no longer have the body of a boy. In learning more about Confession from our Catechism and Confession Guide Book, I knew that the Sixth Commandment covered the waterfront. "Thou shall not commit adultery" included any "impure acts, thoughts or desires." I breezed through confession with, "Bless me Father for I have sinned, I had about two impure thoughts and desires since my last confession, I disobeyed my parents once, I used God's name in vain twice, I had unkind thoughts about my teacher once and that is all Father". I would hear Father's voice saying, "Is there anything else?" I was in and out of the confessional booth in less than three minutes. My penance took about five minutes and I was extremely grateful for the coaching of the good Sisters. To get through the sixth commandment that easily made the Sacrament of Penance seem simple compared to the Eastman Dental Dispensary.

Eighth Grade

In the eighth grade, I wanted to be number one in the class. My Warden wondered why I wasn't. So did I. When the school year ended in 1939, no matter how hard I studied, I was second. Angelo Costanza went on to Aquinas, a well known Catholic High School for Boys and for the second time, Angelo's decision worked to my benefit. As number two, I was awarded a two-year scholarship worth $100 a year to the adjacent St. Joseph's Commercial School. At five cents per basket, my allowed prisoner income, this scholarship was the equivalent of 2,000 baskets collected and sold at the public market, the approximate number of baskets that I would collect and sell in two full summers of work. Also, it represented 333 hours of the minimum wage of

1939. This was a big deal. My mother and Warden were proud and in two years I would be free of my Prison. I looked forward with great anticipation to St. Joseph's Commercial School.

However, as I was turning 14, I had to cope with my seventh year in the summer-winter prison. On Saturdays, the Warden and his Prisoner would continue to get home about 11:00 PM. It was a long 18-hour day. Betty and my mother would still be awake. Their day had been just as long with housekeeping and childcare. The young ones were asleep. My mother would heat up a dinner for the second time that evening to feed the Warden and his Prisoner.

On weekdays in the summer, my prison hours continued from 5 AM to about 8 PM. During the weekdays, when my Warden and I were having a hot meal at home and as he counted the day's receipts after dinner, there always seemed to be a baby in a high chair watching him. The Warden showed great affection for his babies and his children before he drifted off to sleep in his favorite chair in the living room. The children had to be quiet. He would often wake a half-hour later and in a booming voice, say, "Bah", which, in Arabic, meant Father or Pa. It was traditional for Lebanese fathers to address all of their children as Bah even though Bah was the Arabic name for father. In our household, Bah meant the nearest child had to go to him immediately and say, "Yes Bah". The Warden would say, "Take off my shoes" or "Get me a glass of water". The Warden was on his feet most of the working day. His home was his castle and while in it, he was King and anyone within hearing range had to respond immediately to his beck and call and if the children were all in bed, the task fell to my saintly mother.

CHAPTER 11

Age 14 to 16 My Bike, My Typing, My Achievements and My Mabel

It was 1940. I was 14. Betty was 16, Joe 10, Anne 8, Jim 6, Vicky 4, Deanna 2 and Kenny was newborn. In the summer of 1940, we followed the move of uncles, aunts and cousins from inner city Ormond Street to inner city Evergreen Street in Rochester. Uncle Deeb and Uncle Charlie owned a duplex on 11 Evergreen Street. Uncle Deeb rented his half to my father. It had one bathroom, two bedrooms on the 2nd floor and an attic. The boys slept in the attic. My mother, dad and sisters slept on the 2nd floor. Evergreen Street was off St. Paul Street, bordering the banks of the Genesee River. The neighborhood was considered to be better than Ormond Street but it was still occupied by the poor. I had a chance to buy a used bike for $6.00. This meant that I could not give my mother my week's sale of 120 baskets. She said, "Sweetheart, you should have told me how much you wanted a bike, go buy it."

This was the bike I dreamed of from the time I was ten years old. It had a straight bar from seat to handle bars. Underneath the straight bar were two curved metal bars that gave it a distinctive streamlined look — unlike any other bike. The bike had shiny fenders on both front and back wheels that covered the balloon tires. A red reflector decorated the back fender, a battery-operated headlight lit the way at night and a bell on the handle bar operated with the twist of the thumb. It was my prized possession. I polished the frame, spokes and wheels often and oiled the gears for a constantly smooth ride. I kept the nuts on all parts of the bike tightened. It took me to distant places: Maplewood Park and its swimming pool and zoo and a street which wound down to the Genesee River where I would gaze at the wonder of the Genesee Gorge and the men who were fishing in its rushing waters. I would ride the bike throughout the neighborhood surrounding Evergreen Street, to St. Michaels Church on Clinton Avenue, to the YMCA in downtown Rochester and to St. Joseph's Church on Franklin Street.

The bike gave me a new sense of freedom. With great pride, I would take my brothers and sisters for rides. The bike became my transportation to St. Joseph's Commercial School that fall, winter and spring — a 12-mile round trip ride. On those winter days when the milk was frozen and the radio was announcing extremely cold temperatures, my mother would call Norman DeLorme who worked at Shuron Optical Company, a walking distance from St. Joseph's Commercial. Norman also lived on Evergreen Street. He was married to my first cousin Julia. I marveled at the comfort of his bucket front seat, the warmth of his car heater and the car radio that reported the morning news and weather.

Sister Marietta was pleased that I could continue to serve as an altar boy for funerals, Sunday masses and Wednesday devotions to the Mother of Perpetual Help. These services became more meaningful to me. To be an altar boy during these services; to witness the faith of the hundreds of working people who used their lunch hour for prayer; to feel the unison of the inspiring prayers and songs; to hear the magnificent organ in a wondrous church inspired by cathedrals in Germany; to listen to excellent sermons by visiting Redemptorist Missionaries; to feel the unity of the people in attendance — all of this left me in awe and a great sense of peace. The Redemptorist Fathers and the Sisters of Notre Dame were examples of love and goodness. Under the guidance of Sister Marietta, I served these loving Fathers from the time I was 12 until the time I enlisted in the Navy at 18. I shall always remember the Sisters and Fathers as being devoted, loving and committed fully to their vocations. In my memory, there was never an instance or incident with anyone else or me that would have caused this impression to waiver. Of course, there were those times in the sixth grade, when I did doubt the saintliness of Sister Amabilis and her pointing devil stick.

Sister Ludolpha was responsible for the educational program at St. Joseph's Commercial. My sister Betty graduated with honors from St. Joseph's Commercial the year that I entered. St. Joe's two-year course specialized in shorthand, typing, bookkeeping, business arithmetic, business English and business law. There were about 70 students in the school — both first and second year of which seven were boys. Sister Ludolpha was a remarkable and well-organized teacher. For assistance, she utilized the services of two or three graduates who assisted with typing and other assignments. Sister Ludolpha had a clear, soft, gentle and slow-speaking voice with a warm accent that came from her New York City upbringing. If you were disciplined, it was done with kindness and grace. If she lost her composure on very rare occasions, it was justified. Her love for all of her students was obvious in the way all were treated. She found something good to say about every student. She motivated and encouraged each of them to achieve their greatest potential. Students were flattered by her praise. For example, she would take a name like Yolanda Scortino and say, "What a beautiful name Yolando Scortino, it rolls off my tongue like a lovely song." Or, "You have such beautiful sculptured features, Idell Nesser, you could pass for a lovely Indian maiden, like Pocahontas." Or, "You have the voice of an angel, Genevieve Paris." Jimmy Flaherty, with an outgoing and loving personality, was not doing well at St. Joe's. She said to him, "Jimmy, you keep giving your school work your best effort because someday you'll be an outstanding salesman."

My first year at St. Joseph's was a busy one. During the school year, on Saturdays, I continued to take my books with me on my Prison Truck. My warden, who was now selling fruits and vegetables to the St. Joseph Sisters of Notre Dame and the Redemptorist Fathers, met Sister Ludolpha in the convent kitchen during the school year. He inquired about my progress. Sister Ludolpha spoke highly of my sister Betty's achievements in her two years at the Commercial School. She said, "Betty was very smart but Freddie has the potential to do better." My warden took this opportunity to remind me that someday Betty would be married and her husband would provide for her but I would be the bread winner of my family and therefore I should do better than Betty. Sister Ludolpha, who knew this was my warden's feelings and, I believe, in an effort to help me to measure up to my father's wishes, said to me, "I know your parents can't afford a typewriter, would you like to borrow an old Underwood typewriter from the school?" As I wheeled that typewriter home that day in my bike's basket, I knew I had to do better than Betty, and even more so, I believed that the typewriter would somehow become the key to unlocking the doors to my Prison. With the books as my companion, the Saturdays on my warden's truck seemed shorter. In the winter, as my warden had suggested, I studied inside the truck under a kerosene lamp. In the spring and fall, I studied under the street lights that my warden parked under while he went into the Saturday night bars to sell remaining fruits and vegetables and to shake the dice in the round leather holder.

In the autumn of 1941, I went to pick up my locked bike in the hallway of St. Joseph's Commercial School. The precious bike that I had waited years to buy was gone. I was devastated. Sister Ludolpha shook her head with compassion and disbelief. She suggested that I turn to St. Jude, the Saint of Impossible Situations including Lost and Found. Sister Marietta, my altar boy teacher, went even further. She gave me a holy picture of St. Jude and there was a prayer on the back of it. I walked over to St. Joseph's Church and read the prayer several times referring specifically to my stolen bike. I asked St. Jude to help me to find it; that I was lost without it. In returning home on a city bus, my mother held me and shared my grief saying, "St. Jude will help you to find your bike. You wait and see." In my travels around the big city of Rochester, New York, both on the east and west side of the Genesee River, I knew there were thousands of homes, back porches and garages. We had to find my bike while it was being ridden on the street. Our timing had to be perfect. I was aware that the odds for finding my bike were very, very slim.

One week later, on my Warden's truck, I saw a kid riding my bike. Excitedly I said, "Pa, I just saw my stolen bike, turn around." My warden said, "How do you know that's your bike?" With urgency and panic in my voice, I said, "Pa, don't ask questions. I know my bike. It is the only one in the city with curved bars running from the seat to the front and it is the color of my bike." In a first time ever demanding voice, I said, "Pa, turn this truck around and chase him." My father turned into a driveway and the truck stalled for what seemed like precious minutes. He turned the keys several times. The Model T made slow chugging sounds similar to sounds I had heard before when the battery went dead or it ran out of gas. I kept my eyes peeled on the bike and rider as they made a turn on another street. I said to my Warden, who never witnessed such emotion in me before, "Pa get this damn truck started. We're losing them." A quick prayer to St. Jude and the truck started. Around the corner of that street, we spotted the bike and rider moving slowly down the street. My Warden pulled over to the curb in front of the driver. We leaped out of the truck at the same time. The rider had stopped in front of a house. I raced up to the rider, who was about my age, 15, and seized the bike. My father was right behind me, his face flushed with excitement and anger. Before I had a chance to speak, my Warden said, "Where did you get this bike?" The kid said, "I bought it." My Warden said, "That's my boy's bike. You stole it. I want to talk to your parents. Where do they live?" He rang the bell. The boy's father answered the door and stepped outside. The father said that he bought the bike for his son. In a demanding voice, my father said, "Show me the receipt." The father, appearing to be very disturbed, said that he bought it from another boy. My Warden asked for the name of the boy. The father hesitated as if he feared to give the name. With total self-assurance, my Warden said, "Enough said, this is my son's bike. He knows his bike. I am putting it on my truck. Try to stop me and I will call the police. There are many witnesses who know my son's bike." I noticed how much bigger and taller my Warden looked. He had such a commanding presence. While the father ranted and raged, my Warden calmly put my bike on his truck and we drove away. With a feeling of great admiration for the wisdom and courage of my Warden, I said, "Thank you Pa."

My mother and family rejoiced with me when we returned home from a long day's work. At St. Joseph's Commercial, I did not just chain my bike; I received permission from Sr. Ludolpha to chain my bike to the pipes of a hot water heater. At Mass at St. Joseph's and during my special visits to the quiet church, I repeatedly expressed my gratitude and appreciation to St. Jude. To me it was my first miracle.

A year, after we moved to Evergreen Street, we moved again. Uncle Deeb rented us a small single family house he owned on 7 Durgin Street, a few houses from 11 Evergreen Street. Uncle Deeb moved his family into 11 Evergreen Street and we crowded into 7 Durgin Street. My mother took it all in stride. Ormond Street, Evergreen Street, Durgin Street — they were all inner city houses but mother had a special touch in making these small houses into homes and filling them with love.

In our neighborhood, aunts, uncles and cousins surrounded us and love permeated the Sarkis Clan.. I had two aunts living at the duplex of 9 and 11 Evergreen Street, only a hundred feet away from 7 Durgin Street. They spent most of their time in their hot and sweaty kitchens. Both of my aunts were large women. They wore summer dresses, big aprons and bandanas over their hair. Their back screen doors were only 20 feet apart in this duplex. During the daytime, their kitchens were bakeries and food commissaries, open to everyone that entered. The sweet smell of their baking and cooking would seep through the screen doors and any relative who passed knew that was an invitation to come in for a big sweaty hug, a kiss and a treat. In Arabic, they would say, "God welcomes you, come in."

On different days, my aunts cooked or baked kibbee made with lamb, wheat and pine nuts; stuffed squash, stuffed grape leaves and stuffed cabbage leaves. We would wrap these foods in the baked flat and thin Lebanese bread, about 18 inches in diameter or in smaller pita loaves that would be used for holding the prepared foods. The 18-inch bread was skillfully rolled and flipped from right hand to left hand (similar to pizza dough), and would come out of the oven piping hot, brown and puffy in spots. Some of the favorite treats were fried dough that puffed up to a golden brown. We would cover the fried dough with butter and powdered sugar or spread butter on the oven-hot 18" flat bread and roll it up into a long roll for ease of eating. Our Aunts were busy preparing to feed their own families. We did not linger in the hot kitchens. As we carried these treats outdoors to enjoy the taste and aroma, their voices, in Arabic, would follow us out of the kitchen as they said "God bless and protect you. Come again soon. You are always welcome."

I learned that I had to be careful in visiting these side-by-side kitchens in the 9 and 11 Evergreen duplex. It was essential that I visit both so as not to offend either. This held true with all of the neighborhood nephews and nieces. With their kitchen doors open, I sensed a rivalry between Aunt Cecelia and Aunt Regina to entice nephews and nieces into their kitchens using irresistible bakery aroma as bait. It was a wonderful exhibition of love and giving — one that I shall never forget.

As were all of my father's older kin, Aunt Regina and Aunt Cecelia were born in Lebanon. Aunt Regina was my father's sister, married to a cousin, my Uncle Deeb Sarkis. Aunt Cecelia was a Shaheen, married to my father's brother George. They both had large families. They both spoke English with deep accents. One hot summer day, I asked my Aunt Regina where my cousin Paul was. She said, *"He went to the somma bitch."* It was a while before I understood that she was not mad at him; that he had gone to the "summer beach" at Charlotte on Lake Ontario. Another time, when she was canning fruit, I asked her what she was canning. She said, *"I'm cannin' bitches."* Indeed, my Aunt Regina had a problem with the words "beach" and "peaches".

The typewriter did become the key to my freedom. In May of 1941, at the age of 15, I was typing 70 words per minute, the fastest typist in the class. I became an independent wage earner contributing to the support of my family. My father was no longer my warden. I found a summer job with Sam Halaby, Inc. Like my parents, Mr. Halaby, also of Lebanese heritage, had a large family. Unlike my warden, he was highly educated in sciences before he emigrated to the U.S. He was a successful entrepreneur who developed an insecticide that effectively killed roaches and yet was harmless to humans. It was called Kil-Moe. Sam was a great salesman. He would spray Kil-Moe on his babies to prove to visitors that it was harmless to humans. He would have a bartender set up a shot glass; he would fill it with Kil-Moe and would drink it. It hardly ever failed - Sam would not get sick or die and a sale would be made. In addition, Raymond Shaheen, a paint store entrepreneur, paid me for typing assignments which I did at home. My Warden had to free me. The income I earned from Sam and Ray made a far greater contribution to the family household than the empty basket income that I generated.

For the two years of 1941 and 1942, I had the same front desk at St. Joseph's Commercial. When the class was dismissed, I was the last student to leave. The girls had to pass my desk as they left the classroom. My eyes would gaze down at my desk as they passed by as if it was wrong to stare at the back of their bodies. Eventually, I began to gaze downward slightly to my right watching the girl's legs as they passed me by. By the time the first year ended, and mostly because of the publicity generated by the legs of movie star Betty Grable, I was able to identify all 63 girls in the class by the backs of their legs.

In 1942, age 15, my second year at St. Joseph's Commercial School, one of the girls in my class said, *"Fred, you have a beautiful tan"*. That same year in the fall, on a hay ride one cold evening, another girl held my hand under a blanket, gazed at me and said, *"I think you are very handsome"*. As I did when I was in the second grade looking at my pigeon toes, bowed legs, knock knees and dark skin, I went home to check out my body in the mirror. I had been too pre-occupied with my prison to notice physical changes, except for the changes going on in my genitals. I did not seem to be as pigeon-toed; if I held my feet outward, my legs did not appear to be as bowed, my body was skinny but not like a scarecrow. My skin was naturally dark and with many days on the truck-prison, was well tanned. But, I began to wonder about my pimples and my nose. I was beginning to see my nose from the corner of my eyes and was concerned that it would never stop growing. I thought, *"Dear God, just when the rest of me seems to be getting better, now I'm going to end up with pimples and a big nose."*

On December 7, 1941, I was on a stage at Benjamin Franklin High School in Rochester. In competition with every high school in the Region, I was to be given a first place award from the Veterans of Foreign Wars for an essay that I wrote. It was titled "One Nation Indivisible." A General was to present the award to me. Prior to the ceremony, a wire was delivered to a General on the stage. The General read the telegram to the audience. The Japanese attacked Pearl Harbor. With that, he quickly departed saying he must report for duty immediately. The ceremony proceeded without him. A photographer took a picture of me receiving the Award from the Commander of the VFW post that sponsored the Essay Contest. My family left the auditorium that day with mixed emotions. There was great pride in my achievement but feelings were tempered by the reality that America would be dragged into World War II.

On December 8, 1941, the Democrat and Chronicle front page blazed, "Pearl Harbor Attacked." A picture of the Post Commander and me appeared in the local section of the newspaper with a story of the Award. My warden and my mother were in the audience with my brothers and sisters. They were all very proud of this gold medal and $25 War Bond, presented to me by the Veterans of Foreign Wars in a public ceremony. Given to the son of an immigrant and publicized in the newspaper, the honor was quickly diminished by the fears of WWII. Through his Arabic newspaper, the radio and his customers, my Warden was keenly aware of the horror and politics of war. Germany and Russia occupied most of Europe. The United States was lending assistance to Great Britain, under siege by Germany. My father worried that many of his nephews would be dragged into the war and if it lasted a long time, he knew that his sons could follow. In my research for the Essay Contest, I wrote of the totalitarian and atheistic governments of Nazi Germany, Communist Russia and Fascist Italy. My essay questioned the good that would come from an alliance with Communist Russia and Russia's future impact on world peace, if the Allies were victorious. My Warden, familiar with the persecution of Christians by anti-Christians in Turkey, Syria and Lebanon, also feared a pact with atheistic and Communist Russia, as America, on the defensive, was dragged into World War II.

Seven months later, at age 16, I was to graduate from St. Joseph's Commercial in June of 1942. I knew that there were awards in every subject. My goal was to win as many awards as I could. My typing jobs and my intense commitment to homework left little time for any recreation. I was cramming, panic stricken that I would fold under the pressure of separate exams in Typing, Bookkeeping, Shorthand, Business Arithmetic, Business Law and Business English. About a week before exams, much to my amazement and shock, Sister Ludolpha approached me. In her loving voice, she said, "Freddie, you have already won the Award for General Excellence in all subjects. If you get the highest marks in the other subjects, you would also win the Top Award in those subjects. I would like to excuse you from taking the final exams in all subjects in exchange for the Award for General Excellence. In this way, other students will be recognized for their good work. Do you have any objection?" My panic disappeared. My joy was indescribable. My goal was achieved. My sacrifice of fun and games paid off. My hours of studying at home and on the truck were rewarded. My father, mother and family would be proud. I simply said, "Yes, Sister, thank you for the help and encouragement you gave me. I shall never forget it." Then she said, "You realize, of course, that you are to be the Valedictorian at Graduation." Along with my family, I envisioned my former warden in the audience, bursting with pride — we both would know that my life would be different — I would forever be freed from being a Prisoner of the Truck — my warden would now forever be my father.

In June of 1942, I stood before my 70 classmates, my former teachers, my mother, father, brothers, sisters and relatives. I received the *"Award for General Excellence"*, the top honor from St. Joseph's Commercial School. My short speech expressed my gratitude for the support I received from the good Sisters of Notre Dame and the devoted Notre Dame Fathers. I singled out Sister Ludolpha for her inspiration and motivation; my father for the lessons I learned from him on the truck; and my mother for her example of love, kindness and patience. The graduation ceremony was concluded with a song dedicated to me by one of the girls in the graduating class — the one who held my hand on the hayride. She had a beautiful voice. She was an excellent pianist. The song she played and sang was *"My Hero"*, made popular by Jennette MacDonald and Nelson Eddy in a popular movie of the times. I was frightened by the words, *"Come, Come I love you only, I long for You."* and *"My arms now ache to embrace you, my hero mine."* At age 16, with my goals set for my mother and family and with no dating experience, I was just not ready for that kind of smothering thing. I quivered in my shoes.

My Girlfriend Mabel

One evening in May, a few weeks prior to my graduation from St. Joseph's Commercial School, I became overwhelmed with the pressures in my life. The eighteen Saturday hours as Prisoner of the Truck, the long bike ride back and forth to school, the typing jobs from businessmen that awaited me when I returned home, the hours that I wanted to devote to home study were all taking their toll. I threw my books aside. I thought about girls. I wished I had a girlfriend. Yet, I felt that a girlfriend would distract me from my goal. There were now seven brothers and sisters. We were in our third rental home in four years. The recollection of my mother's face when we lost and moved out of our home on Driving Park Avenue was still very clear in my mind. I wanted to give her back the home that she lost. I wanted to help my warden, brothers and sisters. I knew it meant making sacrifices on my part. Girl friends had to be put aside until I could accomplish this goal. Financially, I knew what it would take. I had confidence that I could land a good paying job after graduation from St. Joseph's. But on this particular hot evening in May, there was something inside of me burning to have a girl friend to love. I recalled a few of the daughters of my father's German and Irish customers that made my heart beat a little faster. I found myself attracted to freckles, blondes and red heads. My scholastic achievement had given me confidence. My pigeon toes, bowed legs and knock-knees seemed to be a bit straighter. I developed a better walk to conceal my pigeon-toes. My dark skin was now considered a good tan. Yet, my plan did not allow time for a commitment to a girlfriend.

As I dwelled on all of my concerns on this May evening, I threw my books aside in great frustration. My brothers and sisters were out in the neighborhood except for Kenny who was in his high chair in the kitchen where my mother was ironing. I stormed into the kitchen and shocked my mother with, "Mom, I've had it. I've been working and studying too long and too hard. Something is happening to my body. I need to get away from all of this. I'm going to see my girlfriend." My mother kept ironing as she calmly said, "Oh, that's interesting, I didn't know you had a girlfriend. What's her name?" I reached for the kitchen screen door and said, "Well, I do have a girlfriend and I am going out right now to see her and I don't know what time I will be back." As I slammed the screen door shut, her voice reflecting concern and curiosity followed me to the back porch. She said, "What's her name." I looked back through the screen door and quickly responded, "Her name is Mabel" and I disappeared into the night.

It was about 7:30 PM. I walked to the back of the house through a field of weeds until I got to St. Paul Street. I crossed it to a fence that separated the sidewalk from the Genesee River. I went through an opening in the fence and down a slope to the river. I tossed rocks into the water for about an hour. I wished that there were a Mabel in my life, someone who understood my family situation, someone who would have the patience to wait for me until I achieved my goal for my mother and family.

I returned home around 9:30 that night. I walked through the field that entered our back yard. The kitchen light was on. I stood on the back porch looking through the screen door. The high chair was empty. My brother Kenny was in his crib. My mother was alone in the kitchen. I knew she could not see me as I gazed through the screen door. For her family of ten, a huge pile of clothes was already ironed. There was another huge pile to be ironed. She looked weary from a long day of mothering her flock. Her sweet face was wrinkled and sad. I knew that that she was worried about my strange 15-year-old behavior. I had been gone for almost two hours, something I had never done before without a clear explanation. Tears rolled down my eyes when I thought of her long day, her love, her sacrifices, her patience with my father's temper, her concern about making financial ends meet, her love and devotion exclusively to family. I thought of her sweet nature, her goodness and her saintly characteristics. I reflected on my youth and my opportunities for the future. My troubles, my work and study hours all seemed small in comparison to the sacrifices my mother was making for her family. She never thought about her needs. Her only thoughts were for her children. She made our household into a neat, warm, comfortable, loving, singing and happy place to live. By her example and her words, she wove good character into our lives.

I reached for the screen door handle and opened the door. She looked at me with surprise and relief. I smiled and said, “Hi Mabel. You are my girl friend and I love you from the bottom of my heart.” We embraced each other. Choked with emotion, we cried in each others' arms. From that day forward, it was not uncommon for me to call my mother Mabel even at the age of 95 when she was dying in a nursing home. She told the Mabel story to everyone she knew. Many relatives and friends on many church and social occasions would greet her with “Hi Mabel” and she would smile with a happy remembrance of that very special evening.

CHAPTER 12

Age 16 to 17 Speed Typing Jobs : The Key to Buying Mom a New Home

My cousin, Joseph Sarkis, was a truck driver for Mushroom Transportation Company. Just before my 1942 graduation, he said, "Get over to see my boss, George Cutaire. He's looking for a billing clerk who can type real fast." I asked what was involved. Joe said it was a package of typewritten paper work on every item loaded on the truck. The truck would go from Rochester to another destination where it would be unloaded for delivery to various points in that city.

The hours were from 4 PM to 12 PM, six days a week, and because there was a lot of contact with truck drivers in evening hours, it was not the work for female typists. Also, because of the night hours, it paid more per hour than most secretarial jobs. Seventy-five cents per hour, twice the minimum wage and equal to 15 empty basket sales per hour. At 48 hours per week, this was $36 a week, the equivalent of 720 baskets per week. In one week, I would earn seven times as much as I earned all summer on my father's truck. This was double what I was making with Ray Shaheen and Sam Halaby. This was big time!

George Cutaire interviewed me and gave me a typing assignment. I returned with the work product in a short time. He was impressed. I was hired. I rode my bike five miles to work, down St. Paul Street over the Bausch & Lomb Bridge, and to the offices and docks of Mushroom Transportation. After three months,

I asked Mr. Cutaire for a meeting. I told him that I had three free hours and wanted more work to do. He said he couldn't understand how I could have three free hours when all of my predecessors needed the full eight hours to get the work done. He appreciated my bringing this to his attention and said he would find more work for me to do. I asked him if my hourly rate would increase. He seemed confused. I explained that my typing speed is what enabled me to get eight hours worth of work done in five; that the reason I asked for more work was to earn more per hour. I said that I was playing a major role in the support of my family and my objective was to maximize my earnings for their benefit. George shrugged his shoulders, gave me more work and consented to an increase in my hourly rate. In three months, I was now earning $1.00 an hour x 48 hours - the equivalent of 960 empty baskets per week. This was two times the earnings of a lady typist with five years of experience. I knew because I was constantly searching the want ads.

After six months with Mushroom, I saw a classified ad for a billing clerk for the Universal Carloading Company not far from Mushroom transportation. If I got the job, I would belong to a union called the Brotherhood of Railroad Workers. It paid $1.25 per hour in union wages. The hours were 4 PM to 12 PM, six nights a week, the same as Mushroom Transportation. I was confident of two things. I typed faster than anyone I knew. I had experience in the same line of work. It required a male typist. I could get the job. I met with George Cutaire again. I told him about this opportunity. George's reply was, "Hey, if you can get the job, take it. You've only been here for six months and you're looking for your third raise. Sarkis, you won't be satisfied until you get my job and I'm not about ready to give it up. Just give me two weeks notice if you get the job."

Mr. Young was the manager for Universal Carloading. He interviewed and tested me. I brought his work assignment back in half the time he expected. He hired me. I returned to George Cutaire and gave him my notice. George offered to match my hourly rate. I said that he was too late, that I had agreed to work for Mr. Young. When I discussed this with my cousin Joe he said, "When you shake hands, it's like a contract. If you can make more at Universal Carloading, take it."

At Universal Carloading, I worked in a small room outside of the docks where the trucks were being loaded. My boss was Matt Katafiaz. Matt was about 30. He was the rating clerk; I was the billing clerk. Matt would provide me with my workload for typing. A box full of forms sat in a box behind my typewriter. These forms were continuous feed to my typewriter. When I completed a particular billing from a specific sender to a specific receiver, I would rip off the multi-pages and begin with the next billing. Matt applied a great deal of pressure on me. He wanted to finish early. The trucks were being loaded. Drivers would be waiting for their billing package to take with them. Matt and I were a team to get the job done right and on time. I began to like Matt. If we got the job done an hour earlier, we could go home and still get paid for the full 8 hours.

My typewriter sat next to a coal-operated potbelly stove. It was my job to feed the coal and remove the ashes in the winter. The air in the small workspace was dry. In spite of drinking plenty of water, my throat was constantly parched. In the winter, the room I worked in was poorly insulated. Cold drafts poured from the surrounding four walls facing the outdoors and adjacent to the loading docks. There were times when I felt that half of my body was being roasted and the other half frozen.

After six months, I began to realize that, regardless of the high pay, I was in a new kind of self-imposed prison. The work was tedious and repetitious. The working environment was poor. When other kids my age were free in the evenings, I felt chained to my work. I often wished that I could have gone to Aquinas, the Catholic High School for Boys. I would have had the fellowship of new friends, tried out for the various sports teams and been challenged by courses that prepared me for college. I felt that my education limited my work opportunities to clerical work. However, I focused my attention on the amount of money I was making and saving. I still recalled clearly my mother's sadness when we lost our Driving Park Avenue home. I was determined to earn and save enough to put my mother and my seven brothers and sisters into a home like the one my family lost in the depression. I spent very little on myself. My St. Jude bike continued to be my mode of transportation. In the daytime, I continued to perform odd jobs for Ray Shaheen and Sam Halaby that added income to my goal.

In the hours before my typing job, I continued to enjoy the benefits of the YMCA. Having learned how to swim at the indoor YMCA on Gibbs Street in Rochester, I rode my bike to the swimming pool at Maplewood Park to take a course in life saving. The instructor was 6' tall and weighed a heavily muscled 200 pounds or more. I was about 5'6" tall and weighed a thin 120 pounds. Outside of the pool the instructor spoke of the behavior and actions of a drowning swimmer. He explained how you should never approach the drowning victim from the front. In a panic situation, the drowning person would grab onto you for support, making it impossible for you to stay afloat and you would possibly drown with the victim. He even gave a lesson on what to do if the drowning victim succeeded in grabbing you. We were to remain calm, sink with the victim, put our hands under his armpits and push him upward. In the victim's desire to reach the surface, the victim would release his death grip and you could then circle around him and save him as instructed.

He then gave each pupil a demonstration of how to approach and save the victim and how to handle the situation when we grabbed him. We were instructed to grab him if we could, pretending we were in panic. When it was my turn, he allowed me to grab him. He followed his own instructions and I released my grip. He then performed the maneuver from the back and swam me to safety the full length of the pool.

Then he told the class that he would pretend he was drowning and we should practice the lesson on him. Others before me, somewhat older, succeeded. When it came my turn, I tried to swim around him as he pretended he was in panic. I could not get behind him. He grabbed me. In that instant, as we went down into the deep end of the pool, I panicked and struggled to be free of his grip, completely forgetting to hold my breath, remain cool and push him upwards under his armpits. I lost my breath, swallowed a cup of swimming pool water, kicked him with my legs and punched at him with one free hand. From previous experiences, he released me immediately. Humiliated and embarrassed in front of the entire class, I got out of the pool, rushed to the locker room, got dressed, quickly biked home and thanked God that my life was spared. My God, I thought, in pretending to be a drowning victim, he almost drowned me.

Other than relatives and family I had only a few friends. Indeed, there was so much love and activity in my immediate family and relatives that this absence of friends was not a source of sadness for me. At Christmas time, it was common for Betty and me to take our brothers and sisters to see Santa Claus, decorate the Christmas tree, purchase the Christmas presents and make sure that it was indeed a Merry Christmas for the entire family. The time seemed to go by quickly. I was keenly aware of World War II developments and the fact that I would be of draft age in another year. These realities, as well as my deep belief that the Holy Spirit and his Seven Gifts would sustain me, helped me to cope with the job and its monotony.

Shortly after I turned 17, a job opening was posted on the bulletin board of the Universal Carloading Company. It was a clerk's job for Over, Short & Damaged freight. The hours were 8 AM to 5 PM, five days a week. It was a salaried job and paid more than I was earning as a billing clerk. I approached Mr. Young. He said that I was too important to the company as a billing clerk. He reminded me that the man leaving the job had been there for 17 years. He also reminded me that I would be of draft age soon and should stay in the job for that reason. I returned to my billing responsibility dismayed. That night, I read my union manual. I discovered that I had a right to that job according to seniority. The company was required to consider my qualifications and my seniority. They could not go outside the company as long as I was qualified and in a senior position. I approached Mr. Young with these facts. Within two weeks a billing clerk was hired and I was trained to be the Over, Short and Damaged Clerk by the man who was going into the service.

This new job was more challenging. It involved tracing freight that went from shippers to consignees that were either over or short from the original delivery invoice as well as resolving the problems associated with damaged freight. Phone calls and written communications were involved. I loved the job, the hours, the pay and the free evenings. I rejoined the street gangs who played baseball and football in the streets in the evening. I joined the YMCA evening athletic programs. My bike continued to be my sole means of transportation.

Finally, at the age of 17, for the first time in my life, weeknights and Saturday nights were free. On Saturday nights, I would go out with my altar boy friend, Clarence Pecoraro and George Saikley. George was the only son of Lebanese immigrants. Clarence was the son of Italian immigrants. The three of us had much in common. We were shy and inexperienced with girls. If we went to a YMCA dance, we were like wallflowers waiting for the girls to ask us to dance and none of them did. It was more relaxing for us to go to the pool hall and shoot pool. Telephones were now popular in most homes. We would call each other up on Saturday nights and say, "What do you want to do tonight, shoot pool or go to a dance?" The three of us knew that we were marking time before we were called to serve in WWII.

That summer a great tragedy struck. My cousin Joseph Sarkis, 26, on his day off from Mushroom Transportation went fishing. Joe was a tall and strong man. He projected a tough truck driver image. Very few people would challenge Joe's rough exterior. When I worked for Mushroom, he would ask me if George Cutair was treating me right. He perceived me to be shy and wanted to protect me. He said, "If George gives you any trouble at all, let me know and I'll take care of it, OK?"

A few weeks later, Joe was fishing with two companions in the Genesee River. One of his companions had fallen out of the boat. He yelled for help because he couldn't swim. Without hesitation, Joe jumped into the river and struggled to his friend. In spite of sheer exhaustion, Joe was able to get his friend back to the boat. The man in the boat reached for Joe's friend. He succeeded in pulling him into the boat. When he turned to give Joe a helping hand, Joe was gone. Complete exhaustion made it impossible for Joe to hang on to the boat and he drowned.

At his funeral service, I recall vividly the words of the priest, "No greater love than this, that of a man who lays down his life for a friend." At the funeral mass, my cousin Don Sarkis, Joe's brother, told me that his brother Joe would have survived if he knew how to swim. When he jumped into the water, his only thought was to save his friend. To this day, the sacrifice of my cousin Joe's life to save another, knowing that he could not swim, stands out as the most courageous act I have ever known.

It was about this time that St. Nicholas Church, the only Eastern Rite Roman Catholic Church in Rochester, re-opened with a new pastor, Monsignor Hallak. Monsignor Hallak believed that the future of the church was with the young. He began to make changes in the services. In addition to Arabic and Greek, he introduced English in the services. My sister Betty and I became active in church programs, fundraisers and the church choir. In the young people of that parish, I found a new community of love, respect and friendship. When we arrived at St. Nicholas, parishioners would be impressed with my father's truck and the number of children sitting in the back. Other parishioners arrived by automobile.

My father was a leader in church affairs. The senior men of the Parish held him in high esteem. In family visits to relatives and friends of the parish, Sunday's were filled with good times. While we visited and played with cousins, my father played cards with his brothers and other Church members. It was a highly competitive and spirited event. I could hear my father and Uncle

Deeb raise their voices in Arabic if their partners made a mistake. The smoke was thick from my father's cigar smoke and the cigarette smoke of other players. During these games, it was common for the men to drink shots of whiskey and use raw pieces of lamb's liver as chasers.

My mother and father seemed to be more at ease in these better times. My sister Betty and I were working. This took a great deal of financial pressure off my father. He was more relaxed. At age 17, I had saved enough money to put a down payment on a home. Betty, my mother and I screened the classified ads for a home. We took a bus to 1293 Park Avenue. The house was priced at $9,200. Park Avenue was near East Avenue, one of the most prominent streets in Rochester. We liked the neighborhood, barn, garage, yard, school district and the price. My mother agreed. It was like the home we lost on Driving Park Avenue during the depression. There was a magnificent Chinese Maple tree in front. It had a large living room, dining room and four bedrooms on the second floor. We made an offer of $8,500. It was accepted. I made the downpayment. The owner took back a mortgage. With the assistance of Mr. Young, a carpenter and customer of my father, we converted a large attic into a boy's loft with three more bedrooms. The backyard was generous in size, part of it with a heavy growth of weeds. Part of the yard rose sharply 20 feet to a slope of land. There was a fence on top of the slope. The subway ran about 40 feet below the slope. This section of the subway was above ground. A mature, bent oak tree had grown from the edge of the porch providing shade from the sun. The house had one bathroom. Our family had now grown to ten, including my mother and father, and we took one bathroom in our stride. There was one house rule. The bathroom could never be locked. After we moved in, it was not uncommon to find the bathroom used by three members of the family at the same time. This was particularly challenging when everyone had to get ready for school at the same time. Many times at night, when my sisters occupied the bathroom, the boys of the attic would have to urinate from the attic windows. One day, my older sister, Betty, screamed up the stairs, "What are you guys doing up there? Something is splashing on the porch roof facing my room?" I yelled down, "We've been cleaning the windows and it's only dirty water from the pails."

I was a very happy seventeen-year-old. Within one year of my graduation from St. Joe's, my goal had been achieved. I bought my mother a new home and assumed the responsibility for the mortgage payments. I knew that if I went into the service when I turned 18, my service compensation would cover the mortgage payments. This was the beginning of a golden period in our lives. Park Avenue became a permanent home for our family and a hospitality center for relatives and friends of the family. My father was pleased with my contribution to the family's welfare. He went along with the entire plan without input or objection and he provided our table with ample fruits, vegetables and lamb meat. Betty's earnings paid for many household expenses. My brothers and sisters adjusted quickly to their new school within walking distance of our home. It was Public School #1, a modern grammar school, with a beautiful park-like setting and more importantly, good public school teachers.

From Park Avenue, the ten of us continued our Sunday journeys to St. Nicholas Church in the back of my former truck prison. Kenny was my mother's ninth child. He sat on her lap in the front of the cab with my father. Betty, myself, Joe, Anne, Jimmy, Vicky and Deanna sat on the orange crates in the back of the truck. In winter, we sat on the same orange crates in an enclosed truck, cramped lovingly together near the kerosene lamp.

On Park Avenue, Sundays became the highlight of our family week. It was the only time during the week that we all sat down together at the same time for meals. Our Sunday mornings, after Mass, we usually feasted on Zlabee. This was the same fried dough that attracted me into the kitchens of my aunts on Evergreen Street. My mother prepared and served Zlabee with fresh fruit and fried eggs. After breakfast, my father and the boys would retreat to the sitting room where we shared the Democrat and Chronicle while listening to the radio and visiting.

One Sunday, my father spoke of the dissatisfaction of the founders of the church with Monsignor Hallak. They were talking about seeking his removal. For the first time in my life, I challenged my father. I reminded him that on each Sunday he recited the Beatitudes in Arabic, which I repeated in English. This was one of the changes Monsignor Hallack made to enhance the interest of the young members of the parish. One of the Beatitudes we both recited was "Blessed are the Peacemakers for they shall be called the Children of God." I asked him how he could recite the Beatitudes from his lips and not live them in his heart. I spoke of the seven gifts of the Holy Spirit and how meaningful they were in my life. I asked him to *counsel* with the senior men, search for *understanding,* reach for *knowledge* and *wisdom* in their evaluations, have the *fortitude* to do it and do it in the spirit of *piety* and *fear of the Lord.* He remained very calm. He seemed to be deeply impressed and proud of what I had said. He took what I said to heart and succeeded in getting all of the senior men to make peace with Monsignor Hallack. I thanked God for instilling the seven gifts in me and if they worked with my father, I was sure these gifts of the Holy Spirit would work for me throughout my life.

The Masses on Sunday mornings, and the breakfasts that followed were filled with thoughts and prayers for all those serving our country in WWII, including several uncles and cousins on my mother's Dwaileebe side of the family and many of my cousins on the Sarkis side of the family.

My Aunt Cecelia and Uncle George Sarkis had three sons in the service. John was killed in a major invasion in 1942. Later in the war, Peter was wounded in the South Pacific and Tom was wounded in the European War. I witnessed the great anxiety experienced by my Uncle George and Aunt Cecelia before I entered the service. In the front Evergreen Street window facing the street, typical of parents who had sons in the service, they hung three red, white and blue symbols for each of their three sons. A blue star signified a son in the service. A silver star signified a son either missing or wounded in action. A gold star was for a son killed in action. My Aunt Cecelia and Uncle George had to change three blue stars to one gold and two silver. In writing this chapter, I searched through my Navy files and found this very touching and emotion-evoking poem. I had copied it in long hand and mailed it to my Aunt Cecelia and Uncle George during my first month in the Service, shortly after the death of her son, my cousin John.

"The blue star in our window has changed to silver now,
And although you are so far away, we feel you are near somehow,
Each night in heaven's zenith, we pick a silver star,
Pretend it represents you, no matter where you are.
And as it shines tonight, son, God sheds its beams on you,
And keeps you in his loving care, as when the star was blue.
But should it change to gold son, you still would not seem far,
Each night we'd look to heaven and pick a golden star."

As I prepared to leave home, I felt that I was in God's hands and was confident that I would return home safely. In spite of the possibility that my parents might have to change the blue star in their window to a silver or gold star, I felt an overwhelming sense of patriotism and excitement as the time drew near to my 18th birthday and the draft that would surely require me to serve.

Mike Joseph, a family friend, knew I was approaching the draft age of 18. As a farewell gift, he took me to Sea Breeze Amusement Park in his convertible. Prior to this Sea Breeze trip, I thought I would enlist in the Air Corps to avoid the Army draft. However, one ride on the jackrabbit that day seriously upset my stomach and that was the end of any desire to be in the Air Corps. After Pearl Harbor, December 7, 1941, when I was 15, I saw many pictures of action in the Army, Air Corps and Navy in newspapers and magazines. I was determined that if I had to face injury or death, I would rather await such a fate sleeping in a navy bunk rather than in a foxhole. It was as simple as that when I enlisted in the Navy a few days before my birthday on May 16, 1944. Before enlistment, I offered proof that I had been contributing to over half of the support of the family I was leaving. They granted me the same allowance that they would give to a married man. This allowance would be sent directly to my mother who would pay for the mortgage on the house as well as other household expenses.

I said good-bye to Sister Ludolpha and Sister Marietta. One week prior to my enlistment, Sister Marietta had asked me to serve one more Mass at St. Joseph's. Sister Ludolpha placed her hands into mine and said, "Freddie, I will pray every day that you will come back without harm and I know that God will answer my prayers."

My family and relatives were in tears as I prepared to board the full bus of 48 enlistees on our way to Buffalo, NY, for our physical exam and assignment to a boot camp. No one was more emotional than my father. He hugged me as if he would never see me again. Tears were pouring from his eyes. In front of other enlistees who began to board the bus and those who came to see me off, he put his two hands over my head and for what seemed like five minutes, blessed me reciting loudly prayers in Arabic. In view of the outdoor crowd that gathered near the bus, I was somewhat embarrassed by his blessing in front of others, yet my heart went out to him and my mother. I knew that they would live in constant fear and concern until I returned safely home. I knew that they would read about every battle and every report of naval casualties and wonder if I would ever be among the killed, missing or wounded as reported daily in the Democrat & Chronicle. Overwhelmed with tears and emotions, I hugged and kissed my Mom, Dad, Betty, Junior (Joe), Anne, Jimmy, Vicky, Deanna and my three-year-old baby brother Kenny and boarded the bus.

As I waved goodbye from the window in the parked bus and looked at the worried face of my father, I recalled what he often said to his fruit and vegetable customers, "A rich man has his wealth and I have my family and that for any man is his true wealth". I could not hold back my tears. I just couldn't.

CHAPTER 13

Age 18
Preparation for War -
The United States Navy

As I waved good-bye to my family from the bus, the 48 enlistees settled down for their ride to Buffalo, NY. To help get acquainted, we were all given name tags. Very naively, I made the mistake of carrying a book on the bus. It was a farewell gift someone had given me at the bus station. It was entitled "My Friend Flicka" and was about a boy and his horse. When a fellow enlistee saw the title, I was doomed to be teased and picked on all the way to Buffalo and to Boot Camp that followed. My father's blessing, witnessed by most of them, was another factor in the teasing.

On the bus to Buffalo, an enlistee across the bus aisle in a loud voice said, "Sarky, let me see the palm of your hand." I extended it and he said, "Man, you ain't got no hair on that palm." I stared at my palm, reached for his palm looked at both and smartly said, "Well you don't either." The bus rocked with laughter and I knew not why.

That same day, the occupants of the bus lined up for a completion of our physical examination in the Buffalo enlistment center. We stood naked, side by side, as the Doctor and his assistant prepared to examine our bodies for birthmarks, scars, tattoos or other physical marks for identification purposes in case of death. After inspecting my body the Doctor said, “Sailor pull that foreskin back.” I said, “What, sir?” He repeated, “Pull that foreskin back.” I said, “Sir, I don’t know what you are talking about.” He stared at me in disbelief and said, “Pull the foreskin back on your penis.” I tried and said, “Sir, it hurts.” He said, “I don’t believe this. Sailor, I don’t care if it hurts, pull that foreskin back.” With great embarrassment and discomfort I obeyed. He stared at my penis and said, “My God sailor, pull that foreskin back and from this day forward clean it every time you shower.” I said, “Yes Sir”, as the giggles surrounded me from the 48 men who were also being examined.

I was quickly becoming aware that, as a young man who went to confession weekly, I had led a relatively celibate and sheltered life. Even a week before I entered the Navy, I served as an altar boy for St. Joseph’s. Since we were all headed for naval boot camp, I knew that I would be a constant target for pranks from my future fellow shipmates. I learned to take it in good stride, and I eventually earned the respect of those who teased me. On this day, May 20, 1944, for better or worse, I was sworn into the United States Navy as an apprentice Seaman, - the equivalent of a buck private in the US Army.

After our physical, we were transported to the Sampson Naval Base on Seneca Lake, south of Geneva, NY, for boot camp training. The Navy barbers scalped us. We traded in our civilian clothing for US Navy clothing. Our entire possessions, including clothing and bedding had to fit into one large duffel bag. You could tell a Navy recruit by the "unsalty" way he formed and wore his newly issued sailor hat. It took six weeks to learn the art of folding the hat to look like an “old salt”, the name given to sailors who had months of experience in the Navy.

Navy sleeping quarters are crowded with double-deck-bunks in a large, open area. I was assigned to a barracks that housed 112 sailors and one large community bath facility with urinals, toilets and showers.

Boot camp has always been perceived to be tough on both men and women in the Armed Forces. Civilian life and its many routines quickly faded into our memories as we were inundated with new demands on every minute of our 18-hour days. Our crowded sleeping and living environments had to be kept pristine by frequent scrubbing of floors, toilets, urinals and bathroom floors. Our personal items had to be stowed according to regulations, with clothes folded in perfect order and shoes spit-shined to a mirror finish. We endured early morning inspections in front of our bunks, barking of orders, drilling with rifles, and marching exercises that seemed endless. There were innumerable physical demands ranging from difficult obstacle courses to exhausting physical tests of endurance that included calisthenics and jumping from great heights into a pool (simulating the abandonment of ship). Petty punishments were doled out with abandon, each requiring more drills and calisthenics. Mess hall meals were hardly a luxury as volume-prepared food was slammed onto our metal trays and we quickly ate elbow-to-elbow on picnic style benches. Sleep was frequently interrupted by standing of four-hour watches or endless forms of harassment.

It seemed that out of the112 men in our barracks, I was the only one that did not consider boot camp hell. To me, it was the boy's high school experience I never had, the Boy Scout camp I never attended, the marching parade that I was never in, the long vacation that I never knew. I relished in the comradery of other boys, the sports and exercises, the excitement of learning how to handle and shoot a rifle, the simplicity of choices in food and/or clothing, the order and discipline that would make me a man — all of this made boot camp the most exciting youth adventure I had ever experienced. Compared to my Prison on the Truck and the Pot Bellied Stove of my 4 PM to 12 PM billing clerk job, boot camp was heaven and I savored every minute of it. The United

States of America provided all of my food, clothing and shelter, gave me a spending allowance and because of my role as a major financial supporter of my family, sent a monthly check to my mother. The Navy was not confinement. It was freedom.

I could never understand the gripes about the food. Up until boot camp, I never had steak, pork chops, roast beef, ham, fish, or spam. My father would buy a fresh half of lamb every week. I was brought up on lamb that was cut into small pieces by my mother. The lamb had to last an entire week for a family of ten. This was accomplished with great mixtures of lamb and rice. This mixture was stuffed into grape and cabbage leaves and small green squash. Lamb also went through a grinder mixed with wheat, served both raw and cooked. Green beans were mixed with rice, lamb and a tomato sauce. Green peas were mixed with rice, lamb and a tomato sauce. On Friday's we could not eat meat. Instead, my mother prepared lentils mixed with rice and chopped onions, eaten cold. When served, it was an unappetizing glossy, dark brown color.

On June 11, 1944, my mom, dad, brothers Junior (Joe), Jimmy, Charlie and Lena (Confirmation sponsors) spent three hours visiting me. I learned of the death of my cousin John in the invasion of Normandy. After I recovered from the shocking news, we talked about my Navy experiences. I told them that I was excited and enthusiastic about boot camp. The following week, my sisters Betty and Anne visited along with my cousin Anna. Betty was working for Blue Cross and Blue Shield and said that when I came home she would take me to Lorenzo's Restaurant in Rochester for a very special Italian treat called Antipasto. I wrote home at least three times a week and received mail from the family at least once a week. Mail call was always a special day for all recruits. I noted that my family became even more concerned about me as a result of the death of my cousin John and the wounding of his brother Peter in the Army in the Pacific.

We were required to watch a film on the cause and effect of venereal diseases. It was most graphic. The worst case ravages of untreated venereal disease, both syphilis and gonorrhea were explicitly enlarged and shown on the sexual organs and bodies of women as well as men. The film included methods for protection and prophylactics after sex. In light of my religious background and relatively sheltered life, I was appalled and shocked by the ravages of what I then considered to be "sinful" sex outside of marriage.

In addition to all of the above, in boot camp, men are evaluated for specific experience, training and assignments in preparation for boarding a ship. To provide for these specialties, sailors would be trained as Machinists, Electricians, Radiomen, Signalmen, Aviation Machinists, Aviation Metalsmiths, Cooks and Bakers, Storekeepers, Gunner's Mates, Quartermasters, Fire Controlmen, Torpedo men, Aerographers, Photographers, Aviation Ordnance men and as specialists in countless other activities.

Because of my typing and administrative skills and my service to the Church, I was destined to serve in Naval Administration and Communications and be an assistant to the Catholic Chaplain on board ship. On July 11, 1944, a consignment of boot camp sailors left for the Naval Training Center, Newport, Rhode Island. Prior to our departure, the seaman were divided to serve either on board the new aircraft carrier, USS Franklin or the new battle-cruiser, the USS Guam — all within six weeks of being sworn into the Navy. I was disappointed that I was not assigned to the USS Franklin. If I had been, I may have never returned home. As future chapters will show, the USS Franklin suffered the greatest number of casualties on board one ship in US Navy history.

On September 15, 1944, after two months of team building, the Newport trained crew arrived by railroad and boarded the USS Guam at the Philadelphia Naval Yard, 16 hours late due to a hurricane that swept the Atlantic Coast. In a few short months, I was promoted to Yeoman 3rd class, the equivalent of a Sergeant in the Army. I felt very proud that I had achieved this rank within five months of my enlistment.

THE USS GUAM
1944 - 1945

"She starts - - she moves - - she seems to feel
The thrill of life along her keel
And, spurning with her foot the ground
With one exulting joyous bound
She leaps into the ocean's arms."

From Longfellow's
The Building of a Ship

On February 2, 1942, in Camden, NJ, the keel of the battle cruiser USS Guam CB-2 was laid. It was America's version of the pocket battleship. It would have the fighting power of a battleship and the speed of a cruiser. The armament of the Guam consisted of nine 12-inch 50 caliber guns in three triple mounts; 12 five-inch, 50 caliber guns in six twin mounts, 14 forty-millimeter quadruple mounts and 34 twenty millimeter gun mounts. Her ship's complement would consist of 125 officers, 2000 enlisted men and a detachment of 80 marines. When construction was completed, it would be a small floating city providing decent food, clothing and shelter for all that served on board. On-ship services included a laundry, food storage, preparation and service facilities, soda fountain, barber shop, dental, medical and mail departments, a Chapel for Catholic, Protestant and Jewish services with Chaplains for each. Replenished and refueled at sea, the USS Guam could remain in battle for weeks and/or months as needed.

Three days after the Newport crew arrived, on September 17, 1944, The USS Guam was officially commissioned. Captain Leland P. Lovette, the former Director of Navy Public Relations in Washington, DC, became the ship's Captain. Commander Louis Everett Gunther, assumed duties as Executive Officer. The ship's band stirred emotions of patriotism. Admiral Low read his orders.

"Ever since the design of this class of ship has been generally known in the Navy, so far as I know, all ranks and ratings from Rear Admiral down have been anxious and eager to serve in them. I feel, therefore, that we here and the ship's company of Alaska [the USS Guam's sister ship] *should be particularly gratified that we are to have the opportunity and privilege to take them into their first action. Our specific assignments we do not know, but with knowledge of the military power and toughness that has been rolled into this design we may be quite certain that we will be in the front row — which is where I assume everyone wants to be."* And that is the way the crew felt. The USS Guam, a newly commissioned ship, a fighting machine, was ready for action.

During our stay in the "City of Brotherly Love," a dance was held for the officers and men of the the Guam at a leading hotel. I did not know how to dance. I stood in the background watching the dancing and listening to the dance music of the band that was formed from men on the USS Guam.

Dick Vatter, the son of a Rochester butcher, was serving as a butcher on board our ship. He invited me to a party that his parents held in the hotel. They had rented a two-bedroom apartment for themselves and their daughter. We were to leave shortly on the Guam's first "shakedown" cruise in preparation for battle. This was their farewell party for their son. Mr. Vatter offered me a mixed drink. Somewhat influenced by my awareness of wayward husbands at Hedges Bar & Grill, I said that I didn't drink alcoholic beverages. He said, "Go ahead, your father would want you to drink a toast to your ship on its commissioning." They all had their glasses waiting for me so I took the glass. Mr. Vatter gave a beautiful toast, "God bless and protect your ship and you two boys wherever she sails," and "down the hatch" the drink went. I felt very relaxed and at their insistence I had two or three more drinks. I looked out of the hotel window and said, "Holy smokes, this drinking does tricks to your head. I see smoke coming out of a billboard on top of that building." It turned out to be a Camel billboard advertisement where at intervals the soldier pictured exhaled a giant puff of smoke in the form of a ring. The Vatters exploded with laughter. They checked out of their hotel to head back to Rochester. As they said good-bye to us, Mr. Vatter broke into tears and embraced Dick. Then he embraced me. I felt sadness that my parents had not been able to be with us. The combination of the drinks and the emotions left me dizzy and sick. Dick had a difficult time getting his sick shipmate back to the ship. I resolved that I would never drink again and wondered how many men went home feeling like this in the bar on Joseph Avenue and Leo Street in Rochester. I thought of my father and wondered if this was why I was never permitted to enter that bar-restaurant. Was he protecting me from behavior by men and women that he did not want me to witness?

My promotion to Yeoman 3rd class gave my shipmates even more ammunition for razzing "Sarky." In the US Navy, in various naval offices throughout the world, there were also female Navy personnel referred to as WAVES. Many of these WAVES wore the same two crossed feather-pens signifying Yeomen. The Army counterpart for female service personnel was WACS. The World War II words sung by military men in cadence or rhythm while marching made reference to both WACS and WAVES.

"The WACS and WAVES, are winning the war, parlez-vous,
The Wacs and Waves are winning the War, parlez-vous,
The Wacs and Waves are winning the War
So what the Hell are we fighting for,
Inky, Dinky, parlez-vous,"

For this reason, my shipmates referred to me as a "titless WAVE," or a "ball bearing WAVE," much to my consternation. Here I was, a well-trained recruit who survived boot camp and razzing by my fellow Seamen; who missed ten out of ten rifle shots in boot camp training because I forgot to put my rifle "sight" in an upward position before I fired at the target; who outlasted most of the men in all of the drills, calisthenics, endurance tests, marching and rifle drill presentations — now perceived by my shipmates to be a "Titless Wave."

In October of 1944, in one of the last allowed liberties before the shakedown cruise, a group of three sailors and I caught a bus in the Philadelphia Navy Yard to the center city of Philadelphia. We ended up in a small dance bar. It was packed with sailors and young girls who appeared to be between 18 and 20. Under pressure from my buddies, I forgot my pledge to abstain from alcohol. I limited myself to two cocktails. A shipmate introduced us to a girl he met in the bar. She and three girl friends came to the bar together. He pulled us aside to tell us that one of girls invited us to her home along with her three girlfriends. Her parents were away for the weekend and we would all have a party. He suggested that we meet in the men's room to agree not to split up and to develop a plan. I was in a dilemma. I did not want to break up the party of four couples. In the men's room, there was a coin-operated condom-dispensing machine. I played follow the leader as we each bought a condom. I wanted to be one of the boys. I was a sailor. I had to be a macho, sexy guy.

We piled into two cabs and headed for our hostess's house. Our hostess was very hospitable. She turned on the record player and offered us bottles of beer. We talked and danced until 12 midnight. I was not much of a dancer but did my best to fake it. The hostess turned down the lights in the living room. I sat on the couch with my young lady friend. My attraction was intense. My shipmates disappeared from the living room, going upstairs to bedrooms, one couple at a time, leaving us alone. This was the first time in my life that I was in a situation like this — the first time in my life that I would experience any form of sex. I was extremely nervous. I learned that my date was nervous as well. We shared our feelings with each other. I spoke of my religious background, my four sisters, my feeling that I would not want a sailor to have a one time sex affair with any one of my sisters. In fact, I said, I would beat the sailor up. I spoke of my respect for her as a person and my desire to save sex for marriage. I learned that this would have been her first time as well. We held hands, talked about our families and our hopes and dreams for the future.

About an hour later, my three buddies and their girl friends returned to the living room. We took a cab to the Naval Bus that was to leave at 2 AM from its Philadelphia center-city location. In the cab, my shipmates asked me how I made out. I told them it was the most fantastic sexual experience I had ever had in my life. As we returned to the base, I felt the unopened condom in my pocket. As we passed a waste container, I quickly discarded it. From that day forward, the brunt of teasing diminished. Crazy as it then seemed to me, I was now treated like one of the macho sailor boys. There was no further teasing of Sarky on the USS Guam.

Our shakedown cruise began on October 24, 1944. For me, being at sea on board a ship the size of the Guam was an exciting adventure. The Guam participated in bombardment and other practice exercises with the USS Springfield and Pittsburgh on their way to Trinidad, B.W.I. In boot camp, in addition to our regular duties, we had eight hours off and four hours on watch. The same applied aboard ship.

I was put in charge of the personnel jackets of the enlisted men. These were small folders that contained the background of each sailor. My duties required me to prepare any changes in an enlisted man's record in triplicate involving promotions, demotions, reassignments, health problems, disciplinary action taken for offenses committed, etc. One copy would be sent to Navy Headquarters in Washington, one was kept in the ship's office and the other would be placed in the sailor's personnel jacket.

Offenses included such matters as: AWOL, (Away without official leave), Abusive and Threatening Language, Asleep on Watch, Assault, Breaking Arrest, Disobeying a Lawful Order, Disrespect to a Superior Officer, Drunkenness, Falsehood, Leaving a Station before being Relieved, Missing Ship, Neglect of Duty, Obscene or Profane Language, Resisting Arrest, Scandalous Conduct, Striking another in the Navy, Theft, etc. My responsibility involved the maintenance of personnel jackets for over 1800 sailors. I also took dictation, handled the correspondence of the Executive Officer and assisted him in the weekly Captain's Mast. There was nothing boring about Captain's Mast. This is where USS Guam sailors confronted the Executive Officer of the ship for all kinds of violations, both petty and major. My job would be to record the punishment and enter it into the personnel jacket. Each week I had the names of the offenders and would have their jackets available for the Executive Officer to review for previous offenses.

Standing watch, eight hours off and four hours on around the clock combined with my Yeoman duties left little room for rest and recreation. I would work in the ship's personnel and communication sections from 8 AM to 4 PM; stand watch from 4 PM to 8 PM, have off from 8 PM to 4 AM when I would sleep; stand watch from 4 AM to 8 AM and back to work again at 8 AM.

My assigned watch station was on the bridge, a fourth floor compartment occupied by the navigator and his crew and usually the command position of the Executive Officer and Captain. This compartment was protected with heavy steel for the added protection of the commanding officers on deck. I wore earphones for TBS (Talk Between Ships). On this watch, my job was to listen for and repeat any communications between ships.

My assigned battle station was on the uppermost top of the ship with the sky as my roof. At General Quarters (the alarm for battle), I would rush up the equivalent of ten flights of stairs and jump into my revolving seat, somewhat like a barber's chair. The swivel chair was equipped with a flexible handle bar that could be moved up or down and stationary binoculars at my eye level attached to it. I sat in this "barber's chair" with my two arms grasping the handle bar, my ear and speakerphone attached to my head. In this position, I could swivel and look in any direction, search the sky or sea with my binoculars, listen to messages on my earphone and push a prominent red button to speak. I reported to the Marine Officer who commanded a Marine detachment that specialized in the anti-aircraft guns on board ship.

I assumed (assumed is a very dangerous word in war) that my duty was to swivel and turn, trying to spot an enemy aircraft. In an initial training session, the Marine Officer gave me my only orders. "When I say Commence Fire, you immediately push that

Red Button on your Headset and repeat "Commence Fire." When I say "Cease Fire", you push that Red Button and you immediately repeat "Cease Fire." You got it sailor. I said, "Yes Sir."

That was it. No other training. In combat, that is what I did. Hell would break lose when I said, "Commence Fire." All would be quiet when I said, "Cease Fire." In that sense, as an 18-19 year old combat sailor, away from my typewriter, I felt that I had an overwhelming power to destroy the enemy.

I wondered how I would ever explain to my grandchildren the importance of my Navy fighting responsibility. I had no weapon. I never fired a shot. I never manned a ship's gun. This was not hand-to-hand combat nor was it charging enemy lines, nor sleeping in a foxhole. I was not sufficiently trained to understand a message that came into my earphones such as "enemy aircraft at 10 o'clock." No one ever gave me a course on the "imaginary clock." I did not know where the voice "enemy aircraft at 10 o'clock" came from. In my first day of combat, I would swirl my "barber chair" around in wild circles, looking for 10 o'clock. Was the imaginary clock lying flat on the water, and if so, was 12 o'clock at the bow of the ship and 6 o'clock at the stern? If that were the case, an enemy aircraft would have to be flying close to the water from any direction. If the "clock" was perpendicular to the water, and the enemy aircraft was at 6 o'clock, would it illogically mean that an enemy aircraft is attacking our fleet of ships from the bottom of the ocean?

Since I was not responsible to shoot at the enemy aircraft, I began to feel it was unimportant to know where the "imaginary clock" was. The Marine Officer had binoculars. He gave me my orders. I had to repeat two words when hell broke lose and two words when it became quiet. After our first combat experience, I quickly learned to look in the direction he looked into. I no longer swiveled my "barber chair" in wild circles and I was glad that he did not notice what I was doing in our first day of combat. Otherwise, I might have been put below decks somewhere so as not to interfere with the process of winning a war.

The Marine Officer never criticized me. He never praised me for the efficiency in which I followed his commands. I was never introduced to him so I never knew his name. I don't remember what he looked like. I never met the Marines who fired the guns. The only words the Marine Officer ever spoke to me were "Commence Fire" and "Cease Fire."

I was glad to be on the uppermost top of the ship with a Marine Officer who knew what he was doing. It was better than being below decks, where sailors, involved with important duties, were unable to see the action of war at sea and in the air and who lived in constant fear of a torpedo ripping through sealed compartments where they performed their duties. If I were to die, I wanted to die above rather than below decks.

Prior to our departure for the Pacific Theatre of War, half of the Guam crew had liberty in Trinidad on one day and the other half on another. When I left the ship that afternoon, I was taken in by the excitement of what was once a pre-war tourist destination. The shops, restaurants and bars were full of sailors and Trinidad natives. "*Rum and Coca Cola, way down south in Trinidad*" was a popular hit song in America, and indeed, the rum was pouring. That evening, I came upon a group of sailors standing in line to enter a building. They were entering one door and coming out of another, supervised by shore patrol — sailors who acted in the capacity of navy police officers. I inquired about the line and was shocked to discover that this was a US Navy supervised house of prostitutes planned to protect naval personnel from venereal disease. Condoms were passed out at the entrance and a treatment program at the exit. In light of the film that was shown in boot camp, I was shocked and confused. I could not comprehend how the US Navy could condone such an activity. As I walked away from the scene of volume prostitution, I walked toward the center of restaurant and bar activity passing a group of homes. Young prostitutes were sitting on porches flirting with sailors as they walked by. Several cab drivers stopped and asked if I wanted to be taken to a young lady for a certain fee. I perceived Trinidad to be a city of sin. However, I noted that many sailors merely shopped or drank in bars and avoided the temptation that was all around them. I was one of them. My respect for the Navy diminished somewhat that day. In my Roman Catholic background, I perceived sex as something beautiful that you saved for your wife in marriage. I knew several of my shipmates who shared my views. However, in reflection on what I had observed, I remembered the biblical story of Mary Magdalene when Christ said to those who turned against her, "Let he who is without sin, cast the first stone." I was therefore very careful to be non-judgmental toward my shipmates and the prostitutes. I realized that shipmates had different values and convictions, yet in war, they all had one purpose in common. They were all prepared to give their lives for their country. What supervised government prostitution had to do with the morale of a ship's crew, I left to the questionable wisdom of the Navy. At this time in my life, this was way beyond my innocent 18-year-old ability to comprehend.

As we returned to Philadelphia from our shakedown cruise on December 12, 1944, we were in the teeth of a storm off Cape Hatteras. Gigantic waves ripped life rafts off the fantail. Steel plated gun tubs caved in. 20mm shields were bent. I became so sea sick, I wondered if we were all being punished for the sins of Trinidad. The toilet compartments on our ship contained dozens of rows of removable seats sitting on narrow funnels. Constantly flowing seawater flushed the narrow funnels back into the Ocean. The movement of water was so rapid, it would send up a spray of cool salt water that wet your bottom. Toilet paper dispensers were behind each removable seat. On calm days, it was not uncommon to see two rows of 20 men on each side of the toilet compartment, sitting within inches of each other, reading the ship's miniature newspapers and magazines. On this particular hurricane effect day, all of the seats were removed and on the floor. Sailors were kneeling over the trough. It was difficult to find an open spot to "heave" into. Many sailors did not make it to the troughs. If you were not seasick from the motion, the compartment smell was so intolerable that it sickened you anyway. I wanted to die. I wondered how men could fight in combat when they were this sick and what effect seasickness would have on winning or losing a sea battle. During this crisis of dry heaves, I wondered if I had made a mistake by not enlisting in Army, Marines or Air Corps.

The USS Guam returned to Philadelphia on December 19, 1944. Leave was granted for most of the ship. I returned home to Park Avenue to one of the worst snow storms in Rochester recorded history. My mother was pregnant with her 10th child. Even though I was headed to the Pacific Theater to fight Japan, I found consolation in knowing that my mother was comfortable in her new home. My brothers and sisters were in a good school system. Betty, now 20 and employed, was also helping with my brothers and sisters, relieving my mother of her endless work load. Sufficient income, including my government pay, was coming into the family to provide for their needs. My brother Joe, now 15, seemed to enjoy setting bowling pins for the Elks Club and working with my former warden. Great financial pressure had been lifted from my father. The Allied Forces were turning back Hitler and his forces and the tide was turning in Europe and against Japan in the Pacific. My family was being spared the ravages of war. All of this made me proud to be an American fighting for world peace and freedom. I felt that America was indeed, the "land of opportunity" and I knew that, with patience, if I applied myself in partnership with the Holy Spirit, there was nothing that I could not achieve in this land of the free. I believed that my life, with God's help, would be spared. I firmly believed that the United States of America would be victorious. I would return from the war to further my education, to find work that would help my mother and father and to provide whatever financial assistance I could for the highest possible degree of education for my brothers and sisters. Once I achieved that goal, I would get serious about raising my own family but not until then.

In spite of the Christmas tears and emotions of my departure to the war zone, it was a happy send off for me. In our large living room, accompanied by Betty (now 20 and Anne, now 14) on their guitars, we sang many of the family's most sentimental songs. Many tears were shed while singing them. I nicknamed Vicky, 8 and Deanna 6, "my sunshine sisters." They harmonized perfectly to "*You are my Sunshine*" and other songs of the times. It was especially difficult to say good-bye to my three-year old brother Kenny. I loved and hugged him dearly. The baby of the family always held a special spot in my heart.

In my final farewell, my father again prayed in Arabic as he held his hands over my head to give me his father's blessings. I closed my eyes and deeply felt the presence of God in this blessing. He was no longer my warden. He was my father. I was free of his prison and open to his blessing. My mother was the last in the family that I hugged and kissed good-bye. Within a few months she would be giving birth to her tenth child. The family said that if we got to nine, we'd call it our baseball team. I knew that in spite of the family that surrounded her, she would worry about my safety and the possibility that she would someday have to put a silver or gold star in the window of her 1293 Park Avenue home. I especially thought of all of the mothers of boys in the service and the day-to-day anxiety that they had to live with. I thought of the blue, silver and gold stars in the windows and I prayed for the safety of all those in the Armed Forces and their parents. I was off to the Pacific Theater of War. I was in God's hands.

CHAPTER 14

Captain's Mast, Missing Teeth, Letter Home

Captain's Mast

The severe December snowstorm of 1944 caused many shipmates to be AWOL (Away Without Official Leave) versus AOL (Away on Leave). AWOL required a hearing by Commander Guenther, the Chief Executive Officer. It was called "Captain's Mast." It was my duty to pull hundreds of "jackets" including my own on that particular day. These "jackets" were compact folded, 3"x 9" hard cover pouches with onion skin paper that held the history of each sailor. The CEO was required to review the offense and determine a sentence. Forms were made in duplicate - one went into the sailor's jacket and the other went to Naval Headquarters in Washington. Because it was the storm that caused so many sailors to be late in returning to the ship, this ritual moved quickly. Hundreds of sailors would quickly plead guilty, mention the storm and be dismissed. When one sailor was asked why he was AWOL, he replied, "Well as St. Anthony would say....." He never got a chance to finish the sentence. Commander Guenther said in the presence of the Catholic Chaplain, "Sailor, I don't care what St. Anthony has to say. Ten hours extra duty. You are dismissed." When this two-hour hearing was concluded, Catholic

Chaplain Mahler said to Commander Guenther, “Commander, you really spoiled it for me today. Now I will never know what St. Anthony would have said about being AWOL.”

The weekly Captain’s Mast brought many humorous and serious situations to light. One sailor was charged with “urinating on deck”. When asked by Commander Guenther, the Chief Executive Officer (CEO), why he did this, the sailor from the deep south replied, “Sir, I felt it bad. I had to go. So I went.” The CEO quickly responded, “Sailor you were not at a battle station. Ten hours extra duty.” I recorded the offense and sentence in his jacket. The sailor’s superior officer enforced the extra duty.

Offenses that I recorded in the jackets of sailors were AWOL, Abusive and Threatening Language, Asleep on Watch, Assault, Breaking Arrest, Disobeying a Lawful Order, Disrespect to a Senior Officer, Drunkenness, Falsehood, Leaving a Station before being Relieved, Missing Ship, Neglect of Duty, Obscene or Profane Language, Resisting Arrest, Scandalous Conduct, Striking another in the Navy, etc. In addition, from the Medical Department reports, I had to record any sailors’ infection and treatment of a venereal decease.

The process of advising the sailor of his offense, giving the sailor an opportunity to speak in his defense and the sentencing by the CEO, of necessity, had to be both fair and swift. At the weekly Captain’s Mast, other than the major storm, there would be as many as 40 sailors waiting in line outside of the hearing compartment. In a two-hour period, the CEO would average about five minutes per offense including the paper work involved. On occasions, I thought the CEO was too tough and swift with his justice. However, I believed that in most instances the sailors deserved the penalties they received. I developed a high respect for Commander Guenther and was proud to serve him in this capacity as well as to be involved in the dictation and typing of his correspondence. I felt a kinship and a bond with the CEO that was closer than the Catholic Chaplain Mahler whom I assisted on Sundays. I felt that the Chaplain saw me as a number not as a person. He was callous and indifferent toward me and toward the punishments that were dished out to sailors. The love that I felt for the Redemptorist priests at St. Joseph I felt for the CEO but not for Chaplain Mahler. I learned that other sailors did not hold him in high regard either. Comments were, "He spends all of his time with the officers and is never seen with the crew." As an 18-year-old sailor, I shared that feeling. Nevertheless, I assisted Chaplain Mahler at Sunday Mass. During church services, he was a Priest of God and I was his assistant.

At the Captain's Mast, among the punishments or sentences given by the CEO were dismissal of charges, a few hours of extra duty, confinement to the ship, deprivation of liberty (unable to leave the ship while docked in port), confinement to the brig (ship's jail) for a number of days, solitary confinement in the brig for a given number of days, probation for a given number of months, reduction in rank and bad conduct discharge. I was unfamiliar with the appeal process but there were occasions when these sentences from confinement to bad conduct discharges were remitted and sent to me for insertion in the sailor's jacket.

I do not recall an instance where a sailor was charged with Obscene or Profane Language, unless it was to an Officer of the Ship coupled with disobedience. The use of the four letter word and other profane language was quite common and reminded me of the many times I heard this language in the inner city of Rochester or saw it painted in public bathrooms and other walls in the inner city. Even at meal time, if a sailor needed the salt or pepper shaker, it became common to hear, "pass the f.....ing.salt and the f.....ing pepper to my f....ing end of the f......ing table." (Four obscene adjectives in one sentence!)

As an assistant to the Chaplain, my only duty was to serve Mass with him on Sundays. I developed a tolerance for the language of the ship knowing that these adjectives were being used to put emphasis on a particular situation or subject matter and were not intended to be malicious or vulgar. As the war ended, Chaplain Mahler impressed me with his final sermon. He suggested that if we, as sailors, did not attempt to break the habit in our remaining time in the Navy, we would be faced with great embarrassment if, during a Sunday dinner at home, we asked for the salt and pepper using four obscene adjectives in one sentence.

Missing Teeth

During my time in the Navy, I typed an average of three letters a week to my mother and family. One of these letters was written on March 6, 1945, and made reference to my sadness over my missing front teeth. At the time, we were heading for the Ulithi Islands, which were being used as a major Naval Base, a great distance from land-based Japanese airplanes. Including my own two front teeth, I had five other molars. These two front teeth and five molars supported a bridge that enabled me to chew my food properly and project a nice smile. In December of 1944, my two front teeth broke in half from decay. The Guam dentist said that when we arrived in the Pacific Theater of War, there would be a hospital ship that was equipped to provide a new bridge to correct my problem. He pulled the remainder of my two front teeth. This left me with a damaged bridge, five molars in my upper jaw and two missing front teeth. Eating was difficult. I spoke with somewhat of a lisp. To avoid being picked on by shipmates, I very seldom smiled. However, my shipmates learned why I was not smiling and consistent with "titless wave" they razzed me with a new nickname, "toothless fairy Freddy".

In December of 1944, a Christmas hit song had these words: "*All I want for Christmas is my two front teeth, my two front teeth, my two front teeth. All I want for Christmas is my two front teeth and I will have a Merry Christmas.*" Indeed, this is all I wanted. My appearance then seemed to be more important than eating. I prayed that somewhere in some Pacific Island Harbor, there would be a hospital ship. Indeed, just prior to our arrival in Ulithi on March 13, 1945, there was a communication regarding a hospital ship anchored in Ulithi, which included a sophisticated dental department. It was sent to all ship's personnel. Emergency cases only would be considered. I eagerly waited in a long line to see the Guam dentist. He determined that as long as I could partially chew food, my case was not an emergency and since the line was long behind me, I was quickly dismissed. I was devastated and retreated to my yeoman duties. In fairness to other shipmates, I knew my case was cosmetic rather than an emergency.

I thought of my battle station and my pending duties. When I was alone, I practiced "Commence fire" and "Cease fire", the words that I had to repeat when the Marine officer yelled out these words from our battle station on the uppermost bridge of the Guam. I found that I could repeat these words but with a slight bit of exaggeration, I could make the "S" sound disappear completely and make it sound like "Commenth fire" or "Theese Fire." I wrote a letter to the CEO stating that the missing front teeth interfered with my battle station duties. He called me into his office and he asked me to repeat these four words. I exaggerated the lisp as best as I could. The CEO was about 52. I was 18. He appreciated the good work that I was doing for him. He could have easily had me reassigned to a non-speaking battle station or had me thrown in the ship's kitchen. After all, I couldn't fire a ship's gun. I didn't know how to load the ship's guns. I didn't know how to put out fires. I didn't know how to steer the ship. I knew nothing about engines. I didn't know how to provide medical attention to the wounded. I knew nothing about navigation, nor could I read the stars for navigation purposes. As I spoke to the CEO, I tried to smile as much as I could to show the ugliness of my smile but I was careful to say nothing about my cosmetic discomfort.

My plan worked. That same day, March 13, 1945, I found myself in charge of the detachment of men who were to receive emergency dental care. Armed with a letter from the CEO, the ship's Dentist reconsidered. We boarded a small boat and boarded the hospital ship where I received special attention. My new tooth bridge gave me back my smile and I was prepared to repeat the four important words, critical to the winning of the war in the Pacific. Five days later on March 18, our Task Force was under our first attack by Japanese aircraft. I was at my battle station ready to die for the CEO who gave me my two front teeth. In several battles that day, with my finger on the red button of the phone attached to my head, I quickly repeated the words of the Marine Officer. My voice was loud, distinct and clear as I said, "Commence Fire" and "Cease Fire".

Letter Home – End of the War and Censorship

September 7, 1945

Dearest Team,

Yippee, censorship has been abolished. As you know, at a certain time each day the ship's news commentator on our public address system would give the same news you hear over the radio. The crew cheered almost as much as they did when the Japanese surrendered last month. So here's a history that I kept of the USS Guam (without censorship).

To start off, our floating city, the USS Guam steamed 72,000 miles, approximately three times around the world. Each propeller turned 33 million times. We used 12 million gallons of fuel oil, enough to heat 4,000 six-room houses for one year in New Jersey and vicinity. We generated eight million kW hours of electricity. We were at sea 3,870 hours and at anchor 2,566 hours. How about that? I received a lot of this information from the chief yeoman who is working on the Guam's history book.

We left Pearl Harbor in the middle of February 1945. Our first stop was Ulithi, a big beautiful anchorage in the southwest Pacific. That's where I first got a glimpse of the US Navy in force and power. Everything from tankers, ammunition ships, supply ships, repair ships, hospital ships (that's where I got my two front teeth), LCI's, LCT's (landing crafts for Army and Marine land invasion), destroyer escorts, destroyers, cruisers, battleships, aircraft carriers and many other miscellaneous craft which made my eyes pop with excitement and pride.

My battle station was changed from my safest and heavily shielded spot in the conning tower to the exposed open spot of air forward, on the tenth level, the highest part of the ship. Up there, I sat in a revolving chair with binoculars and a set of speaker-ear phones. I could see the entire fleet and all the action. Besides being the eyes of the ship, air forward was the station where the gunnery firing was controlled. When the air forward officer gave the command to open fire, I would press down on the red button on my headpiece and hell would break lose.

We were in Ulithi anchorage for a few days and then started to pull out in force. Carriers led the way, then the Iowa class battleships, the Guam, our sister ship, Alaska and other destroyers. It was a beautiful sight to be watching from air forward especially when they're in line formation.

It was then that we realized that our training was over and from now on it was going out with a first class bunch of veterans to be initiated into our first battle. After we got underway, the captain announced over our public address system that we were going to strike Japan with the mightiest fleet of carriers and ships ever assembled in US Naval history. We would go under the name of "Task Force 58" , which had previously made history in battles throughout the Pacific.

Most of us were anxious but scared. We knew that we were in for some stiff action as we soon found out. It was about the middle of March when we were within 300 miles of Japan. Then began days of watching planes take off from carriers, 2 and 3 times a day for attacks on the Japanese navy and territory. Usually about suppertime while in the chow line, they'd return, a squad of 3 in each formation. They had a scary system of landing one plane after the other without crashing into each other. The teamwork had to be unbelievable. I saw many wave-offs but they'd usually make it the second time around. Once in awhile, the plane's wheels would refuse to lower or the pilot would have engine trouble. He would then pick out a destroyer and make a crash landing in the water ahead of the destroyer. The pilots always had plenty of time to get off the planes before they sunk and the destroyer would pick them up in no time. The pilots deserve a lot of credit for bravery.

I believe it was the second day of the raids on Japan, about March 15, when our planes were returning from their raids that a single suicide Japanese plane followed the planes back to the fleet. We were all at our battle stations at the time having been warned previously by radar of a "bogey" at so many miles away. A bogey is the name given to an unidentified plane. Radar, by the way, had a big write up in the August 12 issue of Time Magazine so I'm not revealing any military secrets. As you know we receive Time Magazine on board our ship minus any advertising. In miniature form, it is a compact news package. Without radar, we would never have had sufficient time to be completely prepared at our battle stations.

There were pilots in the air around the clock ready to intercept a bogey. On this particular day, when our planes were returning from raids and preparing to land, a lookout in air forward yelled "Japanese" in an excited voice. It was too late. The plane dove right over the carrier, very slowly it seemed from where we were, and dropped a bomb. There was a black puff of smoke on the carrier's deck and as we changed course, she changed right along with us as if to say, "I didn't even feel it." I don't know what I had expected. I thought there would be explosions and expected the ship to go careening to one side and fall out of formation but with her deck still smoking, the carrier changed course in perfect formation with other ships. With the binoculars, I could see the men running around with hoses on her deck and gradually the fire was put out. Their repair crews made quick repairs and the carrier remained in action.

In the confusion of carrier-based planes preparing to land, the Japanese pilot had dropped his bomb without a shot being fired. After the pilot struck, the sky was covered with bomb bursts in an attempt to shoot him down. I was looking through the glasses as the Japanese plane began to fade out in the distance. I was sure the plane was smoking and doubted the pilot ever got back to tell of hitting a carrier. That was my first sight of actual warfare. I didn't like it because there we were with hundreds of planes in the air and a mighty fleet on the sea and this lone ranger hits a ship. That, as I soon found out, was the only time we were caught off guard.

The days following were busy ones. We went to our air and torpedo defense stations a total of 91 times. Once, we had a three-day general quarters, which meant sleeping at our battle stations, eating battle rations, and keeping an alert watch for Japanese planes. In just one day, I believe we hit a record of 12 torpedo defenses, which meant in my case, running up as quickly as possible the 10 flights of stairs to my battle station. If the plane came within 10 miles and our combat air patrol failed to get him, the general alarm would sound followed by General Quarters – all hands man your battle stations. It was in April that we got the two planes and six assists that you read about in the clipping back home.

I remember clearly the two planes we got. This was a demonstration of our power. Every gun was spitting shells. However one of the crippled planes, unable to reach a carrier in his death dive, in smoke and flames, headed for our ship. I could actually see the pilot in his cockpit. There was no place for me to dive or hide. I was on the highest deck of the ship strapped in my revolving barber chair. I thought this was it; I'm dead. In the last few seconds, out of control, he buzzed over our heads and crashed in the ocean within 200 feet of our ship. Yes, Annie Bananie, my former bed wetting sister, I almost wet my pants.

On March 19, from a great distance, I saw another Japanese plane that flew over the USS Franklin. It had escaped a massive amount of gunfire from the entire fleet. It dropped a powerful bomb that led to a series of explosions, fire and smoke that lasted for hours. As I write this I can only say that it is a miracle the Franklin did not sink. It continued to move in formation as many smaller vessels moved in close to assist her. There was no report of the number of dead or injured but it had to be severe. A few hours after the direct hit on the Franklin, in the earphones that I wore during my watch, I heard a message from a destroyer to the Franklin saying that they were picking up men in life preservers they assumed might be alive. The Franklin replied that they had no option except to throw the dead men into the sea as they struggled to put out the fires and assist the hundreds who were wounded. The next day a destroyer transferred a few of Franklin's injured onto our ship. One of them died on board the Guam and we had our first burial at sea since we were commissioned. It had an impact on our crew. It was our first experience with a burial at sea and all felt fortunate that our ship had been spared several or hundreds of burials at sea.

Our sister ship Alaska, the Pittsburgh and a few destroyers were designated to get the Franklin out of the danger zone. All was going well as we moved away from the danger zone. The Franklin was able to get along under her own power. Torpedo defense sounded and we learned a bogey was in the air. Sure enough, a plane came diving out of a cloud cover bent on finishing off the crippled Franklin. We fired with all we had, as did the other ships and even the heroic Franklin managed to shoot. The plane flew over her, dropped a big bomb and I just squeezed right along with that bomb and thanked God as it hit the water just ahead of the Franklin. We kept firing but I believe the Japanese plane got away and without the power of its bomb, headed home. They say our combat air patrol finally got her about 20 miles from where we were. The men on the Franklin went through all of the horrors of war in this very short period of time. How many survived, I do not know. We left her somewhere in the Pacific and she was escorted to Guam Island where she was temporarily repaired for her trip home.

March passed by with many more raids on Japan and Okinawa. We saw nothing of the amphibious forces that made their landing on Easter Sunday but we had first hand information as progress was being made. The planes of the carriers were continually taking off, dropping their load, returning for more fuel and ammunition and taking off again. Finally, after 60 days at sea, taking on our food, fuel and supply of ammunition even at sea, we headed back for Ulithi. The Captain said we broke a record for being at sea without the glimpse of land.

On April 11, I saw a Japanese Kamikaze, out of control and unable to hit a carrier, crash into the starboard side of the Battleship Missouri. The fire was quickly brought under control and I was amazed to learn that the damage was negligible.

From March 18 to April 26, our fleet destroyed and probably damaged 1,103 enemy planes in the air and on the ground. In one battle, in less than 5 hours, our pilots had sunk a Japanese battleship, 2 cruisers and 3 destroyers – the Japanese fleet that had been on its way to help out at Okinawa. It's a wonderful and fortunate thing being with carriers. We never saw the battle that sank these ships, but in our records we have credit for participating in this action.

We pulled into Ulithi on May 14, having been out of Ulithi since March 14, a two-month period. That is when I had my first liberty since leaving Pearl Harbor on my 19 birthday as I described in my previous letter home. We were only there for about 5 days when we got underway again to rejoin our carriers in raids on Okinawa. We bombarded an island near Okinawa with our big guns. We then received orders to go to Leyte to escape a major Typhoon that was expected.

We weren't more than 15 miles from the Pittsburgh when she had her bow ripped off in the typhoon that caught us by surprise on our way to Leyte Gulf, Philippine Islands. Luckily though, as you've probably read, she escaped without a casualty and is now home. She had been with us on our shakedown cruise and had followed us out here from Pearl Harbor. I was on TBS when I overheard the Pittsburgh report that she lost her bow. Seasick as I was, I waited in alarm for the next message. A few minutes later, the Pittsburgh reported that it was proceeding in reverse. I kept thinking, "Were there any men in the bow?"

On June 11, we pulled into Leyte Gulf where we would enjoy night movies, topside, and beach parties, safe from storms, Japanese and trouble. I wanted so bad to let you know where we were so you wouldn't worry and your letters kept coming regularly the same as mine left the ship. We were at Leyte until July 15 when we left. Okinawa was now in our hands and we anchored in Bucker Bay, Okinawa on July 18. We were assigned to the Ninth fleet, separated from our carriers for the first time since we've been out here.

When you thought we were in on the raids on Tokyo, we were either anchored safely at Buckner Bay or cruising in the East China Sea looking for Japanese shipping. That was the way the end of July went by. In our operations in the East China Sea, we saw no Japanese ships, but we knew that we were disrupting the enemy's plans by creating an effective blockade. We were in Bucker Bay, Okinawa, when the first atomic bomb was dropped on August 6 and Nagasaki on August 9. When Hiroshima was announced, the men gathered topside yelling & cheering. My feelings were uncertain. That day and evening I thought of the Japanese mothers, fathers and children and my heart went out to these civilians who were victims of a dictator's insane war.

We were in Okinawa when Japan's first surrender offer was received and it was there that I saw the display of celebration fireworks that I've never seen before. We had beach parties on a little island called Tsunken Shima. It was a beautiful layout, the best we've ever seen in the line of beach parties. The land reminded me more of home than any of those sandy palm-treed islands. The grass was rich and green and there were many gardens growing. The beach was beautiful for swimming and the beer was ice cold. (2 bottles as usual, ahem). We didn't see any native Okinawans but we did see some of their burial grounds and as shown in Life magazine, their burial tombs are better than their homes.

We were in Buckner Bay when the battleship Pennsylvania was hit, while the Japanese were waiting for our reply to their offer to surrender. Torpedo defense was sounded and all ships were prepared but the Pennsie didn't have enough of a warning. She was hit pretty badly in the fantail. We all felt terrible. Here we were on the eve of victory, and our good ship Pennsie was hit by a Japanese pilot, while at anchor, after getting through the toughest part of the war unscathed.

After the surrender terms were agreed upon, we finally shoved off on August 28, going into the East China sea up into the Yellow sea, passing near Tsingtoa, China but not seeing much, up further and passing by Dairen, the big seaport of Korea. We passed Dairen and Port Arthur again yesterday and could see white buildings and homes. We've been flying big American

Flags showing off our power. Last night after supper we passed by a fishing boat not too far away. There were about 10 "Chinamen" in it waving their hats, arms, and one waving a big 3-foot fish. They got in the way forcing the entire column to go around them and yet they waved and waved while we waved back. That was the closest we ever got to seeing Chinese people.

We were sort of sorry we didn't get the occupation of Japan with the Third Fleet because many of our former ships were in on it including the Missouri. It would have been something to write about, sailing up Tokyo Bay in a victory fleet.

Well team, you now know where I've been and where I am now. Get a map of Asia and you'll find it right to the point. You see, since June 11, you really had nothing to worry about for we've seen no action as we first did when we came out here. If there were someway that I could have told you, I would have. The censor cut out the "In port" or "At Sea" part of my letters that I used to put in the upper-right-hand corner.

We're still in the Yellow Sea tonight although there is no land in sight. The occupation of Korea should take place soon and there probably won't be any use for us out here in a while. After this operation, who knows where we'll go or what we'll do? We expect to fuel at sea tomorrow and probably take on mail again, as this letter will go off. You've heard of the Victory Fleet that the Missouri will lead the way into New York Harbor on Navy Day, October 27. Well, we are keeping our fingers crossed hoping and praying that we'll be a part of that Victory Fleet although there is much doubt. It would be the most wonderful experience of my life.

It is getting late and I've been rushing with this letter so excuse all the cross outs. I dream of you every day and just can't wait to be with you again. God bless you team. All my love and kisses enclosed for each of you. Hope to hear from you in tomorrow's mail.

The yeomen have been kidding me all day about censor being lifted. They keep asking me if I've written my diary home as yet. I guess it's because they know how lengthy I make my letters when an opportunity is at hand and from this letter I see they weren't wrong.

Your loving umpire,
Fred

CHAPTER 15

Black Sailors on the USS Guam and the next Millennium

In addition to my responsibility to attend Captain's Mast and to record offenses in a sailor's file jacket, I also had to maintain the medical record of each sailor forwarded to the ship's office by the medical department on board ship. Shortly after the liberty granted in Trinidad, several men were treated for venereal disease. Of the approximate 40 men treated, I was shocked to learn that about half of those treated for venereal disease were black and about half were white. Yet there were 2,000 white men versus 42 black men on board. I recalled the long line of white sailors waiting at the government supervised house of prostitution. None of them were black. I assumed that the black sailors, like many white sailors, engaged in sex without the choice of government supervision.

Like most Americans, I have taken the role of blacks in World War II military service for granted. When I was discharged at age 20 in 1946, I signed up for the history book of the USS Guam that included combat history, stories, cartoons, photographs of the many divisions and photos of men at play, on liberty etc.

As I write this, it is 54 years later. In reviewing this USS Guam journal in the year 2000, I became aware for the first time that of the approximately 2,000 men on board the ship, I could not find one black sailor in any of the photos of church services, topside basketball games, movies or on liberty in foreign ports. Instead, there was only one picture of black men. It was a group picture of 42 black men in the S-3 Division. Posed on either end of the 42 black sailors were one white Lieutenant and one white Division Officer. As I now write this,and reflect on this division photograph, there is the appearance of a "black naval prison", where inmates are responsible for the massive job of washing and drying the utensils used for the 6,000 meals a day for 2,000 sailors and officers, seven days a week. During combat, these men worked below decks ever fearful of a torpedo that might break through the ship's heavy armor.

Simply because they were born black, in a WWII government allowed segregation, none of these men had the opportunity to be a part of another division, regardless of what inherent skills they may have had. If you were black, you were simply assigned below decks for utensil washing duties regardless of any technical or other skills that you may have had. Even the cooks, bakers and food servers photographed in the S1 and S2 Divisions were all white. This was 1944-45.

It is hard to believe that Lincoln's Emancipation Proclamation was issued on January 1, 1863. This freed the slaves in those territories still in rebellion against the Union. The Webster Dictionary defines "emancipated" as "not constrained or restricted by custom, tradition, superstition, etc.," and "freed, as from slavery or bondage." Eighty years after Lincoln's Gettysburg Address on November 19, 1863, at the dedication of the national cemetery at Gettysburg, Pennsylvania, it would appear that the process of the "emancipation" of blacks in the Naval Service on ships in World War II, or in any branch of the US Armed Forces, did not exist.

The Prisoner of the Truck is aware that his boyhood Prison was indeed difficult. Now he wonders how much more he would have suffered, if he were a black sailor in WWII. His award winning typing skills and academic achievements would have been ignored. He would have been assigned below decks with 41 other black sailors to wash metal trays, knives, spoons, forks, pots and pans, three meals a day, for 2000 sailors for the duration of the war.

If he used the salesmanship of the "strawberry story" to demonstrate his superior typing and office administration skills, this would have served no purpose. He would have been assigned to washing pots, pans, serving trays and utensils regardless of what skills he possessed.

About 50% of black sailors contacted venereal disease in Trinidad versus 1% of white sailors. There were no black soldiers standing in line in the Trinidad house of prostitution where white sailors received supervised protection.

If I were black, what impact would this combination of discrimination on and off the ship have on my spirit, my attitude toward my health, my family and my self-esteem?

My God, I think as I write this, World War II was fought to save the world from the madness and oppression of leadership in Germany and Japan. Yet within this War, in spite of its good purpose and its brave men, on board the USS Guam and throughout the US Armed Forces, black men were "constrained or restricted by custom, tradition and superstition". They were not emancipated. They were on-going Prisoners of weak governments that failed them for eighty years (1863 to 1943) since the Emancipation Proclamation. Finally, in the Korean War of 1950, President Truman eliminated segregation in the armed forces but America still had a long way to go for "Emancipation."

In the year 2000, 137 years after the Emancipation Proclamation, our Armed Forces appear to be free of any form of discrimination regarding race, creed or color.

World War II called for a united effort by all Americans. America won it. Nothing should be taken away from the total leadership that resulted in our victory. I realize that I have no right to question the wisdom or lack of wisdom of a war that lead to victory.

Nevertheless, fifty-six years later, in a small way, let me pay tribute to the black men, living or dead, who served on the USS Guam or in our Armed Forces. "You and your families should be proud of the humble and essential role that you played in bringing America to Victory in World War II. I took your service for granted. I was too wrapped up in my own childhood prison to be sensitive to yours. I thank you for your contribution in WWII. I salute you and I ask for your forgiveness."

Let me honor, G.H. Louis, R.E.D. Coleman, H.C. Peters, T.G. Johnson, C.L. Clariday, C.C. Crawford, T. McIver, N. Smith, S. Rice, R.M. Jordon, R.V. Daniels, O.J. Smith, O.W. Bryan, T. Fajardo, H. Trammer Jr, W.L. Brown, F.D. Harris, J. Mazyck, L. Russell, R.L. Roseman, J. McElroy, W.H. Smith Jr., T. Lewis, T.L. Williams, V. Gunn, E. Randle Jr., A. Branch, O. Stennis, W.E. Banks, W. Livingston, W. H. Polk, J.E. Crawford, C.R. Newbolt, R.A. Betterson, W. Johnson, M. Cole, L. Counce, R. Bert, T.C. Smith and the three black men in the photograph who did not have the privilege of being named.

The Next Millennium

Although we have a long way to go to end prejudice completely, times have changed dramatically as we enter the new millennium of high technology. I believe that any human being in the United States of America, regardless of his or her heritage or background, is the captain of his or her own destiny.

For anyone with drive, determination, conviction and faith in God, there is the opportunity to take hardship, adversity and failure and turn it into success in school, at work or at home. These characteristics are inherent gifts from God. How we fuel and energize these gifts in these enlightened times is not in the hands of God. It is in the hands of each individual who understands that nothing comes easy.

Study, hard work, practice and facing reality are an essential part of success. When these characteristics are combined with sincerity, honesty, goodness, patience and an enthusiasm that reflects in whatever we say or do, there is nothing too difficult to achieve, no matter what our heritage, no matter what our background.

Footnote: Any reference to "blacks" is not meant to be offensive. Where I use this term, I am referring to African-Americans.

CHAPTER 16

Aboard the USS Guam Letters to My Family

I wrote home about three times a week. Frequent letters were signals that I was alive and well. All letters were censored on the Guam. Whoever the censor was, he learned about the thoughts and feelings of the men on board. I wonder who censored the censor's letters. Letters that were censored involved a razor cut of a word, a line or a paragraph.

Here are a few of the many letters I sent home. They were saved by mother and given to my sister Ann prior to my mother's death on February 3, 1998, at the age of 95. Two were Father's Day letters. My father carried these two letters in his wallet throughout my two years in the Navy to show to his customers. Fifty-six years later, I discovered that my mother had saved them in the worn envelope that he carried them in.

June 18, 1944

Sampson Naval Base, Boot Camp, first month in the service.

Dear Pa:

You made many sacrifices to raise your family to be good God loving citizens, to be able to serve our country in a free and proud way. I thank you for the days you cradled us when we were babies, missing hours of needed sleep, for buying us our first suits with long trousers, for caring for us when we were sick and when poverty struck.

We took a lot for granted. We never realized what a strain bringing up children can put on parents. You have been God-loving and ever-faithful parents, who brought us through those trial-filled years to our present manhood. And today, many families all over the US have a service flag hanging in their front windows shining as a beacon throughout America, showing the pride that loved ones have for their boy serving his beloved America.

I can say now with a thankful heart, God bless you Dad, Mom too. He will always be with you.

Your loving son,

Fred

P.S. Happy Father's Day Pop.

February 27, 1945

Dearest Lady, (My Mom)

Welcome Home from the hospital. I was thrilled to get my first telegram ever. I loved it. "It's a boy. Your baseball team." Wow, I now have four brothers and four sisters but until I get home, the team is short one player. I know that Western Union charges by the word. The six words in the telegram are another of Betty's gift for writing brevity.

Today I received seven wonderful letters at sea from home. You can bet this sailor was one of the happiest guys on the ship, hearing from the sweetest lady in the world and his brothers and sisters.

Mom, your letters were beautiful and everything I've said about you in every letter I have ever written, I'd like to repeat but that would end up being a book. I really love you. You've been everything to me all of my life, everything that is sweet, kind and good. I want you to realize that always, and someday, we hope soon, I'll be able to sit by your side and read part of this letter to you and then continue on with civilian life proving my love for you is forever. As you said in your letter, you miss me more each day. Well that happens to be just the way I feel too, but I'm kept busy, and there are so many things that keep me busy—a library with all the good books one wants, my study courses for my high school equivalency examination; my work in the communications and personnel office, my friends, our talks at night, drills, etc. Everything keeps me going and the time seems to fly by bringing us all closer to the time we can all go home. I know it'll be quite awhile yet but I'm satisfied and thankful I chose the Navy. I'm not kidding, not saying this to make you feel better. It is the way I feel.

Of course, there are times that I miss you all very much but being occupied makes it a lot easier. I have the picture of our family we took in my civvies (civilian clothes) pasted on my desk. Other sailors post their photographs in their lockers or if sheltered in their work areas. I often glance up during the day, looking at that peaceful scene and wishing that time would travel back to when we were all posing together. It's the picture that I like best except for the fact that Dad isn't in it but I have the other one with everyone in it, except Betty who took it. It is also on my desk. The rest of my pictures are in a photograph book that I bought. I have written comments about each picture that I will show you when I return, many of them humorous.

I, too, for one, Mom, am glad you have our baby Lee to keep you occupied, as if you don't have enough to do. I can imagine how much you missed Kenny while in the hospital and by the time you get this letter everything will be settling to normal again. From Betty's letter she sure had one big time helping you out.

I have the letter mentioning your wedding anniversary. I'm sorry my card didn't reach you at the hospital as I planned. I wish I could have solved your blue feelings by dropping in on you and holding my newborn brother in my arms. Mom, you shouldn't worry about me. I'm fine and in no danger. Worry about taking care of my new baby brother.

Thank the kids for their letters and tell them that I'm sorry that I haven't found time to answer each of them separately. Their letters are precious. They warm my heart. Betty's, Joe's, Ann's, Jim's, and my sunshine sisters, Vicky and Deanna. I love Kenny's drawings. But Ann's take the cake. She's a little peach and I know how much of a help she's been to you, with Betty working full time. Little sweet Ann, more like my Mabel every day. Tell her not to mention this to anyone but she's my favorite sister. I know you will read this out loud so go ahead and tease my other sisters.

Hug my two youngest brothers especially for me. Tell Dad that I'm not neglecting him in these letters. I know how much he'd give to be able to sit down and write his own letter. Thank Betty for her swell letter. Maybe she didn't have the patience of Job but Job didn't have a bunch of kids and a house to run. She's a model. I love her and all of my little custard dumplings. More kisses. I hope that you receive my packages. I sent two air mail and my wrist watch regular mail insured. Mabel, stay beautiful for me.

Always your loving son,

Fred

6 April 1945, At Sea

Dear Brothers Junior (Joe), Jim:

Well Joe and Jim, we finally beat the girls by having our newcomer make the score 5 brothers to 4 sisters. First of all, the prospects of a better spring weather means you are helping with the victory garden again this year.

Betty wrote and told me about you guys setting pins at the Elks club at night, after school, during bowling season and giving most of your earnings to Mom. Boy, is this sailor proud of you.

I guess we all remember what our parents have sacrificed for us. I believe that you know how much we owe Mom and Dad. The war has changed a lot of people and I think it has made kids back home older, more serious about things and more supportive of their Moms and Dads. I also know how all my sisters chip in with their tasks under the direction of Betty and Anneo.

Take good care of Mom for me by doing everything she tells you. When I look back on the days when I was home, busy as I was, I wish I had been more helpful at home. Little things that you can do around the house are big things for Mom. Take the ashes out of the cellar cheerfully. Keep the cellar clean. Straighten out the barn. Go to the store for her. It's a sacrifice but just a little one compared to all that we owe her. When I was home I remember how we would argue about going to the store to buy something Mom needed. I'd say send Junior. Junior would say send Jimmy. Jimmy would say," I did it the last time." So when called on by Mom, do it cheerfully and make yourself a lot happier knowing that it makes our Mabel happy and saves her the headaches listening to the arguments.

Like the two of you, I don't have all the time I'd like to have for myself. I've my work to do in the office, and watches to stand. Orders to take from guys with a higher rank, orders, sometimes I don't like to take, but in the service there's no such thing as arguing. You do it. Of course there are guys who don't like to take orders and usually I see them before the captain and I am the one who has to put the bad news into their record file – a record that holds them back from promotions.

Hey remember guys, I am talking about the lady who is on her feet from the time Pa wakes up until after everyone has gone to bed — all day, washing and ironing your clothes, preparing meals, gardening, working with the girls on housekeeping, getting everyone ready for Church and it goes on. Imagine how happy you make her every time you obey right away without a fuss. It just makes her life easier. I should stop preaching cause I know you are doing more than your share.

Keep writing to me when you can. I love your letters. Give Kenny and baby Lee hugs for me. Study hard. Good luck with June exams. Give school your best effort and be satisfied with the results. Take good care of Mom, my one and only, for me and show her how much you love and appreciate her advise and wisdom. Remember me in your prayers and don't miss Sunday Mass. I'm always thinking of my baseball team. God Bless All.

Your loving brother,

Fred

April 27, 1945

Dearest Mom & Dad & Family:

I expect to be promoted soon to Yeoman 3rd class. In the Army it is buck private, private, corporal and sergeant. In the Navy for me, it was Seaman, Seaman 2nd class, Seaman 3rd class, Yeoman 3rd class. This will mean a bigger check that the Navy sends home to you because of my "major family support" status before I enlisted.

I don't think I can praise the Navy enough for the fast way they get mail to us when we are at sea. It is too bad mail doesn't reach you as fast because I know just how you feel when a week or two goes by without hearing from me. So far, I have not failed to write every single week mostly because I do not want you to worry about me and I know that each letter puts you more at ease that I am OK.

How are all my dumplings today? I'd like to see the Deanna and Vicky, my sunshine sisters, with their glasses on. I hope they make good use of them and comply with the doctor's order on when to wear them. Your eyesight is something precious.

Today, I am on watch from 8 PM to 12 PM. For security purposes, all sailors must stand watch twice a day — four hours on watch and eight hours off watch. That's eight hours of watch in a 24-hour day. In addition, we spend eight hours of regular daytime duties. The loud speaker's blast the wake up calls at 6 AM. Exercise drills in formation begin at 6:15 AM. Breakfast hours are from 6:15 AM to 8 AM, staggered by division intervals, to prevent over crowding. The watches get kind of tough, since you are confined to a station. However, this is war, and in war, it's great to have clean beds, clean clothes, showers and hot meals in a ship that is constantly being washed and polished by its crew members.

During my watch, I was studying by the little red light, as I used to do on Pa's truck under the kerosene lamp. In a previous letter I mentioned the officer who noticed my interest in studying. Well during my watch this evening, he seemed to be half-asleep while I was working on algebra problems. Suddenly, he stood up and said, "Sarky, when are you gonna get stuck? I wanna help you but you never get stuck". Well, one problem did have me stuck so I showed it to him. He explained my mistakes and also a shorter way of doing it. So from now on, anytime I need help, I have him right next to me on the same watch. I can't describe the wonderful feeling I get by his interest in helping me. Isn't that great?

Sheffield, the southern boy who works in my office, and who stands watch on the bridge, came into the pilothouse the other night where I stand watch. He said, "Fred, look at that beautiful sky." It was one of those spectacular sunsets, clouds in sky, and the sun setting in the ocean. He said, "How's about writing a love letter for me, that sky otta give you ideas." I did write the letter for him. He got a reply a month later. He said, "Saaky, you got this girl fallin' in love with me and now I don't know how to write back." I said, "Sheffield, you are on your own from this point on, just be yourself." On the next watch, he came to me and said, "Saaky, we're havin' fradd raace for supper and ahm going down to eat at faave o'clock."

It's getting late. I'm closing for now. Kiss the team for me, from the shortstop to the batter Betty. Love to all.

Always your loving son,

Fred

May 1, 1945

Dearest Mom & Dad & Family:

I wish I were back to the school days when I was a kid playing football, running till I was winded, learning teamwork for fun instead of war. I remember coming home from school, running, jumping and yelling most of the way, glad to be in the outdoors. There were those special school days when I felt happy and free. I knew I would find love, warmth and a delicious home-cooked meal waiting for the team and me. I remember the lady of the house, either outside hanging up the wash, down in the cellar rinsing clothes or upstairs fixing beds, the pots on the stove jumping from the steam of boiling fresh vegetables and the girls helping as much as they could — the table set, ready for the gang to arrive. One by one, you guys would run into the kitchen, usually poking your noses in the pans and yelling "Hey ma, watcha got for dinner?" Mom would reply, "Is school out already?" Those were the days, something we often take for granted as kids. How secure it felt to jump into a warm bed at night, to sleep in quiet comfort and be awaked by that sweet voice, breakfast always waiting.

It was the same daily routine each day, full of youthful fun, something to be remembered as one's happiest times. I know it's mine. I thank God daily for those memories, the days, weeks, and happy years that flew by. Maybe the long hours on Dad's truck were tough, but I thank Him for the home he placed me in, parents that any fellow would rave about, be proud of, and fight for as I do now. I know that's why I'm out here, that's why I'll do my best in every battle, with the strongest faith and courage in God. All I have I owe to my parents and country. They have given me an equal place in the world—a place where I chose my school and subjects; worship in the Church of my choice; be able to compete with anyone rich or poor; discuss opinions of our government and the men who run it, many little things that mean so much to a free people.

Now we are miles apart. I remember the difficult days, as well as the happy days. I have come to realize that one can only place a higher value on happy days, when one recalls what the bad days were like. I had many bad days growing up but I try to focus more on the good ones. Children should be grateful for parents who try their best to be good parents. I'll always love you, Mom and Dad, love you as much as my heart can. I will always remember your goodness, kindness, patience and sacrifice to bring up God-fearing children.

I hope censor allows the following to go through. On a recent night, a Japanese bomber had snuck through our air patrol. We call this air patrol our night fighters. The loudspeakers yelled, "All hands man your battle stations." You probably wonder what that's like. With only a red light to guide us, we have to grope around in the dark for our clothes, or sleep with them on. All ships have excellent radar equipment to warn us in advance of pending danger. It doesn't take long to slip on our stockings, shoes and dungarees. In quick time everyone is at their station, manned and ready, fully dressed, prepared in this case, for the lone enemy bomber. The bomber was about five miles away, according to the earphones I wore at my battle station. Our ship, and other ships, opened fire. It was about 1 AM and you could watch the flaming shells lighting the sky. There was a huge burst of flame in the night sky about five miles from our ship. The enemy plane, that we could not see, was shot down. Sounds impossible but I saw it with my own eyes. Our ship was doing most of the firing and, as far as I know, we were credited with downing the plane. We secured about 2 AM and I slept soundly until reveille. It just seemed like another drill to me.

Kiss each of the team for me. Tell them how much I love them. An extra hug for my shortstop baby Lee and my lovable Kenny. God Bless All and remember to keep your faith and trust in Him, as strong as ever, as I do. Happy Mother's Day sweet lady again. All my love and kisses, from the bottom of my heart, my one and only Mabel.

Your loving son always,

Fred

P.S. Thanks to all my brothers and sisters who send me mail. I love receiving them because they brighten my days. Betty, thank you for writing so regularly. Maybe Anne isn't my favorite sister. She probably told you she was. I will keep answering all letters even though many will be shorter than this one. Love you.

May 9, 1945, At Sea

Dearest Mom & Dad:

I'm well and in the best of spirits, mostly because of the good news of Germany's defeat and the beating that the Japanese have been taking lately, not counting what will be in store for them from now on. If they bomb Japan as much as Germany was bombed, I don't see why there would be the necessity of an invasion. Let's hope and pray for a quick defeat. I recall a picture I saw just before enlisting in the Navy a year ago. "Victory through Air Power," the picture that predicted just how Germany would fall. Air power would smash the hub of the wheel, and the spokes holding the rim would collapse, and the infantry would smash through all sides of the rim. So let's hope for a quick defeat against Japan cause Freddie wants to come home.

Ain't much more to say so I'll close for now with God Bless All. Will write again tomorrow, Ascension Thursday. Kisses for the team and tell them how much I love and miss them.

Always your loving son,

Fred

May 19, 1945, At anchor

Dear Pop:

Mabel has been getting most of my attention in the past so I figured it was about time I wrote a little private letter to you. First of all I want to thank you for those precious words of yours which Mom transcribed in your last letter on May 4.

Hope business is good and that your truck doesn't give you trouble. It seems that used to be your headache always. Either a flat tire, or motor trouble. From the family's letters everyone really is making our Park Avenue yard something to be proud of and I'll be waiting anxiously for the day when I can see it together with my happy wonderful family.

A year has gone by since I first enlisted but still my separation from home into new surroundings hasn't changed me in any way. I've made many friends, fellows that I can rely on when I have problems - decent kids from a home like mine. I've talked, eaten and slept with them in the same compartment of the ship. We encourage each other when we feel down in the dumps. We are there for each other whenever there are problems. While waiting for a movie or while lying in our sacks, we'd talk about home, and the wonderful family we left behind. It seems I can't walk from one ship's compartment to another before I meet a friend and stop for a few words. Someone will show me the photographs he received in the last mail or something his loved one said in a letter, or a picture of a new born baby. Little things like that they take pride in showing to each other, the same as I do.

I'm always bragging about that yard and home, my mom and dad, brothers and sisters, my good old baseball team. I often pass the kids letters around for other fellows to read because children's letters are so sweet and innocent. I can't remember which brother or sister wrote this. "The prayers we forget to say for you at night, we say in the morning".

So you see, Dad, I'm learning something about family beyond ours — brotherly love, friendship and helping one another. The job I have is interesting, the time goes by fast, my friends are many. I've learned to be patient and work out my own problems. My love for home and family grows stronger each day.

In my past letters, I've told you of the action I've seen and how I've felt. I know that makes you worry all the more. I don't blame you for worrying. It's natural as I said once before but don't let it get you down. I'm on a big ship, and a ship that can defend itself. Compared to the boys in the Army, Navy and Marines, I consider myself one of the lucky ones. I have my shower every night, regular good food, warm comfortable bed to sleep in, a good job, and hear from home often - - so I'm thankful. Most of all I have my faith and all those prayers being said for me back home. I know that prayers are helpful and I am thankful for them. I have many advantages, Dad, and I don't take them for granted. So, keep up those many prayers and don't worry too much. All of you are in my prayers as well.

Kiss all the kids for me and tell them how much I love them. Also thank Mabel for her beautiful poem, and give her my special love. God Bless all of you, Dad. I thank God every night for a wonderful father.

Always your loving son,

Fred

FATHER'S DAY LETTER

May 31, 1945, At Sea

Dear Dad:

Last year, things were altogether different. I wrote you a letter, then only 50 miles away from home. Now I'm on the other side of the world. Difference though in the distance doesn't make a bit of difference in my heart

As far back as I can remember, I have always had the same love for you that I have now. In school, I realized that I owed you something I never could repay, something any fellow would be proud of, bringing me up in a wonderful home, sacrificing many things for my sake, always thinking of your home and children before yourself. Easter would come around and practically everyone but you had a new suit or new shoes. And yet you always stood out as a father to be proud of, and I always was and always will be proud of my Dad. You have given me everything I could ever ask for.

I admire you, Dad, because you've done things many men could not do. At 17 years of age, you left Lebanon to come over to America all alone, leaving your family behind, and not knowing a word of English. That takes courage, Dad, something that has kept you going all these years from the day you stormed out of that school room when you were asked to pull up the shade and instead shut the window. I can imagine how you felt and when your business hit the rocks, the business you worked so hard to build, and on top of it all, losing your home that you worked so hard to give Mom and us kids. I haven't forgotten those hard days when you had to move your family from the best to the worst section of the city. And yet your fatherly love and admirable courage kept us going, properly clothed and fed, always working from early morning till late at night to keep things going smoothly, too proud to accept relief from the city.

You know that I was not a happy kid working on the truck but I did learn lessons from you, Dad, that I hope will help me for the rest of my life. You taught me the art of selling during the strawberry season. You told me that if I hated working on the truck, the only way to get off of it was to take my books and bible and study on the truck during the many hours that I wasn't busy. This is what helped me to do better in school. This is what made me number one at St. Joseph's Commercial School when I was 16. I am now 19, Dad, and I think back on that graduation day when I was speaking as the Valedictorian. I remember looking out into the audience. I saw the tears flowing down your cheeks. I knew that I made you proud and it made me so happy.

Dad, I have the education, I did well, but I lack your wonderful qualities. God has been with you all these days. He gave you the holy gift of Fortitude or Courage to cope with your hardships and sacrifices. He gave you the gift of Wisdom in your leadership in St. Nicholas Church. He watched every move you made guarding your family and with His help, you watched with pride your children grow up day by day realizing that you had something money could buy for no man but something that money could spoil. You have the gift of a family and a happy home to be proud of - - the envy of every father.

You came to America, Dad, because you truly believed it was the land of opportunity, a country where you could raise your children without fear of persecution. Dad, you have earned for yourself the most precious of all things in the eyes of God and man— the most wonderful wife and mother and a big family that fills the home with togetherness and joy.

Dad, may God bless and always be with you. Happy Father's Day.

From your loving and faithful son,

Fred

CHAPTER 17

Prisoners of Political Madness

The USS Guam was anchored in Buckner Bay, Okinawa, less than 310 miles south of Japan, when the first Atomic Bomb was dropped on Hiroshima on August 6, 1945. Three days later, the A-bomb was dropped on Nagasaki.

On August 6, 1945, all of the sailors rushed topside when the news of Hiroshima was announced over the public address system. It seemed clear to everyone that the war would soon be over and we would all return home. I stood among my cheering shipmates with mixed emotions. The ship's newsletter included data on the population of Hiroshima and the estimated number of dead and wounded. Hiroshima was about the same size as Rochester, the home of my warden father, my mother, my eight brothers and sisters, our home, schools, hospitals, churches, parks, Eastman Kodak, Bausch & Lomb, Gleason Works, Rochester Gas & Electric, Rochester Telephone Company, Democrat & Chronicle, etc.

The Japanese and Germans had shocked the world with their sophisticated war machine. Hitler had been working feverishly to perfect an A-bomb. During WWII, it was common talk among citizens of Rochester that our city would be one of the enemy's prime targets for air raids. Rochester was the home of Gleason Works, the maker of sophisticated gears, essential to the war effort.

The destruction of Gleason would cripple the country's gear manufacturing capability, essential for the running of our ships, tanks, airplanes etc. 1293 Park Avenue, the home of my parents, brothers and sisters was only 2 miles from Gleason Works.

That night on August 6, 1945, I found solitude in the aft of the Guam anchored in Okinawa. I meditated on the destructive power of the Atomic Bomb. These were my thoughts.

I could not help but think that if Japan or Germany had perfected the Atom Bomb ahead of the United States, Rochester could have been Hiroshima. My entire family, relatives, schoolmates, teachers and friends would have suffered or died. I would eventually return, if at all, to a devastated city to visit the ruins. I wondered where I would erect a memorial to my dead family.

At 19 years of age, there was no doubt in my mind that my country was on the offensive due to the provocative attacks of the enemy. America and its Allies were engaged in World War II in the defense of liberty. Yet, on this night of August 6, I felt compassion for the Japanese military men whose families were in Hiroshima. What mental anguish did these men suffer when they heard that their city and their families were wiped off the face of the earth with a single bomb? Did these Japanese military men come to the realization that their government's fanatic and insane leadership caused such misery and pain?

I tried to put myself in the shoes of a 19-year old Kamikaze pilot and other young Japanese military soldiers who were taught to believe that they were serving their country with honor when they sacrificed their lives in suicide dives to destroy or cripple an American Naval Vessel. I thought of the Japanese soldiers. They bitterly defended the island of Iwo Jima right to the end, in spite of a war they knew they were losing, without thought of surrender. If I had been born Japanese, would I have had the same suicidal willingness to die for my country based on a strong spiritual conviction instilled in me by my country and my parents? Would I have considered it an honor to commit combat suicide for a cause that offered no victory?

I thought that if I had served in the US Army and came into hand to hand combat with the "enemy", I would have fought vigorously to save my life even if I had to plunge a bayonet into the heart of another 19 year old enemy soldier. I wondered whether that would have been an act of self-survival rather than an act of bravery in service to my country. I wondered how sick I would be when I saw an "enemy" soldier, 19 years old, gasping for his last breath as I watched him die. I wondered how I would feel about his parents who spent all those years raising him to manhood.

I was happy that the Atom Bomb would end the war and hasten my return to my family and to my future with them. However, as the former Prisoner of the Truck, I felt a deep compassion for all military and civilian casualties in World War II. Whether friend or foe, my heart went out to all mothers and fathers who lost loved ones, or for the military personnel who returned to a destroyed town to find that their mothers or fathers were killed in the war.

I thought of the Japanese civilians as brainwashed victims of war, victims of an insane political system that sought war in the pursuit of economic or territorial gain. I thought of my father's customers, most of them German immigrants, who were examples of goodness, skills and generosity in the Rochester community. I wondered how many of their relatives in Germany, caught in a web of insanity, had no choice but to bow to the power of Hitler, his Army and Gestapo for fear of death or imprisonment.

I just thought and wondered.

In a long period of peace, from one generation to the next, it is easy to forget the horrors of past world wars. I researched the Internet for the impact of wars for the past hundred years and to give thought, not to winners or losers, but to humanity as a whole.

THE SLAUGHTERS, OPPRESSIONS AND MAN MADE FAMINES

(Matthew White, Historical Atlas of the Twentieth Century, 1999)

Examples of the number of people who died in all the wars, slaughters, oppressions and man-made famines:

Oppressions	**79,000,000**
Military Deaths in War -	**38,000,000**
Civilian Deaths in War -	**21,000,000**
Man-made Famine -	**44,000,000**
TOTAL -	**182,000,000**

These numbers are staggering. We can only pray that reason among world leaders and their people will prevail over insanity in the new Millennium. Otherwise the devastation of the next 100 years will surpass the horror of the last 100 years. How many of those who suffered or who witnessed suffering, were prisoners, "shut up against their will or not free to move"?

Even the Bible makes reference to the insanity of leaders. ".... when David returned from the slaughter of the Philistine, the women came out of all the cities of Israel, singing and dancing, to meet King Saul, with timbrels, with songs of joy, and with instruments of music. And the women sang to one another as they made merry. 'Saul has slain his thousands, And David his ten thousands.' And Saul was very angry, and this saying displeased him; he said 'They have ascribed to David ten thousands, and to me they have ascribed but thousands...' And Saul eyed David from that day on." 1 Samuel 18:6-9

On board the USS Guam, I served with two ships in Task Force 58 that represent the two worst casualties in US Naval History. These following figures represent a very small percentage of 182,000,000 who died in the past 100 years. Yet, they are examples of the human suffering caused by war.

The USS Franklin (CV13)

This is a record of that disaster, taken from the Internet Web Page of the USS Franklin (I mentioned the USS Franklin in my September 7, 1945 letter to my family):

"Headline: *Mar. 19, 1945 - USS Franklin (CV 13), which had maneuvered closer to the Japanese homeland than any other U.S. carrier, was attacked by a single Japanese plane which dropped two armor-piercing bombs, devastating the hangar deck and setting off ammunition. Franklin was enveloped by fire. Casualties totaled 724 killed and 265 wounded. Franklin remained afloat and proceeded under her own power to Pearl Harbor for repairs."*

"The Franklin, which was loaded with fully gassed and armed planes and hundreds of tons of explosives was herself a 30,000 ton floating bomb. After the initial blasts of the two bombs, the Franklin's open aviation lines ignited. The planes warming up on her flight deck turned into raging infernos; their bombs and rockets adding to the conflagration. 40,000 gallons of aviation fuel poured out of Franklin's hangar deck in a flaming niagra. Every last soul on the hangar deck was vaporized in the flash of an instant. Raymond Milner, Smith's best friend on the carrier, had passed into the pages of history along with several hundred other sailors."

Shortly after March 19, 1945, throughout the United States, there were 724 gold stars and 265 silver stars that were hung in the front windows of the homes of parents and wives — all caused by one Japanese pilot — all in a matter of minutes.

USS INDIANAPOLIS

The USS Guam served with the USS Indianapolis in pre-invasion raids on Okinawa. The Indianapolis was damaged in this invasion and returned for repairs.

After repairs, while on another assignment, having just completed a special mission, the USS Indianapolis was torpedoed by a Japanese submarine on July 30, 1945, only six days before the 1st bomb was dropped on Hiroshima. The ship's compartments were not sealed and it sank in 12 minutes. The USS Indianapolis website records the event of 883 dead out of 1,199 on board. There were 331 sailors who survived after spending 4 to 5 days floating in life jackets in shark infested waters. There was a major error in communication regarding its departure & arrival. It was fortunate for the 331 survivors that they were spotted by an aircraft that was not engaged in a search.

Another 883 gold stars in the windows of parents throughout the United States — all caused by one Japanese submarine eight days before America dropped the first A bomb on Hiroshima.

Note: *For ships at war, the Franklin and the Indianapolis suffered the worst casualties in US Naval Military History.*

Hiroshima and Nagasaki

Japanese estimates placed the total number of dead from the two Atomic bombs of Hiroshima and Nagasaki at 240,000. The pre-raid population of both cities totaled 450,000 people. The deaths, not counting the injuries, represent 53% of the population of these two cities.

To comprehend the destructive power of the A-bomb, the US sustained 292,000 battle deaths throughout six years of WWII. Whereas, within three days of each other, in a matter of seconds, 240,000 Japanese people died from two Atom Bombs.

Cost of the War

(Free Concise Encyclopedia — An Encarta Article titled World War II)

"World War II's basic statistics qualify it as by far the most costly war in history in terms of human and material resources expended. In terms of money spent, it has been estimated at more

than $1 trillion, more than all other wars combined. The human cost, not including more than 5 million Jews killed in the Holocaust, is estimated at 55 million dead—25 million of those military and 30 million civilian. The human cost of the war fell heaviest on the USSR, where more than 20 million were killed. The Allied military and civilian losses were 44 million; those of the Axis, 11 million. In terms of global politics, the most significant casualty was the world balance of power. Britain, France, Germany, and Japan ceased to be great powers in the traditional military sense, leaving only two, the United States and the USSR."

There were others wars after WWII. I salute the US military forces of *all wars* in the past 100 years, both living and dead, who fought for democracy and peace.

I pray that the next century will be one of peace for all nations; that hunger, famine and disease, including the growing threat of world AIDS be wiped out; that the rulers of all nations become rulers of peace instead of power and madness; that the people of every nation, for the good of humanity as a whole, never again allow themselves to become prisoners "kept shut up against their will or not free to move"; that future generations of men, women and children of all nations be spared the fear and the destructive power of War.

Prejudice

Hitler's persecution of the Jews was a Living example of insane prejudice. In the United States, the discriminatory treatment of African-Americans since Lincoln's Emancipation Proclamation of 1863 is a sad example of justice moving too slowly. The World Book Dictionary for the definition of prejudice — *"an opinion formed without taking time and care to judge fairly; applies to an opinion or judgment, usually unfavorable, formed beforehand with no basis except personal feelings."*

It is time to end prejudice against one's race, creed, color, physical appearance or sexual orientation. It is time for all of us to come together as good neighbors. It is time to "Love your neighbor, as you love yourself". It is time for the Golden Rule to flourish, "*Do unto others as you would have them do unto you.*"

CHAPTER 18

The War Has Ended!

The war ended. On May 26 of 1946, at age 20, I returned to my 1293 Park Avenue home to my mom, dad and eight brothers and sisters. While I was on the USS Guam, on February 28, 1945, I received my first six-word telegram. It simply read, "It's a boy. Your baseball team." He was named Lee Charles. My mom and dad now had nine living children. My new baby brother Lee was now a year old, twenty years younger than me. The entire family and many relatives welcomed me back home at the New York Central train depot on Central Avenue. It was a joyous reunion. I could not wait to hold my brother Lee in my arms. My brother Kenny was four and the second to jump into my waiting arms. My sunshine sisters Vicky and Deanna were ten and eight. Jim was twelve. Anne was 14 and my brother Joe was 16. Betty was 22. My mother and father cried as they held me while the others happily circled us with embraces. I was no longer the skinny, bow-legged, knock-kneed, pigeon-toed,dark-skinned boy who was mocked by his classmates. I was no longer a Prisoner of the Truck or a Billing Clerk working next to a pot-bellied stove from 4 PM to Midnight six days a week. I was a US Navy Veteran, a survivor of World War II. I truly believed that America was the land of opportunity and I would pursue opportunity to the best of my ability. I had received a high school equivalency diploma in the Navy. I believed that with perseverance and hard work, there was nothing I could not achieve. Congress had passed the GI Bill of Rights. It would give me an opportunity to focus on getting a Regents High School Diploma and completing courses in college that would give me a degree in Business and in Law.

In two years, the family that I called my team had been very supportive at home. My sister Betty was working for Blue Cross Blue Shield of Rochester. She was also mom's major assistant. She organized tasks for all of the children that contributed to disciplined and orderly household. Vicky, Deanna and Ann had perfected their singing harmony. Ann and Deanna, self-taught, were playing the guitar. I thought the three of them were better than the famous Andrews Sisters who starred in movies and entertained the troops overseas during World War two. Joe was attending Monroe High School. Joe, Jim and Betty were making major contributions to the support of the family. All were doing well in school.

Junior was now Joe by his own decree. He was Wady Joseph Sarkis, Jr. but he chose to be Joe Sarkis and there was no arguing about it. Joe was the 8-year-old boy who was naturally gifted with the art of selling strawberries. Joe had a positive self-esteem and it showed in everything he did. He was not afraid of work. He worked at the Elks Club on Clinton Avenue in Rochester in the evening. The Elks Club had eight bowling alleys and a swimming pool. During the 33 week bowling season from September to April, Joe set bowling pins from 7 PM to 11:30 PM from Monday thru Friday. He also set pins from 1 PM to 10 PM on Sundays whenever there were tournaments at the Elks Club. When Jim turned 12, Joe got him a job as a pinsetter. The Elks Club was on Clinton Avenue, in the downtown area of Rochester. My brothers used the transit bus system to get back and forth from work. They earned $8 a night, $40 a week. They kept a $1 a night for themselves and gave the rest to my mother — a significant contribution to household expenses.

Each pinsetter took care of two alleys, jumping from one to the other to pick up and reset the pins. It was a demanding job. In league play, bowlers were well organized. There were no idle times. When one bowler finished, the other was standing up to take his turn. The pin setting had to be coordinated so that there was no delay. Pin setters would hang on to the high end walls of each pit and lift their bodies to avoid being hit by flying pins. They reset the pins by putting their foot on the device that raised the spikes. Each bowling pin had a hole at its base. To insure that pins were lined up in proper order and in accordance with league rules, the ten pins were placed in the permanently placed spikes. Setting bowling pins was an art that had to be learned. Each pin weighed two pounds. Beginning pinsetters could pick up only one pin at a time to reset them on the spikes.

After a month, the pinsetters would master the art of picking up two pins in each hand, doubling the speed of resetting the pins as you jumped from alley to alley. A pinsetter had to learn how to pick up more than one pin at a time, bundle them in your hands for quick pin setting, and jump from alley to alley. There were two leagues the 7 PM to 9 PM league and the 9:30 PM to 11:30 PM league. The only break in pin setting was between league play and that was no more than 30 minutes. In 1947, a year after I returned from service, my father went to the Elks Club to observe his two sons at their work. He went back to the pits. He heard the noise and echoes of eight alleys in full swing; bowling balls rolling down the alley; the smash of the ball against the pins, the noise of the flying pins colliding with each other, the effort his sons had to make to remain high from the pit in order not to get hit. He was shocked. He told Joe and Jim that when the season ended, they could never set pins again. His word was final. They never set pins again.

In the writing of this book, and what will be a shock to all of the old time bowlers, who remember the days of pinsetters, Joe allowed me to tell this story of pin setting.

Many times a right-handed bowler will hit the pocket perfectly and the ten pin will remain. Left-handed bowlers would hit the pocket perfectly and the 7 pin would remain. This required the bowler to shoot the 2nd time extending the time it took to complete ten frames. Pinsetters were interested in speeding up play. This would give them a longer rest period between two shifts as well as allow them to get home earlier after the 2nd shift. Therefore, if the bowling ball hit the pocket perfectly, as the pin setter raised his feet to prevent being hit by flying pins, his foot "accidentally" kicked the ten pin for the right handed bowlers or the seven pin for the left handed bowlers. For all the older timers who remember pinsetters, it has now been disclosed that this was a common practice among pinsetters. What impact did this have on legitimate bowling averages or league champions will forever remain unknown.

Joe also had built a newspaper route. Since he worked late at night as a pinsetter, he made a deal with my sister Ann, who was then 12. If she took over his paper route, which included a lot of easy drop-offs in an apartment house in the neighborhood, she could keep 25% of the money earned and turn the balance over to him. Joe was a born salesman, not only in the selling of strawberries but also in the art of turning over his business for a 75% commission of the profits.

In the summer, Joe also worked three days a week on my father's truck, including Saturday nights, while Jim worked the other three days. Possibly because of the financial contribution that Betty, Joe and Jim were making to the household or because of health reasons, my father began to get home earlier during the week — around 6 PM. However, on Saturday nights, he continued to stop at Hedges Bar and Grill to sell left-over vegetables to bar patrons.

Neither Joe at 16 nor Jim at 12 seemed to resent working with my father. Joe never complained about cold winter nights in the back of the truck. Possibly, I thought, it had something to do with my father's shorter hours and a limit of three days a week for each brother during the summer months. (Joe, Jim and I really never talked about it until the writing of this book when Joe and I discussed old times. I will deal with that in later chapters.)

It was good to be home. I finally held my baby brother Lee in my arms. We were a united team of nine again. After many prayers, I had returned home safely. There was much joy at 1293 Park Avenue and my mother and father were at peace, knowing that their sailor son had returned unharmed.

I immediately set my education and work goals. I joined my three brothers in the third floor attic where we all slept. My baby brother Lee slept in a crib in my mother's bedroom. The girls occupied bedrooms on the 2nd floor. There was still only one bathroom for eleven of us — a toilet, a sink, a bathtub, a shower curtain. The open door policy prevailed.

1940 - Graduation from St Joseph's Grammar School. I'm up front on the left.

1942 - Graduation form St. Joseph's Commercial School. That's me on the left.

1943 - On my bike with sister Betty and baby brother Kenny

1943 - 1293 Park Avenue - The home I bought Mom when I was 17.

1944 - Home on leave with family.
Mom pregnant with soon-to-be-born brother Lee.
Betty missing.

1945 - USS Guam - a Battle Cruiser!

1945 - USS Guam - Using the typing skills that bought my freedom and my mom a home

1945 - USS Guam - My battle station - "Open Fire!" Cease Fire!"

In Rochester, N.Y., Fred Sarkis, President of K.O.R. Inc., and family gather 'round for a song after a picnic on the lawn of his beautiful home. "We're really a family within a family—the family of Rudd-Melikian dealers", he explained.

Mr. Sarkis checks sales records with one of his men. "R-M's advertising, plus the hard-hitting, local merchandising has certainly paid off for us", he commented.

The Sarkis family cuts K.O.R.'s 6th anniversary cake. "Rudd-Melikian field engineering and location sales help have helped us to increase our business 30% every year," Mr. Sarkis said.

Accepting award from Lloyd K. Rudd (left) and K. C. Melikian (right), Fred Sarkis and his sister, Betty, register their pleasure with smiles. "The R-M franchise has sure put us in the chips," says Sarkis.

1955 - Success in the coffee vending business

1956 - Helen Margaret O'Hara and me on our wedding day

1957 - The Kwik-Kafe coffee service team

1958 - Rochester Cafeteria Services, Inc.
My partner John O'Donnell and me

1967 - Bristol Mountain Ski Area - "Rocket Run"

1967 - Bristol Mountain Ski Area - "Aerial View"

1967 - Bristol Mountain Ski Area - Bobby Kennedy and me.

Community Chest Campaign 1968
ISD Chairman on Safari
("Insipida Sarkisa Dumdum")
and friends.
SPECIAL
COMMITTEE

1968 - Community Service - Having fun raising funds

1970 - A Tribute - Congressman Frank Horton honors Mom with a flag that flew over the White House

1970 - The Start of Bristol Harbour Village
the skeleton of a possible failure

1972 - A Joy to Behold
A special picture of Helen and Fritz

1969 - Christmas - Josh, Gina, Fritz, Wade and Greg
The last vear at the Ambassador Drive mansion

Bristol Harbour Village

Vision Becomes Concrete Reality

Articles and Photos

By

W. C. DANNENBRINK

A VIEW FROM the balcony of a cliff-side apartment shows the southern portion of Canandaigua Lake. The apartments in Bristol Harbour Village are in several five-story buildings that line the cliff above the village's marina and swim area below.

THE DEVELOPERS hope that by this time next year, an 18-hole course on the Bristol Harbour Village property will be ready for use. The course will be for members and guests when it is fully operational.

From cocoon to butterfly. The full-fledged metamorphosis is not complete. But the transition from a man's dream to reality now appears assured.

Bristol Harbour Village, once just a vision to its originator, Frederick W. Sarkis, apparently has overcome a rather tumultuous beginning and with the help of major financial transfusions is becoming a reality.

In July 1968, Sarkis, then a resident of Pittsford announced that he was planning a $12 million, 200-unit condominium development on 145 acres of land which included a 2,000-foot frontage on Canandaigua Lake. The development was to be located just north of Seneca Point in the Town of South Bristol.

In the ensuing months, Sarkis and his associates were confronted with tremendous opposition. Residents of the area, environmentalists and others protested the planned development.

Hearings were held by state agencies, state legislators were contacted, and civil action was taken in the courts. Actions like a lengthy hearing before state public health department agencies, what Sarkis once described as a "tough money market," and other factors stretched his resources to the breaking point.

By August 1970, work on the first of a planned 16 condominium buildings stopped because of the fiscal squeeze. Two months later it was announced that arrangements had been made with a Maryland mortgage investment firm and work was ready to begin again.

The following January, the State Department of Environmental Conservation announced that it would approve a 120-boat dock to be placed at the foot of a 120-foot cliff below the condominiums. (The decision was fought by Canandaigua Lake Pure Waters Ltd., a lake area environmental group, but the courts ruled against the group in November 1971.)

By January 1972, Bristol Harbour was growing — at the site and on the drawing boards. It was now planned to be an 867-unit development on 242 acres. Fourteen of the now-constructed condominiums had been sold. Total cost of the development was estimated at $25 million.

In May 1972, the development got a major boost when Connecticut Mutual Insurance Co. joined the venture and, in Sarkis' words, "insured proper financing." The company is a limited partner and owns 35 per cent of the stock. It has committed $12 million to the first phase of development of what is now described as a $60 million development.

By September 1972, plans were pretty much what they are today: 874 units on 490 acres; an 18-hole golf course; riding and hiking trails; tennis courts; 462 condominium apartments in 19 buildings that rise from the cliff on the shore of the lake; other dwelling units in town houses and "clustered" residential units scattered around the landscape.

An estimated $750,000 is being spent on water and sewage treatment facilities. In the future a "mini-commercial center" will be built, a club house for the golf course, a 200-unit hotel or guest house; and other features.

As can be imagined, living in Bristol Harbour Village will not be cheap. Fees, memberships in clubs, and incidentals such as utilities and exterior maintenance cost the owner of a two-bedroom condominium an estimated $200 a month. This is in addition to any mortgage payments the owner may pay for his unit.

And these payments can be high. Units cost from about $30,000 or more for studio apartments to $80,000 or more for multi-bedroom units.

There still are objections to the development from some who fear it will lead to environmental or other problems.

But the butterfly (that's the symbol the developers have adopted for the complex) is emerging from the cocoon. What was once an idea has moved from drawings on paper, to models, to the real thing.

THE MAN WHO conceived the idea of Bristol Harbour Village is Frederick W. Sarkis, chairman of the board of the development firm and a resident of the village.

OVER

1974 - Bristol Harbour Village - A concrete reality

A UNIQUE FEATURE of Bristol Harbour Village is a vertical gondola which carries residents and guests from apartments 120-feet above to the marina and swimming area on the shore of Canandaigua Lake. The village owns boats — and limits the number of power boats — which can be rented by residents.

THE VILLAGE is self-sufficient in many ways and one of them is the treatment of sewage. The existing treatment plant can handle 65 thousand gallons per day and eventually will have a capacity of more than 300,000 gallons per day. It will provide tertiary treatment and when weather permits, fully-treated effluent will be used to spray irrigate an 18-hole golf course nearby.

SOME THINK THE Bristol Harbor Village condominium apartments fit in well with the surroundings. Others feel they are usurpers and should never have been allowed. Zoning laws have been passed by towns around the lake to prohibit similar developments. This photo shows four of 16 buildings that the developers plan to build along the lake. Other units will be away from the shore on parts of the 140-acre development.

1974 - Bristol Harbour Village - More concrete reality

1975 - A family of smiles in spite of my business problems
Bottom Row L to R - Josh, Fritz, Wade and Mom
Top Row L to R - Me, Helen, Greg and Gina

LIKE THE U.S. HOCKEY TEAM...

We're Number One
in Quality, Experience, Spirit, Innovation & Performance

#1

Our game is the professional management of cafeteria and vending services to business and industry.

Our expertise as coach/consultants is national in scope.

Our 1980 Game Plan is to expand our unique services throughout Western and Central New York.

TEAM PHOTO (left to right) - 1st row; Fred W. Sarkis, Charbel Sarkis, Joseph J. Tascione, Toufik Sarkis, Wayne E. Wilson - 2nd row; James Sarkis, Douglas P. Sarkis, Ray A. Cross Patrick L. Artuso, Donald E. Waddell, Randy B. Stoner - 3rd row; Elias T. Sarkis, Kevin G Blakely, Daniel R. Kennedy, Paul P. DeMeyer, Joseph P. Tomasso.

Company Team Players not pictured are:

John J. Cantatore
Douglas A. Eichorn
James A. Kryger
Gary W. Saffran
Donald Sarkis
Oscar T. Sarkis
Richard W. Sarkis
W. Joseph Sarkis, Captain
Richard J. Shea
Craig V. Urisuoli
Carol A. Audin
Diana L. Kennedy
Caroline L. LaRocco
Linda C. Sarkis
Susan Sarkis
Irmgard Burley
Cheryl A. Toscano
Nancy M. Yannello
Shirley A. Bell
Mary A. Bell
Sherry A. Grandin
Janis M. Kern
Nancy A. Marrow
Mary R. Padiak

If superior quality is the Game Plan for your people in the 1980's, put this team to work for you by calling Joe Sarkis, Captain, at 716-647-9050.

SMS SARKIS MANAGEMENT SERVICES, INC.
454 LEE ROAD ROCHESTER NEW YORK 14606
716 647 9050 24 HOUR SERVICE

1980 - Sarkis Management Services
A comeback after losing the ski area

Photo courtesy of the Democrat and Chronicle - Rochester, New York

1999 - A hug of thanks after a talk to kids at risk in Canandaigua, New York

Photo courtesy of the Democrat and Chronical - Rochester, New York

1999 - A happy and content retired man
Blessed in so many ways -
a loving and supportive wife, five entrepreneureal children,
eleven terrific grandchildren, a close and wonderful family,
so many great friends and a sustaining faith in God.
And still busy helping and motivating others.

Photo courtesy of the Democrat and Chronical - Rochester, New York

2000 - A five-minute clown act before a motivational talk

CHAPTER 19

Age 20-23 Work, High School, College and the Death of my Father

In the summer of 1946, right after discharge, I entered Franklin High School. Franklin offered a special accelerated program for WWII veterans, who sought a high school degree, under the GI bill of rights. I chose an intense and continuous twelve-month period of study in order to earn a New York State Regent's High School diploma. This was the equivalent of completing two years of regular high school courses in twelve months.

My only means of transportation was the subway near Park Avenue that would take me to Franklin High in 20 minutes. The hours of school were from 8 AM to 2 PM.

At the same time, I ran an advertisement in the newspaper. Little did I realize what an impact this ad would have on the rest of my life. It read, "20 year old WWII veteran seeks part time office work. Shorthand, bookkeeping, typing, what have you?" My address and phone number were in the ad.

A week after I started the Vet's program at Franklin High, I was working out in the back yard of 1293 Park Avenue. My mother had expanded the rock garden on the slope that lead to the above ground subway. At the top of the slope there was a fence. One could walk up a flight of rock stairs and look down several feet at the subway bed that traveled underground when it reached the city of Rochester. I was working on that part of the flat land in the back yard that was heavily weeded. My plan was to convert this large space into a lawn to allow more room for playing, especially for the tossing of a football.

My mother came out to the field excitedly and said, "There's a distinguished looking man here to see you." It was Mr. Maro Hunting, the President of the Hunting Company. He owned a wholesale plumbing and heating supply company (the largest in Rochester) that serviced the plumbing and heating contractors in the area. I was sweaty, dirty and somewhat embarrassed about my appearance. I was surprised that Mr. Hunting did not phone me for an interview in his office. He quickly explained that he lived off of East Avenue and had to drive by Park Avenue so he thought he would drop in. He said he served in WWI and was surprised to see an ad from a WWII veteran with office experience. I told him about my educational plans. He said that was fine. I could work from 3 PM to 6 PM taking shorthand and typing letters for him and various salesmen in the organization.

He asked me to come to the office on Railroad Street for a trial. Railroad street was adjacent to the public market where my father purchased his fruits and vegetables. I passed the shorthand-typing evaluation with flying colors and was quickly hired at an excellent hourly rate. Mr. Hunting was impressed with the amount of time it took me to return letters for his signature as well as my determination to get a high school diploma while helping my parents to support a large family. He explained that I would also be taking dictation from others in the office including the salesmen.

The Jefferson Veteran's program was intensive, challenging and different. During one examination, one of the teachers would walk up and down the aisle, looking over the shoulder of a Veteran and say, "Want a drag on my cigarette". Then she would say,

"Are you stuck on that question?" She would give a hint or two to help the Vet solve the problem, and then move on to the next Vet with her lighted cigarette.

The bus ride to the Hunting Company took 20 minutes. Unlike the repetition and intensity of the 16 to 18 year old billing clerk job in a poor and stuffy working environment, the office of the Hunting Company was open, bright and air conditioned. There were about 30 employees in all departments and they were all friendly to this young WWII veteran who could take dictation rapidly and deliver the correspondence quickly for signature. One of the salesmen was Raymond O'Hara, the father of a young lady that I would meet years later and marry. Joe Daily was the Office Manager. Ed Reininger was the Operations Manager responsible for stocking and deliveries. I enjoyed my work and the people I related to. I did not believe it was possible to have fun on a job but there was plenty of it. At about 6 or 6:30 PM when Mr. Hunting finished his work, he drove me home to Park Avenue. Years apart in age, from one world war veteran to another, I had a high respect for the behavior and goodness of this company president.

Mr. Welch, one of the salesmen, dictated a letter one day and I proudly returned it to him for signature. I noted that he was taking the letter around to all of the salesman and they would roar with laughter. In the plumbing business, there are many male and female and human connotations such as: nipples, elbows, male coupling, female coupling etc. There was a boiler in those days called Weil-McLain. I kept looking at the shorthand from Mr. Welch and pondered over a word regarding the boiler. I kept thinking about the male and female couplings and I determined that the word after Weil-McLain was "circumcised." In my mind I saw a boiler with threads on it that screwed onto another large part. I assumed the threads were referred to as "circumcised." Finally, Mr. Welch let me in on the laughter and said the word after Weil-McLain was "Certain-Sized."

Mr. Daily was a fun maker. When I took dictation from him, it was common for him to shake the file on wheels adjacent to his desk. This would help the files to settle. Mr. Hunting was only a few desks away from this open office. There were no partitions separating any of the individuals in this space. Mr. Daily had hired a young 19-year-old college student. She was a very attractive buxom blonde. One of her jobs was to place documents in a mail file while standing up. When she was tired of standing in one position, she would shift her weight from one foot to another, throwing her hip to the left or right as she filed. Each time she shifted her weight Mr. Daily would vigorously shake his files. I would have to muzzle my laughter so that Mr. Hunting, whose desk was nearby, would not hear it. I often wondered why Mr. Hunting did not put a stop to this but he pretended to be busy with his work and not notice. This behavior went on for months and each time it had the same effect on me.

I thought of dating this hip swinging blonde but my mind was focused on my goals. I had this notion that dating was a serious matter. If you dated a girl, it would lead to a serious relationship and then marriage and there was no way I could help my mother and family if I were married and left home. Also, I wanted nothing to interfere with my educational goals. When I was satisfied that my mother, brothers and sisters were secure in their needs and their future, I would start dating.

As my father's work slowed down, due to problems with his health, my sense of duty and obligation to my family grew. Under the GI Bill of Rights, I had picked out a six-year program at Notre Dame University with full tuition and part subsidy for living expenses. At the library, I had reviewed every subject Notre Dame had to offer. I selected subjects that would earn me a degree in business administration and law. However, I decided that this would mean that I would have to leave home and weaken the support that my family needed.

Instead, Mr. Hunting allowed me to work full time from 8 to 4 PM Monday thru Friday. This allowed me to attend the University of Rochester night school on Prince Street, not far from the Hunting

Company. My two-year subjects were Business Law, World History, Accounting and Economics. Between my job at the Hunting Company and these courses, my plate was full.

In my second year at the Hunting Company, Mr. Hunting hired Donald Mack, another WWII veteran with a degree in Accounting. After a few months, Mr. Mack asked Mr. Hunting to allow me to become the bookkeeping machine operator. He hired Stella Kielson to take over the expanded secretary services. Stella was a devout Jew and I was a devote Christian Arab. She radiated joy and sweetness every moment of the day. We developed a respect and friendship that lasted many years. She grew to love my family and for many years, at Christmas, she would buy a small gift for everyone of my brothers and sisters and deliver them to our home wrapped in one big package.

Based on the quality of my performance, Donald Mack increased my salary. I handled all of the accounts receivable records for every contractor including billing and payment records. Don asked to have my father stop by after he left the adjacent public market in the morning. I never told Don about the four hours I spent locked up in the truck on winter Saturday nights outside of Hedge's Bar & Grill.

Don spoke highly of my father. He said he was impressed by the fresh presentation of fruits & vegetables, my father's warm personality and his devotion to his large family of nine children. He asked my father to stop by three times a week. He would leave the office to go down to the truck to hand pick the produce. He never asked about the prices. He pleased my father when he raved about me as an outstanding student and good worker. He became one of my father's best customers.

Don was married but had no children. I often wondered whether Don shared his large purchases with his neighbors and friends. I became a Donald Mack admirer. If asked, there was nothing that I wouldn't do for him. And ask he did. As I completed my two years of courses at the University Extension and two years at the Hunting Company, I began to think about Notre Dame again.

I had had saved enough money to pay off the mortgage at 1293 Park Avenue. I thought that between my father's earnings and Betty's on-going support, I could pursue my dream for Notre Dame while the GI Bill of Rights was still in effect.

As I was completing my second full year at the University of Rochester night school, Don Mack said to me, "I want you to read this Reader's Digest Article about these WWII veterans, Rudd & Melikian. I want to get your thoughts on the product. I sent away for information and I want you to read what they sent me. I'm thinking of getting a franchise on this product for the Greater Rochester area." I thought to myself, I'm only 22 years of age and this brilliant accounting chief and business manager, who completely reorganized the Hunting Company, wants my opinion on a franchise product? I was overwhelmed.

That night I spent four hours reviewing the Reader's Digest article and data supplied by Rudd-Melikian. It was a coffee vending machine invented by these two GI's, who had degrees in engineering and who served as engineers in WWII. The most interesting part of the article was the story of the development of a frozen coffee concentrate that would serve a better cup of coffee then instant coffee.

A customer would insert 5 cents into the machine. A cup would drop out and the hot water would pour into a heavy weight paper cup at the same time as the liquid coffee was being dispensed. A customer would press a button for the liquid sugar or cream or both. A wooden stick, similar to that which held a popsicle would come out of the machine for stirring the coffee. The machines were serviced daily. In the package of information, there were testimonial letters from companies speaking highly of the quality of product and service. Coffee breaks were popular in the military service. Rudd-Melikian believed that millions of veterans, returning from the war, would influence coffee breaks in worksites via the use of this automated service. In 1944, drinking coffee during working hours was considered a form of loitering. Thermos bottles for lunch boxes were acceptable.

My evaluation was simple. It was an easy conclusion. It would be new to Rochester. Not a single organization had a coffee vending machine. It was a new invention pioneered by two enthusiastic WWII veterans with a strong educational background in engineering and business administration. If the frozen coffee quality was superior, I thought it would be an easy sell in a market that had unlimited potential. I thought wherever there was a Coke machine, there could be a coffee vending machine. The market potential seemed huge. I excitedly told Don that it was a great idea but it was important to sample the product. We received a frozen can of Kwik-Kafe. We thawed and refrigerated it. We measured the 6 cubic centimeters required and poured it into a china coffee cup. It was a delicious product, hard to tell from freshly perked coffee.

I anticipated that Don Mack would leave the Hunting Company and become an entrepreneur. That would be a big loss for me. His attitude toward my father, his respect for my work, my increase in pay, his scheduling my work to fit my college courses, and now this respect for my opinion - all combined to earn my love and respect for him.

He listened intently to my views. My voice was full of excitement and enthusiasm. I said that I had no experience in these matters but in my opinion, this was a great idea with potential for great success. He shocked me with this reply, "Good, I'm glad you are enthusiastic because you are the one to start and run this new company. You will leave the Hunting Company. We will call it Kwik Kafe of Rochester. I plan to put four investors together, myself, Mr. Reininger and his nephew [22 year old Ken Reininger, who also worked at the Hunting Company] and you. It will take $15,000 to get the franchise." I said I did not have $3,750. He said it didn't matter. He would loan me the $3,750 and I would own 25% of the company and I was the best choice to leave the Hunting Company to start the business.

He set up the paper work. I became a 25% owner of a start up business. I resigned from the Hunting Company. Mr. Hunting wished me luck. I did not know how much Mr. Hunting knew about Don Mack's plans. Everything happened so quickly. It did not matter. Don was my hero. I would follow him to the moon.

The Capital Airlines flight to Philadelphia, the headquarters of the Rudd-Melikian was rough. It was a two-engine plane. I threw up into the paper bag until I had the dry heaves. It was worse than the sickness I experienced in the typhoon on the USS Guam. I wanted to die. I was picked up at the airport by George Schulhamer, an engineer involved in the product. We drove to a brand new headquarters with a big Rudd-Melikian sign on the building. I met both Cy Melikian and Lloyd Rudd. They were young, confident and self-assured. They gave me a few hours to recover from the plane ride. I had soup and crackers for lunch and my first cup of Kwik Kafe in a heavyweight paper cup. I took cream and sugar. It was consistent with the cup of coffee we made back at the Hunting Company.

That afternoon, George opened the machine to show me its various components. I saw the compressor that refrigerated the compartment that held the stainless steel canisters of coffee and fresh cream. Flexible tubes were connected to the spouts on the bottom of each of the canisters for coffee, cream and sugar, in the form of a simple syrup – all canisters of equal size and connected to dispensing valves directly over the cup well. The cup dispenser had six circular compartments. Each compartment held 50 cups. When one compartment emptied, a switch would rise to turn the cup dispenser and the next row of cups would drop into the chamber turning off the movement switch. There were six tubes in the cup dispenser that revolved, giving a capacity of 300 cups. When the last tube was used, the switch would pop up and the machine would read sold out and it would not accept the 5-cent coin. A hot water heater had an extension valve that was positioned over the cup well. The cup would slide down a stainless steel section into the cup well and a holder would protect it from bouncing out onto the floor. An electrical box on springs contained holding relays, delivery relays and timers. Cams on the cup dispenser came in contact with micro-switches that opened up the separate solenoid valves that allowed water, coffee, sugar and cream to flow. There were small screws in the stainless steel valves to adjust the flow of all these liquids and to increase or decrease the centimeters of coffee, cream or sugar dispensed. An ultra-violet light, shielded from the user's eyes, kept the cup-well compartment free of insects and germs.

George reviewed the operating manual and wiring diagrams with me and spoke of all the things that could go wrong and how they could be fixed. I had no idea what he was talking about. I was exhausted from the airsickness. My brain was fried. Fear gripped my heart. How could I possibly keep a machine this complicated working? Three investors back home were relying on me. How could I have made such a stupid mistake? Why did I forget what my father always preached, "If you go into business, you could fail and lose it. If you get an education, you can never lose it. So if you ever have a choice, choose education."

George dropped me off at a crummy hotel near the factory. Roaches were crawling all over the place. I pulled the sheets away and saw the bed bugs. I tried to comprehend the operating manual, drawings and wiring diagrams that were given to me by George. Fear again gripped my heart. I did not study to be a technician. But I knew I had to be the technician until there were enough nickels to support a headquarters, a vehicle, an additional technician and me. Fifteen machines had already been shipped and paid for. We had no customers. We conducted no marketing studies as called for in my economics class at the U of R. Would business be as generous on coffee breaks as the military was? Would they allow employees to hang around a coffee machine, smoke cigarettes and gossip? I threw up again. I had the dry heaves. I wanted to die for the second time that day. Why was I a hero worshipper? Wasn't that for kids? Had I been immature and impulsive in my decision? Did I warrant the confidence Don Mack had in me? How long would it take me to repay Don Mack if it failed? What would that do with my plans for Notre Dame and our family needs? I did not sleep. I showered, shaved and met George who picked me up at 8 AM.

I told George about my panic. He assured me that the trouble-shooting manual merely pointed out every possible thing that could go wrong. That it was possible that 90% of the potential problems would never occur but they had to be referred to. When you have a problem you check the operating manual. He said I did not need to know how to trace wires. I just had to learn how to replace components when they broke down. He said warranties on the machine would allow me to ship the electrical box on springs back to the factory for repairs at no cost. He explained that the electrical box was on springs to prevent activation when people kicked or shoved the machine. I was able to down a bit of lunch that day. The plane ride back was smooth.

The 15 machines arrived in crates at 1293 Park Avenue in June of 1948. They were put into our barn. I bought a 1929 Reo in my second year of college to help me get from home to work, and from work to school and back home. Don Mack found our first location. It was at the Rochester Transit Company in an old building on the 2nd floor. It was primarily for use by the bus drivers who spent their full day on a bus. I rented a truck. My three partners struggled with me to carry the machine up a long flight of stairs. It was back breaking. I thought, "What have I gotten myself into? How am I going to do this alone in the future?" There was no elevator that would have made it easy with a hand truck. The Reiningers were experienced at plumbing so the water line hook up was a snap. Putting the electrical outlet in the wall was a snap. Putting all of the cleaned containers, tubes and valves where they belonged was a snap. Filling up the canisters with the ingredients was a snap. Measuring the ingredients with a test tube to be sure they were dispensing the recommended cubic centimeters was a snap. The adjustments with a screw driver were easy to make. I closed the door on the machine and locked it with the wrench provided with the machine. I inserted the lock that offered access for the wrench. I put the key in my pocket and we waited for the water to get hot. In ten minutes, I took out a nickel. I put it in the machine. The cup dropped, a thin stream of liquid coffee went into the cup. There was no hot water. The stirring stick was sticking out where it was supposed to be. I pushed the cream and sugar button and liquids and both worked. Now we had a cup with everything in it except the hot water. One of the Reiningers said, "What's wrong, why are we not getting the hot water." I pulled out the operating manual. It said nothing about not getting water. Another Reininger question was, "What the hell did you learn in Philadelphia in the two days that you were there? The anger that I showed my father when I was twelve poured out of me. I said, "I did everything I was supposed to do. I don't know what the hell is wrong." I used my key to get access to the wrench. I put the wrench into the machine. I opened the door. From the inside of the machine, I tripped the 5-cent coin switch that activates the machine. It was a repeated failure. Everything worked except the water. I took the back of my screwdriver and tapped madly on the solenoid value that opens up for water. I tripped the switch. Everything worked. We were in business. I closed the door and we poured nickels into the machine for the office personnel who were waiting for their first cup of coffee. History was made. The first cup of coffee from a vending machine occurred in Rochester, New York, in June of 1948. Kwik-Kafe was born. It was a cause for celebration. I did not let my partners down. Don was proud. The Reiningers were relieved. I began to think that in my extensive toolbox, all I needed was a screw driver and a rubber hammer to fix a machine.

Our direct mail program lead us to a few small business locations. Follow up phone calls to Eastman Kodak, Bausch & Lomb and other major manufacturers generated no interest. The rejections were common. "People are here to work." "This is not the military." "We don't want our employees loitering around a hot cup of coffee socializing."

We moved from my home to an empty barbershop on Clifford Avenue. We needed room for the storage of paper cups and other supplies. We had a two-car garage in the back of the barbershop where we could store machines. I would change uniforms during the day as needed. One uniform to clean stainless steel canisters at our headquarters and make simple syrup, another brown uniform, shirt, tie and cap to service the machines and my business suit, shirt and tie to make sales calls.

I sought letters of recommendations from our first group of small customers. I began using the strawberry sales strategy – enthusiastically offering to place a coffee machine on every floor or every other floor. I avoided the negative sales approach, "You aren't interested in a coffee vending machine, are you?" I quickly learned that it was easier to sell strawberries than coffee-vending machines, regardless of my enthusiasm.

My enthusiasm did get us into Fasco Industries, thanks to Leo Kruze, the personnel manager. Fasco made electric fans for home, office and factory use. Their pay scale was lower than the bigger industrial plants like Kodak and Bausch & Lomb. Leo wanted his employees to feel like they could take a break for a cup of coffee whenever they wanted to, unlike the companies with higher wages and no coffee breaks. He located the machines in the center of the plant rather than in hidden alcoves. Employees were reluctant to gossip around the machine under the eyes of supervision. They took their cup of coffee back to their work areas and consumed it there. It was a morale booster. Mr. Kruze added a few more machines. The four Fasco machines were outselling the other eleven machines combined. One day Mr. Kruze saw me filling a machine. He said, "Are you going anywhere near the Chamber of Commerce. My car broke down." I said, "Sure, I'd be glad to give you a ride." I took him to my 1929 Reo. The Reo had window shades. I had them pulled down in the back and sides. Leo said, "Is this what you service your machines out of Fred?" I said, "Yes, Leo and this Reo runs well. The only problem I have is with the fuel pump that freezes up overnight in the winter and I have to pour hot water on it to get the thing started." This was in 1949. The 1929 Reo was an antique. Mr. Kruze, who was about my dad's age, made no comment. The next day I received a phone call from Leo. He wanted to install another coffee machine in another part of the plant to have coverage throughout his entire company. On that particular day, I believe that the 1929 Reo got us a new location.

I continued to put in long hours attempting to upgrade the business by moving the low volume locations to higher volume locations. Before the first year was up, Don Mack surprised all of us with an order for 10 more Kwik Kafe units with a Lincoln Rochester bank loan before I had completed my upgrade program. He also had a contact at Kodak that agreed to try a canned fruit juice machine. The trial was successful. Don ordered 20 fruit juice machines that were installed at Kodak with another bank loan from Lincoln Rochester. At this point, it was necessary to bring Ken Reininger on board to assist me with the operation of the business. We added Huther Bros, saw manufacturers on University Avenue in Rochester and the Haloid Company – long before it became Xerox Corporation. The fruit juice units were an instant hit with Kodak employees. Ken had to keep filling the machines to prevent sell out. It appeared that Don Mack had come up with a winner – one that could possibly lead us into Kodak with coffee machines. However, within a month, the fruit juice machine sales plunged so significantly that we had to remove the machines. Fruit juices in cans proved to be a novelty that Kodak employees tried in the initial installation. The novelty wore off and they went back to the regular cola beverages that were also available in vending machines.

A year after we began, the Reiningers and I asked Don Mack for a financial statement. I had created a form for each service that recorded the meter readings, the refunds and the amount of cash deposited by machine. All of these sales records were given to Don. He handled the checkbook for payroll, products and parts. Don failed to supply a financial statement. With my knowledge of bookkeeping and my courses in accounting at the U of R, I could not understand why Don could not produce a statement. I was concerned about our loans from Lincoln Rochester for the extra ten coffee machines and the 20 fruit juice machines. The cash from the machines just covered payroll and supplies needed. I approached Don directly. His face was flush with anger. He said, "Do you trust me or don't you." I instantly backed off. I said, "I'm sorry Don. I was just worried about our bank loans." His reply was, "That's my worry. You keep doing a good job. Understand?" In spite of my common sense and knowledge of accounting, I knew very little about financial loans. I said, "Sorry Don. I did not mean to upset you with my questions. I do trust you. I'll keep working hard to move our low volume machines into higher volume locations."

In July of 1949, about 13 months after we started our business, I was at my desk in this operating space, the size of a small barbershop. I was surrounded by cartons of paper cups, a freezer for our frozen coffee and other needed supplies. Our landlord was Mr. Ken Knox. He was handicapped and needed crutches. He lived above the former barbershop. He was able to sit at a stainless steel sink where he washed and sterilized the containers and valves for the coffee machine. I was servicing machines as well as making sales calls. Ken Reininger was our route man and technician who took care of service calls.

A car pulled up in front of the barbershop. A well-dressed man got out of the car. He introduced himself as Alfred D'Amanda, the attorney for Mr. Hunting. I offered him a chair. He said, "The Hunting Company has just discovered that the machines that you are responsible for were paid for by the Hunting Company. Mr. Mack wrote checks from the Hunting Company account for $60,000." If my dark skin could turn pale, I would have been as white as a ghost. I was stunned. I explained the original investment plan of $15,000. I explained that Don had loaned me 25% of that for my investment. I told him that Mr. Mack told us purchases beyond our original investment were Lincoln Rochester Trust bank loans. Mr. D'Amanda said that there were no loans from a bank. He said there would be a meeting at his firm's office the next day and I was to be there with Ken Reininger. He had already spoken to Ed Reininger. I phoned Don Mack. He was not at the Hunting Company and he was not at home.

For the first time in my life, I found myself sitting in a big conference room of a law firm's office. Mr. Hunting attended along with attorneys from his firm. Don Mack was there. Mr. D'Amanda said that there was not only $60,000 traced to Kwik Kafe of Rochester but other large sums were taken by Don Mack that could not be accounted for. Don denied the charges, saying if they wanted to call in the District Attorney, they could. He left the room saying that he was going to see his lawyer.

Mr. D'Amanda said that a great injustice was done to Mr. Hunting. Mr. Hunting wanted me to continue to run the coffee business and report directly to him. Ken, Ed and I had to surrender our 25% ownership and each of us had to be accountable for 25% of the missing funds. Totally devastated by this betrayal of Mr. Hunting, I signed anything that was put in front of me. In my naïve hero worshipping heart, I felt a deep compassion for Don Mack and wondered if his actions were caused by some kind of mental illness. Did he think the business would do so well that we could generate the cash flow to borrow from a bank and pay it back to the Hunting Company before it was missed in the 12 months preceding the Hunting Company audit? I will never know what Don Mack was thinking.

I was further shocked a few weeks later when Mr. Hunting called a meeting of Don Mack and myself in his office. He said that he was putting Don Mack under me. If we believed so strongly in the business, he would allow a certain amount of time for Don Mack to find new customers and to move forward with a plan to move poor sellers into better locations. This only lasted two weeks. Don Mack was not productive. The plan for him to begin the selling process did not work. After a private meeting with Mr. Hunting, Don Mack was gone. I never saw Don again. Mr. Hunting called me to his office. He said that he did not know what to do with the coffee vending business that he now owned. He said that I would be reporting to him as general manager of Kwik Kafe, working toward improving the performance of the company by constantly upgrading the losing accounts into winning accounts. He said that he trusted me and the explanations that I had given to Mr. D'Amanda. I went back to my job thinking that I had a moral obligation to Mr. Hunting to make the business a success.

After two months, the business was stabilized. It was able to meet payroll and all expenses. It was not able to generate sufficient cash for payments to Mr. Hunting. Mr. D'Amanda appeared again, parked in front of the former barbershop. I offered him a chair again. He said, "Fred, we are missing more than the $60,000 traced to your business and I think you know where it went. How could you let so much money go into your business without knowing where it came from? I want your full cooperation, do you understand?"

I became the 12-year-old boy who slammed the door of my father's truck. However, I tried to remain calm rather than emotional. I looked Mr. D'Amanda straight in the eye and sternly said, "I know nothing about what Don Mack did with funds beyond Kwik Kafe. Furthermore, how could the Hunting Company let so much money disappear from their business without knowing where it was going? And Mr. D'Amanda, the answer to that question is Trust. Mr. Hunting and I had absolute trust in Don Mack. We both erred. And further more, I will not allow you to ever ask me a question again. I signed all those documents in your office because I thought an injustice had been done. I had no attorney to represent me. From this day forward, Mr. D'Amanda, any questions you have must go through my attorney." It seemed as if Mr. D'Amanda accepted my answers with some respect as he said, "Now you are talking smart. Who is your lawyer?" I said, "I don't have a lawyer but I will get one. Oh, but yes I do have a lawyer. I took a course in business law from him at the U of R extension school. His name is Mr. Jack Conway. I intend to tell him about our meeting a few weeks ago in your office and about the questions you have asked me today." Mr. D'Amanda said, "Good, I'll wait to hear from him."

I made an appointment with Jack Conway and disclosed the facts in a half-hour conversation. He said, "Fred, what did you learn in my class about signing documents without an attorney." I said, "Mr. Conway, I know you are Catholic as I am. I loved Mr. Hunting. I felt a great injustice was done to that trusting old man. He came to my home. He hired me. He made my hours flexible so that I could go to the U of R. I sat in Mr. D'Amanda's conference room looking at Mr. Hunting and feeling a deep compassion for him. I was in shock, thinking that I was righting a wrong." Jack said, "But Fred you don't even have a copy of what you signed to show me, do you?" Feeling kind of stupid, I said, "No." He said, "Wait here I'll be right back." I said, "Do you have another appointment?" He said, "No, I'm going over to D'Amanda's office. I'm going to find out what you signed and threaten to have him disbarred if he does not cooperate."

Jack Conway returned in less than an hour. He held documents in his hand. He said, "Now here's the original note you signed for $60,000. Here's the agreement that you signed pertaining to this note. As far as your 25% ownership is concerned, that is gone," I sat there stunned as he tore up these two documents in front of my eyes. I said, "How did you do it." He said, "I told you, I threatened to have him disbarred for not telling you that you should seek legal counsel in a case involving the embezzlement of funds." I had a new hero whom I stayed with as long as he practiced law. And Mr. D'Amanda never again parked in front of my former-barbershop headquarters.

The Conway action had no impact with Mr. Hunting on my job as general manager of Kwik-Kafe. I worked diligently to grow the business as best I could. I developed low cost direct mail advertisements that generated leads. I followed up every lead with a product demonstration. I had excellent letters of recommendation from well-known Rochester organizations that I used in my calls. Many of these letters stated that the service was a morale booster to employees and that properly located in the plant, the productivity of the worker was improved rather than impaired.

In addition, I kept excellent monthly records. My two years of bookkeeping and accounting were paying off for me in this regard. I was in control and I honored that control with customers and Mr. Hunting. I prepared monthly operating statements for Mr. Hunting. I encouraged an audit anytime he wished. He allowed me to freely maintain control over all receipts, deposits and withdrawals needed to run the business. Without interest costs, I began to develop a positive cash flow. Mr. Hunting called me in one day and said, "You are doing a good job. I talked to an important person I know at Kodak. His reports say that you are a very impressive young man and an excellent salesman. However, he also said that Kodak is not ready for coffee vending machines and, if they were, they want one vendor to handle all their needs and that vendor would most likely be the Canteen Corporation of America, a company on the New York Stock Exchange."

I was aware that a coffee-vending competitor had arrived on the scene in the form of a giant national corporation. It was a coffee vending machine with all powdered ingredients. I was attending national vending machine trade shows sampling coffee from all coffee machine manufacturers. I knew that in a controlled side-by-side test, our cup of coffee would be the overwhelmingly choice of Kodak employees. This was a difficult sell. The "package deal" was what all companies wanted – one service for all of their vending needs from one supplier. In addition to Canteen Corporation of America, other competitors were entering the field in Rochester offering the total package of vending products – cold drinks, hot beverages from dry ingredients, candy, snacks, milk and ice cream.

1949 – 1950 Events at Home with my former Warden

During my intense involvement with Kwik Kafe, my father was not feeling well. It all began after Joe's accident. He was in the back seat of a friend's car on a double date. The accident caused his back door to open. Joe fell out of the car. His head hit the curb.

He was in a coma for three days and three nights. My father never left his side. Either the stress of the accident or for other medical reasons, my father was slowing down. He had diabetes and high blood pressure and was seeing a doctor.

After graduation from Monroe High School, my brother Joe took over my father's business. On occasions, depending on how he felt, my father would go along. When he wasn't with Joe, he would spend his afternoons on East Avenue playing cards with friends or on church matters involving the new pastor or watching the wonder of the new invention — television. He was especially interested in world affairs and politics. He kept fairly busy and occupied. However, being at home made it difficult for my mother, who was still smoking. She continued to fear his temper. He constantly expressed his dislike for women who smoked. There was no way my mother could change his mind and she wished, above all, to avoid a confrontation. He created enough disturbances in the household without dealing with this one. She patiently coped with this reality and would sneak in a cigarette whenever he wasn't home. The children continued to be the eyes and ears of the household warning her of his coming and shaking the towels to clear the air.

My father would occasionally go to the public market early in the morning to check up on Joe's buying habits. Joe had bought a 1936 olds for $100. He used Joe's car to get there. Joe would get his public market job done and visit his first customer at 9:00 AM. He did not linger at the public market restaurant as my father used to. On his return to the public market one day, my father collided with another vehicle on East Boulevard and he was at fault. No one was hurt. Joe's car was destroyed. Joe asked my father to replace the vehicle. My father said it was not necessary. Joe had the truck. He could use that. Joe was angry. He took his problem to Uncle Deeb, the elder of the Sarkis family. Uncle Deeb said to my father. "You wrecked his car. You must buy him another one." At a used car dealer, Joe wanted a 1940 Nash to replace his car. The price was $175. My father offered him $100. The dealer would not budge. My father excused himself and went to the rest room. While he was away, Joe handed the dealer $75 and said, "tell my father you will take it for $100. I want that car." My father came back and continued the negotiation. The dealer pretended to bargain further. Then the dealer threw up his hands and said, "Take it for a hundred and get out of my hair."

Betty was 25. Ann was going on 18. Everytime one of his two daughters had a date, my father had to know every detail of that date. Fortunately, Ann was a baby sitter for the Fargo's, who lived next door. If Ann had a date, my mother would say to my father, "Ann is baby sitting for the Fargo's." Betty, who worked days, had no alibi. When her date arrived, Betty, somewhat embarrassed, waited in her bedroom while my father would interview her dates. He would want to know something about their family, where they worked, how much they made per hour, what their intentions were in dating his daughter, where they were going, what time they would be back. As they stepped outside, he would see them to the front porch and say, "Don't forget. She must be home by midnight. I will be waiting."

One of Betty's dates was with a doctor from the University of Rochester. Ray Shaheen, who was an active and close member of St. Nicholas Church, called Betty for a double date. Betty's date was a well-educated English speaking doctor who had a Moslem name. My father asked my mother, "Where is Betty?" My mother said, she was with Ray Shaheen. Ray Shaheen was introducing her to a doctor at the University of Rochester. When my father heard the last name of the doctor he went into a rage. He waited impatiently for Betty to return. Ray Shaheen, knowing my father's temper, thought it would show good manners to bring her to the front door. My father stepped out to the porch and wrestled Ray Shaheen to the ground as if to beat him. I pulled my father off of Ray Shaheen, grabbed his arm and took him into the house. I apologized to Ray. He said he understood. I went in to confront my father in the living room. Betty went crying to her room.

As he sat in his favorite chair, recovering from his emotional outburst, I stood in front of him and said, "Pa, I fought for my country for freedom and for peace, yet there is no freedom or peace in this household when you behave like you do. Your daughter is 25 years old but she does not have freedom or peace. You make her live in fear. You upset my brothers and sisters. You upset my mother. I don't like it. I will not stay in this house if you continue to take away the family's peace. What are you thinking? Are you thinking of the bad behavior between men and women that you saw in Hedges? Do you think that is what American dating is all about? To go out to a dinner, to go out to a movie, to go to a dance is not the same as spending all night in a bar. You only make your daughters feel like they cannot be trusted. Why do you get so upset? Why do you cause pain to my mother and our family by your violent anger and behavior? Tell me what you are thinking."

For the first time in my life, he saw me in a different light. He did not get angry with me. He tried to explain why he behaved as he did. He explained that in the old country, Christians were persecuted by Moslems. He said, "It was a crime to steal from or rape another Moslem, but if a person was not a Moslem, he was an infidel and it was not a crime to steal from or rape a Christian. That is why so many Christians fled Lebanon."

I told him he was talking about 1915 when he left the old country. I told him the world was changing. I told him that he had to change with the world. I asked him how he would feel if Betty had a date with a Jewish doctor. He said, "The Jews and the Christians have the same Ten Commandments and I would not be as upset if Betty had a date with a Jewish Doctor." I said, "Pa, you have to think in modern times; the next time this happens, I am going to pack up my clothes and leave this house. Believe me."

Unfortunately, there was another episode. My mother was crying in the kitchen. My father hit her. In heated anger, I said, "Pa, I told you I would leave if you broke peace in our home. Hitting my mother is the last straw. I am leaving and I am taking the family with me." I told the family to pack. Nine of us packed our things and we went to Uncle Charlie's, my father's oldest brother. It was a two-day, two-night stay. My brother Jim refused to go with us. He stayed with my father. Uncle Charlie visited my father to get a new commitment about his behavior. We returned home.

From that day forward, dating by my sisters Betty and Ann became easier. I had counseled with my father. I reached for his understanding. I had the fortitude to speak up. It did not work the first time. It did work the second time. The gifts of the Holy Spirit worked again as they did with my warden-father when I was twelve-years-old.

1949 was a difficult year. I felt trapped in a business that had soured. My father was having health problems. As the year was coming to an end, after Christmas, I put on my Navy winter jacket, walked up to the Park Avenue rock garden stairway to the overlook of the subway. I thought about my future. What plans did God have for me? My WWII, GI bill of rights would expire in the months ahead and I would not be able to pursue my dream for a degree in business and law. I believed that with this degree, I could get a job at Kodak and with years of experience, I could even become a top executive. I knew about their excellent employee benefits and retirement plans. I knew that Kodak executives were encouraged to be active in the community.

I also thought about the frustrations of business. The pursuit was material. You render a service. Profit is the motive. An aptitude test that I had taken after my discharge from the Navy showed a strong inclination for social work. I felt that I would make a good priest. It was not too late to consider the priesthood. I was only 23. If I didn't have family obligations, an alternative would be to enter the seminary. I thought that if I put the same effort into the priesthood as I was doing in business, I would be able to spread the word of God more effectively and creatively than many priests that I knew. Betty, 25, Joe 19 and Ann 17 were all working. The house was free of a Mortgage. Now would be the time to choose between Notre Dame and the Priesthood.

I shivered as I looked up at the clear sky without clouds or a moon. I gazed at the stars and found myself quietly saying, "Jesus, if you want me to be a priest, show me a shooting star and I will enter the seminary." I stared at the sky for at least a half-hour. There was no shooting star.

Instead, a voice broke the still of the night. It was my father standing at the foot of the rock garden. My brother Joe, who graduated from Monroe High School in June of 1949, had taken over my father's truck and business until my father felt well enough to return. With concern in his voice, my father said, "Bah, what are you doing up there?" I didn't know exactly how to respond. I simply said, "Thinking about my future, Pa." He started to come up the dozen steps to the top of the rock garden. He had not been feeling well at Christmas. He was taking the steps slowly and breathing heavily. I was leaning on the fence that served as protection from falling into the subway bed, about 40 feet below me. He stood beside me and rested his arms on the fence, looking up at the sky. He stood there silently for a few minutes as if to catch is breath. He said, "If you are up here thinking about your future as you said, I must tell you something." "First,", he said, "I am sorry that you went into business. I told you when you talked about going into the coffee vending business that you could lose that business. I told you that you should get your education first because that is something nobody can take away from you." I said, "Yes, Pa and I think you are right but I do what I think God wants me to do and I accept whatever happens." He said, "You are a good boy. You have God in your heart. I must tell you something that is difficult for me to say. I saw my doctor last week. He said that I have high blood pressure. He said that it is very serious and that I could get a stroke or die instantly of a heart attack without warning. He said it could happen anytime within the next few months. You just said, you were thinking about your future. I must tell you what your future is. You are a good son. You are my oldest son. In the old country when the father dies the oldest son must take care of his mother and his younger brothers and sisters. That is your future."

I choked up with emotion. Even though I knew he was not feeling well, I did not want to believe what I was hearing. I said, "No Pa, don't talk like that. It can't be true. Doctors can give you medication. You cannot die. You are only 56. You are still young." "Fred", he said, "I can feel sickness in my body. I know it will happen. You must listen to me." Tears flooded my eyes, as they are now, as I write this 50 years later. In the cold of the night, we embraced. He kissed the tears on my cheeks. We held each other close. My body and cheeks were chilled. I could feel the warmth of his cheeks and the heat from his body. Still in an embrace, I whispered in his ear, "Pa, if something happens to you, you can count on me. I will take care of the family. Nothing will get in the way of that Pa. As God is my judge, I give you my word." I could hear a sense of relief when he said, "I knew I could count on you. You are a good boy." He hugged me tightly — the hug that I wanted in the back of the truck outside of Hedge's Bar & Grill when he did not notice me. *Thank God, my former warden hugged the Prisoner of His Truck.*

We did not talk about this again. I kept busy with my job at Kwik Kafe.

To pass the time away, my father played cards with friends on East Avenue in the backroom of Hershey's Smoke Shop, within walking distance of our home. March 11, 1950 was the last day on the truck for Joe. He got a job at Fasco Industries, our largest coffee vending account. My father was preparing to go back to work. Two days later, on March 13, 1950, my father, my warden, the man who taught me how to sell, who urged me to study to escape the truck, died instantly of a heart attack in the backroom of Hershey's Smoke Shop. It was only two and a half months after he prepared me for his death.

On that day, I became the anointed head of the house. There was no longer any confusion of what I wanted to do with the rest of my life. I would stay home. I would forget Notre Dame and thoughts of the priesthood. My life became simple. I had only one choice. I would continue to manage Kwik Kafe for Mr. Hunting and to work with my brothers and sisters in providing a happy and peaceful household for my mother and family.

[Note: On October 13, 1952, after my father's death, in one of his frequent visits to our home to see how we were all doing, my Uncle Charlie Sarkis, father of my cousin Dr. Richard Sarkis, while watching a Friday night boxing match on television, with a sudden gasp for air, died in my father's rocking chair. My sister Ann was holding his hand as he drew his last breath.]

CHAPTER 20

A New Family Beginning & Miracles

1950-51

On March 14, 1950 my father was laid out at home in the living room. Relatives had taken over the kitchen, preparing food and refreshments for all those who came to pay their respects. There was nothing our family had to do except to stand in line to receive the condolences of relatives and friends. For two days, there were afternoon and evening hours. First the visitors paid their respect to my Father with a silent bow of the head or a knelt prayer. They then expressed their sympathy to the family. First, to my mother, then to Betty, Fred, Joe, Anne, Jim, Vicky, Deanna, Kenny and Lee who was then four years old. It was a very emotional scene for those expressing sympathy. In the kitchen, the women who prepared the food were talking and laughing as if they were catering a party. In the living room, all was quiet and sad. I could tell that Lee and Kenny were hurt and confused by this contrast. Several times in those two days, I would kneel down to Lee's level and give him a kiss and a hug to comfort him. Kenny was 8. I did not have to kneel for Kenny but in between the great number of visitors, I managed to hug him as well.

Both sides of Park Avenue for a half mile were crowded with parked cars. We were all surprised by the number of our father's customers who paid their last respects. We learned that he was well loved by all of his German, Irish and Scottish customers, many of whom remembered me as a little boy. They wanted me to know how much my father loved me. They said that he carried my Father's Day letters in his pocket so that he could show them to his customers. A countless number of them said, "He was so proud of you." Others had saved the newspaper clipping of one of my Father's Day letters that he had taken to the Democrat and Chronicle for publication.

After the Mass at St. Nicholas church, all ten of us, my mother, my brothers and sisters sat closely together in one funeral van. It was a cold March 16. Monsignor Hallak, the pastor of our church and frequent visitor to our home, conducted the ceremonies at home, in Church and at the cemetery.

After the cemetery services, shivering with cold, the ten of us huddled closely together in the funeral limousine, gathering warmth from each other. We were very silent. No one was speaking. My father's death seemed to bind us together more closely than ever before. It was as if it would be a new beginning for all of us. In my mind, I felt that my mother's life would be easier. I loved my father but I never liked the frequent hurt that his unpredictable moods and temper caused her, especially since she valued peace in the household. I especially remembered the times before I began my first full time job, at age 16, when they would speak in Arabic. His tone of voice seemed to be filled with anger. I assumed it had something to do with her needs for money for groceries and household expenses. Yet, In spite of his faults, she always defended him and encouraged us to forgive him because of the pressures he had to live with.

The day of his burial, I not only resolved to keep the promise made to my father but I was determined to go further. I would do everything possible to insure that my mother lived in a house of predictable peace.

The Big Business Events between 1950-51

In April of 1950, Kwik Kafe was two years old. Mr. Hunting sent potential buyers of Kwik Kafe to see the barbershop headquarters and to meet me, his manager, to answer questions. I could see that my future as a manager was limited. I knew that the business, as it was, did not justify a purchase at $60,000, the amount Mr. Hunting sought to recover. The return on investment did not justify this value. In addition to Canteen of America, there were local, highly competitive companies beginning to offer the complete package of vending including the powdered coffee unit referred to in a previous chapter.

In May of 1950, just past my 24th birthday, I asked for a meeting with Mr. Hunting. I told him that I knew he wanted to sell the business and that he had received offers for less than $30,000. If sold, I told him that made my continuity as his manager seem uncertain. I said that I would like to be considered among the parties interested in buying the business. I advised him that anyone who bought the business would have to either run it or hire someone for a higher salary than I was receiving, a salary that could very well wipe out the cash flow that I was generating.

He asked if I had an offer. I said, "Mr. Hunting, if I gave you $30,000 for your business, you would have a $30,000 loss. You could take this loss and deduct it from Hunting Company profits and save $15,000 on taxes. You could then wipe your hands completely of this bad experience with a $15,000 loss instead of $60,000. Please consider that I have been responsible for running the business for one full year and accumulated $10,000 in cash. If I had not remained involved, it is very possible that this business would have folded and you would have taken a $60,000 loss."

Suspiciously, he said, "Where on earth do you suppose you can get $30,000? I said, I have generated cash of $10,000 that would go to you; you would take a two year note from me for $10,000 backed by collateral on the equipment and I will raise $10,000 by getting a mortgage on my mother's house." Mr. Hunting said that this was a very poor offer and was unacceptable. I then gave Mr. Hunting a choice of selling the business to me or finding a replacement for me within 90 days. Again, it was the strawberry story — a choice between one or the other. I explained that I still had six months to take advantage of the GI Bill of Rights and I wanted to enter Notre Dame University in September of that year. Mr. Hunting continued to politely refuse the offer. I thanked him and said I would do my utmost to train a new manager in the next 90 days — and I meant it.

In the latter part of May of 1950, Mr. Hunting sent his son to "look over the business" and to take an inventory. I spent a week with Mr. Hunting's son reviewing the management systems that I developed for the control of cash and product in every machine. I reviewed all of my sales records and promotional efforts. When he took inventory for audit purposes of the products in the former barbershop, he put a half filled box of pencils on a table and preceded to slowly count them one by one. I knew then that he was not cut out for this business.

In early June of 1950, one month after my talk with Mr. Hunting, I received a phone call from Mr. D'Amanda. I said, "Mr. D'Amanda, I will not talk to you. If you want to speak to me you must speak to my lawyer, Jack Conway." He said, "Fred, as you discussed with Mr. Hunting, you just tell Mr. Conway we will take the $10,000 from Kwik Kafe's account, we will take your $10,000 note if you show up with $10,000 in cash within the next two weeks. He can handle the paper work for our approval."

I hung up and stood on my head on the desk, supporting my body with my feet on the wall. Mr. Knox said, "Are you going crazy?" Still upside down, I said, "No Lester, I just had a miracle. I'm going to own this business. It is a miracle. Thank you, Carmelites."

Since my dad's death, I promised to give a dozen eggs a day to the Carmelite Nuns on East Avenue, not far from where I lived. This was a cloistered order of nuns who prayed for world peace and for the intentions or petitions of those who came to them. They were not allowed to talk to or to see outsiders, except to acknowledge gifts that were hand delivered to them within the small entrance. There was a bell and a revolving platform. A donor would ring the bell and speak through a screened device. The object would be placed on the revolving platform. The sister would respond by asking, "What do you seek from our prayers?" The donor's answer could pertain to health problems of the individual or a loved one, or success in business, education or simply for a special intention.

I rang the bell. I heard a voice say, "Yes?" I said, "Sister, I made a promise to deliver a dozen eggs a day to the sisters." She advised me to put the eggs on the platform. She revolved it and said, "What do you seek from prayers?" My answer was, "Sister, I am the manager of a business that I want to own. I need prayers to help make it happen." The routine was the same every morning. I'd say, "Here are the eggs, Sister." She would say, "Same intention"? I'd say, "Yes Sister, same intention " and be gone.

When I was 12 years old and we lost our home on 470 Driving Park Avenue for failing to make the mortgage payments, the memory of my mother's tears and sadness were still fresh in my mind. I remember thinking, "Maybe when I grow up, I will buy my mother a new home and pay off the mortgage quickly".

It was only 6 years later, before I turned 18, that I bought 1293 Park Avenue for my mom and family and paid off the mortgage. How could I possibly ask Mother to risk a $10,000 new mortgage on our Park Avenue home? Her response was one of joy and enthusiasm. She simply said, "Fred, I believe in you. I know you will make it a success. Do it." I was only able to get $8,800. I cashed my $500 in war bonds. Betty had enough saved for the remainder. I rushed to Jack Conway with the $10,000 in cash. The deal was quickly closed.

Right after the closing in June of 1950, at age 24, I went back to the Carmelites with my dozen eggs. "Same intention?" the sister asked? I said, "No Sister, I want the good sisters to pray that my company will be given a chance to test our coffee machines at Kodak." Each morning, I would drop off the eggs. "Same intention?" "Yes, Sister, same intention."

In March of 1950, my brother Joe turned over my father's business to my cousin Paul Sarkis. Leo Kruze, the Personnel Manager of Fasco, hired Joe for $1.50 per hour. After I bought the business from Mr. Hunting in June, Joe left Fasco Industries to join Kwik Kafe. Joe relieved me of the hours I spent servicing machines so that I could spend full-time selling — a plan that did not have the approval of Mr. Hunting prior to my purchase of the assets.

In July of 1950, I made my periodic phone call to Gordon McKay, the Personnel Director at Kodak Park, a division of the Eastman Kodak Company. I saw Mr. McKay at least four times a year. He was always gracious enough to give me an appointment. At each appointment, I would fill him in on our progress and present letters of satisfaction from companies that we were serving. I always asked him for another appointment. Again, as in the strawberry story, I would say, "Can we meet again in six months, say June or July?" In our July meeting, I told him of the new ownership of Kwik Kafe. Again, I politely asked if we would be allowed to have a side-by-side test either in August or September. Mr. McKay had checked our references from companies we were servicing and received good feedback. He respected my enthusiasm for our product. In addition, every time we signed up a new customer in competition with Canteen, I would tactfully write to Mr. McKay to advise him of our growth. However, at this July meeting, Mr. McKay repeated, "Fred, things have not changed. We are happy with our service. Canteen is doing a good job. There are no complaints from our employees. Stay in touch and we welcome any news of your progress." I kept dropping off the eggs to the Carmelites on East Avenue every morning. "Same intention?" "Yes, Sister, same intention."

In October of 1950, Paul Sarkis gave up my father's business and joined our company as a coffee service man. My full time effort in sales and a bigger risk-budget for direct mail advertising began to pay off. We successfully converted all of the 25 coffee vending poor sellers into good sellers. In addition, we purchased 20 new units through a payment plan with a local bank. It was no different than purchasing an automobile. For each machine purchased, I had a separate payment book of 48 monthly payments. I would clip coupons each month for each machine and send a check for the total to the bank. We were generating sufficient cash flow to make the payments.

In trade magazines, I advertised the 20 fruit juice machines that had been gathering dust in the garage. These machines had cost $1,000 each but Mr. Hunting would not let me sell them for less than $700. I sold them for $500 each. In October of 1950, I went to Mr. Hunting with a check for $10,000 to pay off the note. He was shocked and somewhat suspicious. He said, "Where did you get the $10,000." I told him I found a buyer for $500 each for the 20 fruit juice machines that you wouldn't let me sell. He smiled at me, signed the release of collateral prepared by Jack Conway and said, "Fred, I know you will make this business very successful and I wish you the best of luck."

I continued to drop off the dozen eggs. "Same intention?" "Yes Sister, same intention? On November 1, 1950, All Saints Day in the Catholic Church, at 9:45 AM, I received a phone call from Gordon McKay. He said, "Fred, I want to talk to you about a side-by-side test, when would it be convenient for you to come to my office?" Consistent with the strawberry story, I tried to keep my cool. I politely asked, "This morning or this afternoon?" He must have known the strawberry story. He said, "No, I can't do it today. How about tomorrow or day after tomorrow?" I chose tomorrow. I again stood on my head on my desk with my body supported by my feet against the wall. Mr. Knox said, "Now what?" Again, upside down, I said "Another miracle. We get a side-by-side test at Kodak Park."

At my appointment with Mr. McKay, he told me that Canteen had, without Kodak's permission changed all of their heavy weight paper cups to light weight paper cups. The result created havoc. Coffee cups were leaking at workstations, on executive desks, in containers that held multiple cups, on the production lines, etc. Drippings of coffee on the floor were a hazard for a slipping accident. This change represented a savings of one-half cent per cup. At 5 cents a cup, this represented savings of 10% on the sales price. This was a major blunder by a national company on the NY Stock Exchange. It would have been far wiser to increase the volume of sales by a better quality than to save dollars with a reduction of quality. We were spending a penny for our heavy weight, plastic-coated paper cups to eliminate a cardboard taste to protect the flavor of our coffee. Canteen quickly converted back to a heavy weight cup but they were not plastic coated.

We had our first trial in building 6 at Kodak Park. Unlike most companies with staggered breaks, certain departments in film production had to take 15-minute breaks at the same time in the morning and afternoon. My brother Joe was in charge of service. He and the Canteen service man were allowed to watch the 15-minute break but were not allowed to speak to the employees. The first few days were not measurable since curiosity would attract people to our machine. But at the end of a two week period, employees would wait in a long line to use the Kwik Kafe machine. The only use of the powdered machine came from people who were too impatient to wait. Kodak ordered several other trials in other buildings. The results were the same. On average, Kwik Kafe was outselling Canteen seven to one.

I dropped off the daily dozen of eggs to the Carmelites. "Same prayer?" "No, Sister. We won the trial. Pray for all of Kodak."

The word spread throughout the various divisions of Kodak. The results were the same. Kodak management decided to centralize their decision making process. We were asked to bid on all 268 coffee vending machines for all 36,000 employees at Kodak Park, Kodak Office and Camera Works. We bid at 5 cents a cup and a realistic 10% commission on sales. We won the bid. Our superior quality resulted in a 28% increase in vended coffee sales at Kodak. It was a win, win situation for all. Kodak employees enjoyed a better cup of coffee. Because of the increased volume, the monthly commission checks to Kodak were higher.

I dropped of the daily dozen of eggs to the Carmelites. "Same Prayer?" "No Sister, just prayers in thanksgiving for intentions favorably received."

The Kodak experience led us to believe that we should be different from our full line competitors. We did not need to offer all products through vending machines. In the fields of medicine and law, there were many specialists. We picked up on this theme and aggressively promoted ourselves as quality-control specialists in the consistent delivery of the best cup of coffee available from a vending machine. We guaranteed every coffee drinker his money back if he or she was not satisfied. In addition, we wanted every service man, every machine and every vehicle to look neat and clean. We installed a full-length mirror in our new Portland Avenue headquarters. Each man had to pass that mirror every morning before he departed on his route. A sign above the mirror read, "This is how I look to my Customer." Consistent with the policy, procedure and training manual, the service men had to sign when hired, there were questions on either side of the mirror which read: Are my shoes shined? Are my shirt and uniform clean? Am I wearing my tie and cap? Is my hair cut? Are my finger nails clean? Am I clean-shaven? Do I daily check the amount of liquid coffee, cream and sugar dispensed, to insure consistent quality? Do I check for the proper temperature of the water? Do I empty the over flow bucket daily and sanitize it properly to prevent odors? Do I keep my station wagon and advertising cup on top clean? Do I record the meter, tests and refunds properly to assure an honest monthly report to the customer on every machine?

We beat our competition in many ways. One significant cost saving was related to the cost of operating a fleet of trucks. We required each coffee service man to purchase his own station wagon to be used for business and for pleasure. Kwik Kafe rented the vehicles from the service man for a sum equal to the monthly payments, plus a reasonable estimate for gas, oil, maintenance and a small profit. In addition, if expenses exceeded the rental income, they were tax deductible and the servicemen had a family vehicle for nights and weekends. Each service man was required to strap a large metal Kwik Kafe Coffee Cup with our phone number on top of his vehicle, serving as advertisements for Kwik Kafe day and night. This also eliminated the need for a large parking area for trucks.

Another important cost saver was my family's involvement. We added fresh doughnut machines to our coffee service in several locations. The bakery delivered the donuts to 1293 Park Avenue. In the basement of our home, my young brothers and sisters would get up one hour earlier in the morning before school to pack the doughnuts in sealed bags. Joe would take them in his service vehicle to the office for distribution to the other Kwik Kafe service men. Our family was united with one goal — to grow the business and to pay off the $10,000 mortgage on our house. No one could match our total service program, high volume, good quality, honest count, low labor and operating costs and a reasonable selling price.

My sister Ann was another key person in the growth of the business on Portland Avenue. Ralph Clausen was the manager of the Rochester division of Canteen Company of America. We were to meet at lunch to discuss the threat of license fees on food and beverage machines. He arrived at our headquarters. I was ten minutes late in returning to our headquarters. At lunch that day, Ralph Clausen said, "You have no parking lot. All your men own and maintain their own vehicles, therefore, they are well cared for. You have family members working for you in all departments. I watched your sister Ann while I was waiting for you. A delivery of cups arrived in this freezing weather. Ann put on her overcoat, opened the door and told the delivery men where to stack the huge delivery of paper cups. She was counting money from each vending machine and keeping a record of sales for that particular machine. She was answering the phone. She locked the money in a safe. She excused herself for a few minutes to go down to the cellar to throw some coal in the furnace. She kept the entire working area clean. My God, Fred, be reasonable, how the hell can I compete with you guys?" (Ralph Clausen joined our company a few years later to assist with our rapid growth into other products and services.)

On October 3, 1951, on the occasion of my mother's 48th birthday, the family presented her with a beautiful plaque showing a scenic view of a home that read, "God Bless Our Un-Mortgaged Home." She lost her home in the depression. She would never lose it again. It was a day of joy and peace. Ann and Deanna brought out their guitars. Kenny and Lee were now harmonizing songs together, as were Ann, Betty, Vicky and Deanna. Joe and I entertained with a comical "Dem bones, Dem Bones, Dem Dry Bones" and joined the others in favorite family songs, including of course my mother's favorite. It seemed as always, when we sang these words, we would direct our united attention to Mother and would watch the tears of happiness flowing from her peaceful face.

"You are my sunshine, my only sunshine,

You make me happy when skies are gray,

You'll never know dear how much we love you,

Please don't take our sunshine away".

In our singing, we included religious songs in praise of the Lord who gave us this wonderful family gift of joy, love and togetherness. This was a very special time in the life of Frances Sarkis and her children. She was at peace. I was only 25 and full of creative ideas for our growing business. In partnership with the Holy Spirit and an assist from the Carmelites, I felt that nothing was impossible to achieve. It was only five years ago that I ran an ad that read: "20 year old WWII veteran seeks part time office work, shorthand, bookkeeping, typing, what have you?"

CHAPTER 21

Age 24 to 37
Building a Business
Becoming Rich

1952 to 1963

In 1952, Kwik Kafe was featured on the front cover of a national trade magazine for the perfection of the first computerized system in the nation to report sales by each coffee machine to a customer. In cooperation with the local IBM service bureau, we developed a "marked card system" for our service men to use. These cards were fed to a super computer at the IBM center. For each machine, it recorded the daily meter readings, the number of tests and refunds given, the amount of cash collected and the shortage or overage. This report accompanied the monthly commission check paid to the customer.

In the vending machine business, a customer relies on the cash sales and commissions, as reported by the Vendor. If the Vendor reports sales less than actual, the customer is denied his rightful commission. The combination of our high quality, good service and professional computerized reports served to give us an image of impeccable integrity in our operations.

From 1952 to 1956, we remained coffee-vending specialists. In the national Kwik Kafe franchise system, we achieved the highest penetration of market for six consecutive years. The combination of market penetration, excellence in quality control, sanitation and superior service by our personnel lead to six consecutive First Place National Awards at the annual convention of franchisees. I took my Mother to these annual meetings and she assisted me in accepting these national awards. Rudd-Melikian, our manufacturer, in a national trade journal featured a picture of our family around our home picnic table. Ann was playing the guitar and we were all singing. When the picture was taken, Betty, Joe, Ann, Vicky, Jim and myself were working either full or part time in the business.

In the vending industry, we were the first in the nation to introduce a profit sharing plan for all employees that equaled the 15% maximum allowed by IRS. We had no employee turn over. Most of the service men and technicians, including Joe and I, bowled once a week and played euchre afterwards. There was a great family spirit.

By 1958, we had 35 employees and over 450 coffee vending machines on location. We were selling over 15,000,000 cups of coffee a year. We were Rochester's "King of Coffee". Personnel managers, who were not satisfied with their full-line-vending providers, asked us to take over all the vending machines in their plant including candy, snack, cold drink, cigarette, milk and ice cream.

In 1958, we moved to a new headquarters on Maple Street, opened up Rochester's first commissary for vending food products and introduced the first automatic cafeterias for those companies that did not have manual cafeteria operations.

From 1958 to 1961, we were the first company in Rochester to develop a complete package program for our clients. My associate, John O'Donnell was a key man in helping us to build a new division that specialized in cafeteria and other food service programs for business, hospitals, schools and colleges. John was a graduate of the Cornell Hotel School with extensive executive experience in what was called manual food service programs. There were other key men in the organization too numerous to mention.

Our business continued to rapidly grow. We operated over fifty vehicles and had over 600 employees. We were early birds in the development of a computerized center that produced professional monthly reports for our food & vending customers. We built a strong chain of command with excellent training, motivation and supervision programs that focused on maintaining high employee morale while meeting the wants and needs of our customers with high quality products, in a cost effective manner. The Golden Rule applied in our organization. "Do unto others as you would have them do unto you."

With the assistance of what was then the Association for Retarded Children, we earned a national award from President Eisenhower for the employment of the handicapped — the largest employer of handicapped in the Rochester area. The program worked because one or two handicapped adults were assigned to non-handicapped co-workers in each of our cafeteria operations for side-by-side motivation and training.

Our work with the handicapped included the employment of a blind salesman. From his commissioned earnings, he would pay for a driver and escort. The man was Matt Katafiaz. In early chapters, Matt was the man I worked for when I was a 16-year-old billing clerk at the Universal Carloading Company. Sugar diabetes led to his blindness and ended a brilliant career. He was the Southern District Manager for Universal Carloading Company before he went blind. At Universal, his performance was outstanding and he was being considered for the national Presidency prior to the loss of his vision. I ignored the criticism of competitors who accused me of using sympathy to get sales. Once Matt began his dialogue with the prospect, they forgot that he was blind and respected him for his listening skills and brilliance as a salesman.

My mother was an important part of our business entertaining. When we introduced the first automatic cafeteria, we impressed our customers and prospects with Lebanese food prepared by my mother and vended at the drop of coins. In addition, we held annual parties for customers and served Lebanese food prepared by my Mother. She was an important part of building public relations with our customers.

My work, in our national and state trade associations and in the Rochester community, was extensive. I received major recognition awards from the Junior Chamber of Commerce, the National Automatic Merchandisers Association, the Greater Rochester Chamber of Commerce and the United Way. I also served on the Board of Directors of these Organizations and several others. I served as Chairman of the United Way's Speaker's Bureau and was an invited speaker for food service seminars, American Management Association, Kwik Kafe Conventions, National Automatic Merchandisers Association, Boy Scouts of America, Junior Achievement, Danny Thomas Fund Raising and many other Civic and Church Groups.

The volunteer work that I loved the most was working for Richard P. Miller, the executive director of the United Way Campaign. He allowed me to bring fun and humor into the campaign. There was a full week of reporting toward the end of the campaign. Over 600 volunteers would attend the reporting luncheons. Massive display boards reflected how each Division was doing. As Chairman of the Individual Subscribers Division, I developed a theme for each day of the luncheon that brought laughter and a competitive spirit between various divisions of the United Way. These themes were so popular that Carl Stevenson, Treasurer of Kodak, asked me to come up with a plan that would add spice to the pledge that Kodak would annually give to the United Way. At the luncheon, Carl announced that Kodak's pledge was so significant that they had to retain someone who could guarantee it's safe delivery. With the pre-planned background music, I rushed into the heart of the large hall of the Chamber of Commerce dressed as Batman carrying the pledge card in my hand.

As Chairman of the Speaker's Bureau, I traveled and gave talks to company employees who were responsible for soliciting their fellow employees. Mr. Miller loved the strawberry story of the Prisoner of the Truck. He encouraged me to tell it to these volunteers. I would conclude my short talk with, "Never ask, do you plan to give again this year? Ask if you will increase last year's pledge by 5% or 10%."

I cherished my role as head of house, as anointed by my father. I found my job and my community activity to be exciting and challenging. This left little time for dating. During these years, every Sunday was family day. My family would squeeze into one car and go to St. Nicholas Church on the corner of Leo & Remington Street in Rochester. It was a small church. My father was one of the 1927 founders. Monsignor Hallack was our pastor and very close to our family. He joined us on Park Avenue frequently on Sunday's following the Mass. Mass was said in Greek, Arabic and English. We were Eastern Rite, Roman Catholics. I sang in the choir and served as President of the Youth Council.

In 1955, when I was twenty-nine, on our way to Church, my sister Ann wanted me to stop and pick up one of her girlfriends, Helen O'Hara. This was not too uncommon. It seemed as if we always had a friend of a brother or sister who wanted to join us for Church as well as for the delicious Sunday "Zlabee" breakfasts that my mother prepared. Zlabee was made from flour and yeast. The mixture had to rise overnight at the right consistency. Next morning, it was removed by hand in portions, fried and served with butter and syrup. Accompanied by fresh eggs and fruit, it made for a wonderful Sunday event, and was usually followed by everyone singing in the living room.

While eating breakfast, my hand hit a full glass of milk and because Miss O'Hara was across from me at the table, I was somewhat embarrassed by my clumsiness. My brother Joe had attended Monroe High School with Miss O'Hara, but they were not in the same class. He knew Miss O'Hara by her looks. I was surprised to learn that Miss O'Hara's father was one of the Hunting Company salesmen that I took dictation from. My cousin Richard, who was studying to be a Doctor, was also at our breakfast, which was not too uncommon because Joe and he were very close cousins and had many double dates together. After our songfest, Miss

O'Hara and my sister Ann went up to Ann's bedroom. While they were there, Joe and Richard made remarks about Helen's attractiveness. When Miss O'Hara came down the stairs again, I took a much closer look. I did not know this but Ann had brought Miss O'Hara home, hoping there would be a connection between Miss O'Hara and me. Disappointed in my lack of attention, Ann announced that they were going bowling and off they went.

Suspecting that Ann had brought Miss O'Hara home to meet me, I asked Ann for her phone number, which Ann readily provided. I caught Miss O'Hara at the wrong time. She was on her way to Ft. Lauderdale with friends. Miss O'Hara was a graduate of Brockport State Teachers College and was in her first year as a teacher of Physical Education and Health at Monroe High School, where she was popular with her students. My father once said, "Fred, if you don't marry a Lebanese girl, you should marry a German or an Irish girl. But first meet her parents. If you fall in love with her mother, then you should think about marrying the girl." I thought, "Well, if I date Helen, I'll meet her mother and then take one step at a time."

I found myself taking time to evaluate my commitment to my father. I was so wrapped up in building the business and so heavily involved in community affairs that I had little time to think about dating or marriage. There was a young German girl on Portland Avenue that I dated. She came from a large family but she showed no interest in a second date. I must have been a boring klutz. I kept remembering the seven-course dinner she ordered at a fancy restaurant. For each course, she would eat about a third of her serving and the waiter would take it away. That included the dessert she ordered as well. I kept wondering why anyone would order more than they could eat. In our household, that was a major offense. Then there was Lorraine Hajjar, our choir leader at St. Nicholas Church whom I faced every Sunday in the choir. She was four years older and more like a sister than a potential marriage partner. There was the girl that my cousin Richard introduced me to but that date was a major failure on my part for reasons I cannot mention.

Lee was now eleven, Kenny fifteen, Deanna eighteen. Vicky was twenty and married to New Jersey's Bud Rosa, who had asked me for her hand in marriage. Jim was twenty-two and at a major seminary. Ann was twenty-four. Joe was twenty-six and married. Betty was thirty-one and I was twenty-nine, both unmarried. Mr. Melikian, the inventor of the coffee machine said that I should get rid of my marriage checklist for dating a girl and just date for fun. My checklist was something like this. I must love her parents; be sure she wants to have all the children that God will send us; not be wasteful about anything and eats what she orders; be fairly attractive; have a lovely figure; be outgoing, warm and friendly, intelligent and have a strong belief in God.

I decided I would try to date Miss O'Hara for fun and get rid of the checklist. My fatherly role as head of the house was diminishing and I could still care for the needs of my mother and younger brothers if I were married. I did not plan on getting married like Joe did and bring his wife to our home to live until they found a place. Josie would go to the only bathroom and lock the door. That completely disrupted the routine of the household. One night I tried to use the bathroom. Josie was still in there and I had to go outside in the back yard and wash up in the kitchen sink. I woke up the next morning and she happened to be there again with the door locked. I knocked on the door and said "Josie, when are you going to give the rest of us a chance. You've been in there all night. My God!"

Nor did I want to play pranks like I did with Josie. Joe suggested that I get in their bed and cover my head with a sheet while he hid in a closet. I went along with it. I was getting extremely nervous when she got into the bed and cuddled up next to me. I turned around and she screamed, fleeing the room in panic, Joe, in the closet, was rolling over with laughter.

It was spring break and Miss O'Hara was going on vacation to Ft. Lauderdale. I asked if I could call her for a dinner-date when she returned. She was friendly and said "OK." She returned. I made the date. I went to her home. I met her mother and father. Her father and I spoke of the days at the Hunting Company and the people who were no longer there. I fell in love with her mother (Checklist). I brought surprising news to Miss O'Hara. I forgot that it was bowling night and wondered if she would mind watching us bowl and we would then go out to dinner. She was delightful in her reaction - a good sport. She seemed to enjoy watching the boys bowl and the boys enjoyed meeting and watching her and whispering to me about what a hot chick she was. The bowling ended. We went to dinner. Miss O'Hara ate everything she ordered. I drove her home, walked her to the door and said goodnight. "I'll be calling you again, if you would like." She said, "OK".

We continued to date. We were having fun like Mr. Melikian said. I was very attracted to her and loved every moment I spent with her. She said she liked my reaction when I spilled the glass of milk at my mom's breakfast table. She was sweet, gentle and loving. She had class. My sister Ann knew what she was doing. My best date was the summer of that year when Miss O'Hara was the Waterfront Director at the YMCA Camp Onanda on Canandaigua Lake. I drove down from Rochester for a breakfast date. I asked for Miss O'Hara. No one seemed to know who Miss O'Hara was. Suddenly someone said, "Oh, he means skipper, the one who takes us for overnight stays in the river south of the lake." Wow! I was impressed. The area south of the lake was full of wildlife, mosquitoes and even snakes. They found Skipper and we drove to Canandaigua for a breakfast. Skipper ordered a heaping platter of pancakes, eggs and home fries. I thought she was going to lick her plate. We were having fun like Mr. Melikian said and my checklist was working well except I didn't know how many children she wanted to have if this fun dating got serious.

We were engaged on Christmas 1955, six months after our first date. Miss O'Hara and I spent New Years Eve with my mother, Kenny, Lee and Deanna. They all loved Miss O'Hara. Photographs of our New Years Eve Party reveal the joy of that evening. A few months later, as we were heading for the Springhouse on Monroe Avenue for dinner, I started talking about a wedding date. Miss O'Hara became nervous and thought it was premature. I spun around the parking lot and took her home.

Seriously wounded, I said something like, "I'm going to be 30 years old. I've been respectfully courting you with the intention of marriage and a family of our own. I don't know what you were thinking when we got engaged but that is what I was thinking."

We had made a previous commitment for dinner with my cousin Amelia and her husband Faye Reynolds, for the following night. Before I left the curbstone, I said I had to live with the commitment and would pick her up. She said, "OK". After the dinner at the Reynolds home, as I parked in front of her home, she tenderly and sweetly reached over for my hand and said, "I'd be honored to be your wife." I said, "You'd better think about it a bit more" and swiftly drove away.

On our next date, she shared her feelings with me. There were good reasons for her concerns that helped my understanding. She said she had confronted her reasons and they were not justified and not only that, she would have as many children as God sent us. So I had fun as Mr. Melikian said I should, and my checklist was complete. Helen Margaret O'Hara and I got married on June 30, 1956, bought a house on Pinnacle Road in Rochester. Our first born in December of 1957 was named Regina Marie. Our second child Gregory John was born in May of 1960. (When Gina was two and Greg was three months old, I overheard a conversation while shaving. Gina asked, "What's that?" Helen said, "That's Gregory's penis." Gina's reply, "Why can't I have a peanut?" Her mom said, "Because only boys have penises." In a disturbed voice, Gina said, "Well, if I can't have a peanut, I want some chocolate candy!")

In 1961 Mr. Fishman, a co-founder of a company called Automatic Retailers of America (ARA), with $18 million in sales, flew into Rochester. Our sales were $3 million. After an evaluation of our books, he and an investment banker made an offer to buy our company. I told them that I was only 35 and had no thought of selling. They said, "At 35, you could become our national president when Mr. Davidson and I retire. Mr. Fishman was 48 and Mr. Davidson was 52. I turned the matter over to Jack Conway, my attorney and Brendan Meagher, the Managing

Partner of Price Waterhouse in the Rochester branch. ARA offered $1.4 million. I told them to ask for a non-negotiable $2 million, thinking they would go away. ($2 million equates to $20 million in year 2000). After much haggling between my accountants and attorney, they met the price. Both advisers, aware of our financials, highly recommended that I proceed with the closing.

I became the Vice President of ARA for the Northeastern United States. I was put in charge of acquisitions and the development of the northeastern part of the United States. Helen and I bought a home on 199 Ambassador Drive. It was a magnificent 6,000 sq. foot home in an exclusive neighborhood, plenty of room to raise a family, with good schools and a Catholic Church and School nearby.

I could not be a happier man. The skinny, bow-legged, knock-kneed, pigeon-toed, dark skin boy who grew up to run a "situation wanted" ad in the newspaper at age 20, was now, at 35, a multi-millionaire with a wonderful mother, wife, brothers, sisters and children, all happy and healthy. Praise God. What a blessing. (Little did I know of the trials and tribulations ahead of me).

News of the sale traveled throughout the Rochester community. I was on Rochester's hit list for contributions. I was a Rochester young man's success story from rags to riches. High level executives and bankers along with other prominent Rochester people invited Helen and me to parties. Early after the sale, the only major contribution I made was to Lebanon. Relatives from Lebanon were all seeking money for various reasons. I resolved the Lebanon requests, with the help of a Bishop in Lebanon. I donated sufficient funds to build a medical clinic in my father's village that continues to serve the village and its surrounding communities.

I knew I needed to make a major contribution to the Rochester community in which I was raised and in which I was successful. It had to be different. It was in my nature. I had this track record of creativity, of being a pioneer in the first coffee vending machine, the first central commissary for the preparation of packaged foods, the first automatic cafeteria and the first to offer industry a total package including vending machines, employee cafeterias, executive dining rooms etc. In my volunteer efforts, I developed ideas and programs that raised a greater number of dollars for the United Way and other fund raising campaigns. In addition, these efforts helped to significantly increase membership in organizations such as the Rochester Chamber of Commerce.

With my newfound wealth, I wondered, what financial contribution do I give back to the Rochester community? I needed time to think.

In the meantime, I focused on my goals as a corporate vice president of ARA. Other Kwik Kafe dealers in New York State and New England became aware of my merger. We knew each other from national meetings of franchised dealers. They had a great respect for our 1st place achievement as Kwik Kafe dealers. From the time of my merger with ARA in 1961 to 1963, through acquisitions and an aggressive marketing and sales thrust in this ten state area, my responsibility for Business & Industrial food service operations grew to close to $100 million in sales, and 4000 employees. This involved 1500 individual customers of all sizes. Our success at Kodak sparked the interest of many major corporations, including the major IBM plants in NY State.

Our "Northeast Area" headquarters was expanded on Maple Street in Rochester. I had an excellent group of regional vice presidents who reported to me. To assist the regional vice presidents, I had a staff of area dieticians, chefs, cafeteria and vending design specialists, computer experts and an administrative aide. They provided major assistance to the Regional Vice Presidents for the opening and operations of all profit centers under their control. For example, in Rochester, we assisted Xerox with the design, construction and operations of all of their cafeteria and vending services.

In 1963, I had received the top national award from ARA for my operational achievement and community activities. At these national meetings, at the closing dinners, for entertainment purposes, I was allowed to humorously impersonate the various speakers including the ARA President and other corporate officials. Somehow I was able to accomplish this without offending any of them. If I missed a few top officials, I discovered that it was a disappointment to them.

At 37 years of age, I could not be happier. I was happily married with three children. My mother, brothers and sisters were cared for. Tuition was available for any brother or sister, if they chose to further their education. My older brothers and sisters were not burdened with the need to support my mother. They were free to move to the vocation of their choice.

I lived in Rochester's most exclusive neighborhood. I was one of Rochester's success stories, "from rags to riches." Parties held at my home for business entertainment or community fund raising were publicized in the Democrat & Chronicle. My staff of catering professionals was available to make these parties unique in every respect.

The invitation for one party read, "Join us for an Arabian Night". On a perfect warm summer night, a Turkish rug ran from the curb to the front door with a mini-tent over the entrance. A seven-foot giant dressed in colorful Arabic clothing with golden slippers greeted guests. The three-car garage was converted to a tent decorated with Arabic art. Inside the tent, two Turkish pipes were available for guest smoking. A lady relative experienced in palm reading and dressed in Arabian clothing read the palms of our guests. A photographer took photos of couples smoking the Turkish pipes. Flaming torches lit the back yard and patio area. Arabic food was plentiful, identified in Arabic with an English translation.

My loveable mother, with humble pride, stood next to the serving table, introducing herself and answering questions about the preparation and ingredients of the Arabic food. She won the hearts of all of our guests and her memory for the names of clients was remarkable. The Arabic food was prepared in our central commissary. My mother supervised the preparation. On the large patio area that surrounded the side and back of the house, stations of flaming mini-grills awaited the guests, who chose their food as desired and cooked on them. After dinner, a belly dancer entertained with a group of Arabic musicians from Utica, NY. My wife and I entertained our guests with Arabic dancing that we practiced together for our wedding, seven years before. Guests were from all walks of life – government officials, clients, relatives, community leaders and friends. A Democrat & Chronicle reporter called it the "party of the year".

This skinny, bow-legged, pigeon-toed, knock-kneed boy, teased for being black, having his pants ripped off, spending seven of his boyhood years as the Prisoner of the Truck, was destined to become the national president of a $2 billion dollar company. My family would move with me to the Philadelphia national headquarters. I would take the lessons I learned as Prisoner of the Truck and in my service to the Rochester community and apply them to worthy national rather than local causes.

I went to bed after the Arabian Night Party wishing that my father had been there to celebrate the success of his son — to see what patience, study, hard work, education, integrity, salesmanship, human relations skills and excellence in product and service had achieved — all seeds planted in the Prison of the Truck.

At the age of 37, I had a new dream for my future with ARA. I would become its Chief Executive Officer. I would move to Philadelphia, grow the business and serve on national committees. I was committed to the Creeds espoused by the Junior Chamber of Commerce. Among them were, "Service to humanity is the best work of life." "Earth's greatest treasure lies in human personality." And, "Economic justice can best be won by free men through free enterprise." The sky was the limit. I was convinced that nothing was impossible to achieve if I put my mind to it.

Little did I realize that I would soon be in another Prison, one that I would impose upon myself, serving a 27 year term for which I had to accept full responsibility.

CHAPTER 22

Age 37 to 45 New Prisons Self-Imposed Becoming Poor

How do you measure success or failure? Happiness or sadness? Are they measured by the amount of wealth you can amass in a lifetime? Or by the entrepreneurial spirit that leads to those riches? Is it by facing defeat and turning it to victory? Or by how much perseverance and patience you can muster in the face of adversity? Is it faith that sustains you in your trials and tribulations? Is it knowing that you gave it your very best? Is it in searching for the good that comes from failure and turning it into success? Is it a sense of inner peace and trust in God that sustains you in good or bad times?

Bristol Mountain Ski Area

In 1963, at age 37, I decided to take the after tax $1.5 million dollars in the sale of my company and invest $300,000 in a project called Bristol Mountain Ski Area. The mountain land was located in the Bristol Hills, 30 miles south of Rochester, NY, in the Finger Lakes Region of New York State. With local financing, this new one million dollar facility (equivalent to $10 million in year 2000 dollars) would be my payback to the community. It was not a hospital wing or school addition. It was not a get rich quick scheme. It would be profit motivated because only through profits can a regional recreational facility grow and flourish in its service to the total community. Like the 1500 profit centers that I was responsible for in ARA, I would be highly dependent on the management skills of the individuals involved. I would take great joy in developing school programs for children at discounted prices, special programs for the handicapped, and establishing an exciting new winter recreational facility for family enjoyment. Our team would work toward affordable season passes and flexible skiing hours for day or night, seven days a week.

The news media found the plans to be very exciting. I was invited to speak to several luncheon meetings about the plans. My ski area associates had created a brilliant slide show for presentation of the plans. One luncheon involved the Chatterbox Club of Rochester. This was a group of affluent ladies who were active in service to the community. They were the wives of the leaders of the community. I asked my mother to attend the luncheon. The group reflected great excitement in the plans. My presentation involved humor and laughter. The response was rewarding. During the question and answer period, one of the ladies asked me how I got started in the coffee business. I traced the events including the $10,000 mortgage on my mother's home that led to a $2 million company sale eleven years later. A lady stood up and said with a bit of humor in her voice, "That was a courageous gesture by your mother, Fred. I would never mortgage my home for my 24 year old son, no matter what business he wanted to start."

At that point, I introduced my mother, who allowed me to mortgage our 1293 Park Avenue home for $10,000 and who, indirectly, made it possible for me to speak to their group about our ski area plans. I asked my mother to stand up. She was a sweet and loving five-foot tall lady. She was greeted with a big round of applause and shyly bowed to the audience. Another lady remarked that her son had been interested in the Kwik Kafe franchise but after discussions with family attorneys and accountants, the family was discouraged from making the investment. (I was glad that I could not afford either an accountant or a lawyer when I entered the coffee business). When the meeting concluded, I found more attention given to my heroic mother than to me. I was as proud of her as she was of me.

Shortly after this talk, I went to inspect a new cafeteria that we designed and were operating at Xerox Corporation. As I was about to enter the door, a group of Xerox executives were leaving the cafeteria to greet a bus occupied by several men of Japanese heritage. I stood to the side to allow room for the meeting. Joe Wilson, the founder of Xerox, recognized me. I spent several years with Joe Wilson working on United Fund Campaigns. He was familiar with the laughter that I brought to the campaign lunches as well as my performance in the Chamber of Commerce Membership Campaign. Joe stopped short of the bus to quickly greet me and said, "My wife was at the Chatterbox Club a few weeks ago. She heard your talk and liked your plans. She gave a brochure to me. I used that brochure to convince two key IBM executives, who were close to the ski areas of Vermont, to come to work for Xerox. Your plans for the ski area did the trick. It's a great contribution to the community." I said, Thank you, Joe", as he moved on to welcome the bus group.

The Bristol Mountain Ski Area was proposed to me by two bright young men, Ron Ratnik and Larry Demarse, ages 30 and 27, professional engineers at General Motors in Rochester. They put together the land package. They did their homework. They knew that snowmaking was the key to the success of the plan. They needed an investor. Their timing in talking to me was right. They were willing to leave General Motors to work full time to make the ski area a success.

Before I committed to an investment, I took a two-week vacation and visited every ski area in the Northeastern United States. Of all of the ski areas that I visited, there were two that stood out in my memory. One was a three-day meeting with Cal Coniff, the young manager of Mt. Tom, a ski area in Holyoke, Mass. The average snowfall was 48" compared to 82" for Rochester; the average winter temperature was 3 degrees warmer than Rochester, yet Mt. Tom operated 90 days a year. Mt. Tom was a small ski area with a vertical rise of only 400 feet. The vertical rise of ski areas in Vermont were over 2000 feet. Bristol Mountain's rise was 1200 feet. During my visit, Vermont ski areas were closed for lack of snow. Mt. Tom was operating from top to bottom because of its snow making system. Skiing conditions were from good to excellent. The entire mountain was lit for night skiing. I watched the long lines at night and during the weekend. Cal was open enough to show me his financial results for the previous years. The cash flow was not encouraging for a return on investment but the operations for the three previous years were in the black. Cal was encouraging with our plan. He felt that Bristol Mountain with its higher vertical, snowmaking, night-lights and close proximity to a much larger city had great potential. His night group programs for schools and colleges were a great success. He believed that ours would be too.

The other memorable, but opposite, experience was with Walter Schoenknect, the owner-developer of a major ski area called Mt. Snow in Vermont. Walt was about 55. I was now 37. Walt was well known in the industry as a pioneer in ski area development. Mt. Snow operated only in the daytime and did not have snowmaking. The only way I could get to see Walter was at 6 PM in a hot tub at the Snow Flake Lodge where I stayed. He said he could only budget 30 minutes and could not have dinner with me. Typical of Walter's creativity, was the lodge that provided a cable ride over the roads right to the base of the ski area.

After I explained our plans for Bristol Mountain and my visit to Mt. Tom, while we were up to our chins, submerged in the hot tub, Walt asked, "What business are you in now?" I told him. "Why do you want to build a ski area? They are not good investments." I said that I was not seeking big profits; that I believed we could develop a positive cash flow to take care of annual upgrades and improvements. I spoke of our proximity to Rochester and our plans for day and night skiing — getting twice the mileage out of the same investment. I said this would be my way of giving a portion of my wealth back to the community that gave me the opportunity for success. Walt said, "Frankly, I think you should stay in the business you are in. You are going to underestimate your investment requirements and discover that you will be constantly pouring more money than the $300,000 limit that you have established. If you want my opinion, I think you're crazy, but it sounds like you have already made up your mind. So, good luck, I have to go." The last I ever saw of Walt was the back of his red body as he emerged from the hot tub. However, as events turned out in future years, I never forgot his comments.

Otto Schneibs, a professional ski area designer was retained to layout the slopes and trails. Otto promised a trail and slope design that would "pamper the beginners and intermediates". We all believed that this was the market to pursue. This was also the recommendation of the ski area managers that I visited.

Bristol Mountain Ski Area, when completed in 1964, was referred to in publications as the most modern ski area in America with the most advance technology in snow making, lighting and food service systems. My two associates earned high praise in the ski industry for completion of this complex project in time for December 1964 opening.

In its first year, the design did not succeed in serving the intended market of beginners and intermediate skiers. The snow making capacity was too small for a long season or a quick recovery from major thaws. The ski area had a significant loss in its first year. I faulted the famed designer, Otto Schniebs. We did not meet the income projections. The narrow trails and slopes created a crowded feeling. Skiing conditions were too variable due to the need for greater snow making capacity. Families were disappointed. The first year failure was not unlike the opening of a restaurant or business cafeteria. First impressions are most important. If a restaurant or cafeteria food service gets off to a poor or a good start, the news spreads rapidly. So it was with the Bristol Mountain Ski Area. Regardless of the good planning, the first year's experience for beginners and intermediate skiers was bad and that impacted skier use and confidence for the balance of the year and the few years that followed.

The design failure lead to the development of Ski Valley and Hunt Hollow, two nearby private clubs and another public ski area called Swain. These Rochester developments used the technology of snow making pioneered by Bristol. Swain and Hunt Hollow were carefully planned for the novice and intermediate market. The impact of this new competition had a negative impact on Bristol's share of the market. Our bank was disappointed with the results. In the second year of operation, I had no alternative but to invest another $300,000 to cover losses, expand the snow making system and to widen the trails and slopes.

Ron Ratnik left Bristol to successfully market his expertise in snow making systems to other ski areas outside of the Bristol Mountain market. Larry Demarse was determined to turn the huge first year losses into a gain. With the expansion of snow making facilities and the widening of trails and slopes, the season of 1965-66 was an improvement over the first year but not enough to generate sufficient capital for improvements. In 1967, a $100,000 new slope for beginners significantly improved the image of the ski area for "pampering beginners" but reasonable profits were still not attained. Fierce price competition from the Swain ski area also had an impact on profitability.

Robert Kennedy

In 1964, while he was running for the Senate, Robert Kennedy could not appear for the ribbon cutting ceremony as he planned. However, he promised to visit us another time. In early March of 1967, I received a call from one of his assistants. He said that Senator Kennedy would keep his promise to return on March 18, 1967. It was a cold sunny day, excellent for skiing. Larry Demarse arranged for me to ski with the Senator. We took eight rides up the chairlift together. Each ride took approximately 10 minutes to get to the top of the mountain, a total of 80 minutes of one on one conversation. Senator Kennedy skied with wild abandonment. Had it not been for his falls, I would have been unable to keep up with him. One dramatic fall was caught on film and years later his wife, Ethel, requested a copy.

I was 41 and the Senator was 42. At first, Senator Kennedy talked about my family, mother, brothers, sisters, wife and children. He became aware that I became head of the household when I was 24 and the success that I achieved. We found similarities in the large families we came from. We were closely knit. We played football. We had many family gatherings. We were Catholic and devoted to our religion. Then his conversation shifted to questions. When did my father die? What was my first business venture? What got me into the ski business? What did I want to do with the rest of my life? Are you interested in government service?

I did not hesitate. I answered his last two questions, "I would like to take the management experience that I gained in the tightly-controlled food and vending business and put it to work in government service. I would like to be the man in charge of seeing that food for hungry nations actually gets to the hungry, and is not intercepted somewhere by corrupt politicians or governments." The Senator replied, "Fred, I will remember this conversation".

I firmly believe if he had become President, I would have been called to serve. If called, I would have ditched my investments as well as my job at ARA and moved my family to Washington. Senator Kennedy was shot fifteen months later on June 4, 1968 in California on his way to becoming President of the United States.

The Beginning of Bristol Harbour Village on Canandaigua Lake, NY

In 1963, shortly after the sale of my company, I had purchased 3 acres of land and 450 feet of cliff waterfront on Canandaigua Lake, 15 minutes from the ski area. The cost was $42,000. Helen and I rented a boat on the north shore of the lake and pulled up on the beachfront. I said, "Surprise, this is where we will build our tennis court! We will build a vacation home up on that cliff. A stairway will bring us down to the tennis court and waterfront for boating and swimming." The surprise backfired. Helen was not enthusiastic about a vacation home where she would spend all of her time worrying about children on the edge of a cliff. Nor did she care to be down at the waterfront, entertaining visiting relatives all summer long. So this land remained vacant for four more years.

In the fall of 1967, I read an article in Ski Area Magazine, the national publication for the ski industry. The article stated that ski areas needed to expand into resort property development in order to enhance their potential for profits, using the ski lodge as a marketing center.

On a winter Sunday in 1967, after attending Mass at St. Januarius Church in Naples, New York, I needed to get away from the pressures of my work at ARA and the Ski Area. In order to get to the lake property that I had purchased in 1963 for a vacation home, I walked the long right of way at the foot of Seneca Point hill to the beach portion of the property. Canandaigua Lake runs north and south. It is 17 miles long, about a mile wide and over 200 feet deep. The waters are pure and clear. The city of Canandaigua is on the north shore and Naples is close to the south shore. The hills surrounding the lake are over 1,000 feet high. The winter view was picture perfect. The unfrozen waters rippled onto the shoreline. In the quiet of this environment, I counted my blessings. My mother, brothers, sisters, wife and children were all happy, healthy and doing well. Yet, I was troubled with the great drain of my financial resources, my responsibility to ARA and my commitment to make Bristol Mountain a success.

I thought about the ski area's struggle to make snow, only to watch it melt on warm and rainy days, and then to start over again when cold weather returned. In many ways, running a ski area was not much different than running a farm — both were vulnerable to bad weather cycles. I thought of the grape farmers and the frequent local newspaper reports of weather that threatened the quality and quantity of the harvest. I became sensitive to the uncertainties that all farmers faced, both in crop production and financial variability. The quiet meditation in this winter setting seemed to refresh my spirit.

I walked back to my car and headed up the steep hill on Seneca Point Road. As I approached the top of the steep hill, I saw a "For Sale" sign in the woods adjacent to my property. It read 24 acres and 2,000 feet of cliff frontage. I parked my car along Seneca Point Road to walk down the sharp slope. I partially walked and slid downward on slippery snow, through the forest of trees to the edge of the cliff. The views to the north, east and south were among the most beautiful I had ever seen in my travels or on TV or in magazines. A tree, near the edge of the cliff, had formed a bench for me to sit on. In the silence and privacy of this God-created environment, where Seneca Indians once resided, my hand felt the St. Januarius Missalette that I had put in my ski jacket at Mass that morning. I checked the index for "How Great Thou Art." Mesmerized by the magnificence of the views, I sang aloud:

"O Lord, my God, when I in awesome wonder,
Consider all the worlds thy hands have made,
I see the stars; I hear the rolling thunder,
Thy pow'r throughout the universe displayed.
When through the woods and forest glades I wander,
And hear the birds sing sweetly in the trees;
When I look down from lofty mountain grandeur
And hear the brook and feel the gentle breeze;
Then sings my soul, my Savior God to thee;
How great thou art! How great thou art!

The following day, I thought that this wondrous location, combined with frontage I already owned, could be divided into twenty-six 100 foot lots for the construction of 26 homes with a commonly owned stairway to the beach and 26 boat slips. I had no experience in land development. I naively thought that this could very well be the land development mentioned in Ski Area Magazine that could generate significant cash flow for Bristol

Mountain. I would reach for a profit of $10,000 per lot and hand $260,000 over to the ski area. Again, in year 2000 dollars, this would be comparable to $2,600,000.

I phoned Herb Ellinwood, the broker. The California owner was asking $47,000 for the property. I told Mr. Ellinwood that I would like to put in a purchase offer. He phoned me a few days later and said that a "group" of lakeside property owners from Seneca Point heard about my interest in this property and also wished to submit an offer. The "group" was aware that I was in the ski business and they suspected that I was purchasing the cliff for development purposes.

They wanted to block me from buying this property for fear that I might create some kind of development that tied in with the ski area. Mr. Ellinwood said that he was obligated as a broker to submit all offers. In 1967 dollars, I estimated the combined wealth of Seneca Point, Canandaigua lakeside property owners at $50 million or more. I had no intention of starting a bidding war. I earned many friendships from several of these property owners for my success in business, my community activities and in the development of the ski area. I was an accepted member of the "group" and invited to play in the annual Seneca Point tennis tournament.

With this in mind, I advised Mr. Ellinwood to simply submit an offer for $1,000 over the full asking price. The "group" submitted an offer for a sum less than the full asking price. I was shocked to learn that the owner, in California, accepted my offer.

Little did I realize what a dynamic and harsh impact this purchase and building plan would have on the next twenty years of my life, requiring me to significantly borrow from the Seven Gifts of the Holy Spirit – Wisdom, Understanding, Counsel, Knowledge, Fortitude, Piety and Love of the Lord. These gifts, always alive, helped me to survive the Prison of the Truck. And with God's help, they would help me to survive the feeling of being trapped - the self-imposed "Prisoner of a New Venture."

Shortly after closing on the sale of the land, I toured the property with a surveyor to lay out the lots. He shocked me by saying that rocky condition of the cliff could not handle 26 separate septic systems. I retained Paul Russell, a sanitary engineer from Harnish & Lookup. He confirmed the opinion of the surveyors. He said it would require a modern sewer treatment plant to serve 26 lots. I asked him what the cost would be. His shocking answer, "$250,000." I asked about the capacity of such a plant. He said it would serve 250 housing units.

A Bigger Plan for a Village

After several meetings, we concluded that it would be feasible to build five-story buildings totaling 250 units on the cliff's edge. However, he said that we would need additional land for the sewer treatment plant. I reasoned that if we could build chairlifts for ski areas, we could also build a vertical lift from the edge of the cliff to the beachfront to service 250 units. We could also build the necessary number of boat slips. Larry Demarse, a remarkable engineer and President of Bristol Mountain, knew how to put the engineering and construction team together for such efforts.

At a profit of $5,000 each in 1967 dollars, this would eventually generate $1,250,000 in cash for the ski area as well as repayment of loans that I had to make to keep the ski area going. Our sanitary engineer said that the sewage treatment plant would require 10 acres of land and suggested that I inquire about the land for sale across the street from this Cliffside property. We were not worried about zoning approvals. The Town of South Bristol did not have a zoning ordinance.

I spent the next weekend negotiating with the landowner across the street from the Cliffside property. He owned 110 acres of land, with many great lake views. In the middle of this acreage, he had built a magnificent home with a dramatic lake view to the south that eventually became our operational center. He agreed to trade his land for stock and a plan to put the ski area and land development into one package and to sell shares of stock to the public. In addition to this purchase, Mack McCabe, a local realtor and friend, handled another land purchase of 110 acres called the German parcel. This would be for a future golf course.

Resigning from ARA

In 1968, when I was 42, I was called into Philadelphia for a meeting. In spite of my outside investment pressures, I was actively involved in my responsibility to ARA during the week and actively involved with the ski area on weekends. During the weekdays, I met regularly with my key ARA regional vice presidents and staff. Our ten-state area performance was the best in the United States. Based on this, I was asked if I would assume the Presidency of the Business & Industry Division of ARA, a division that was approaching one billion in sales. It was made clear that as President of ARA, I should expect to be traveling at least 60% of the time. I would have to conduct performance reviews at the headquarters of the six area vice-presidents of sales in the United States. I would be involved in the opening of cafeterias of any of the Fortune 500 cafeterias in the United States. I knew that the next step could be the CEO of all of the ARA Divisions approaching $3 billion in sales. The founders Bill Fishman & Davre Davidson were keenly aware of my ARA national achievement awards for exceptional profit performance, excellent team building skills and award-winning community service.

I now had five children, ranging in age from one to twelve. I shocked Ralph Globus who was retiring as President of the B&I Division when I very reluctantly said, "Ralph, I cannot take the job for two reasons. One, I must be close to my family and two, my investment in a ski area and in resort planning are consuming my capital and both will need more of my time. I am honored by your offer but I find myself in a situation that is a conflict of interest and I believe I should resign. Ralph asked me to stay on for another year to allow the new area president to determine my replacement. This was a difficult decision. I believed that if I became CEO of

ARA, I would be able to make community contributions on a national rather than local scale. My heart was always into maximizing whatever community service I could render.

Moving Forward with the Plans for Bristol Harbour Village

In 1968, I still had sufficient funds to retain professionals for the development of the 258 acres and half mile of Cliffside lake frontage we now controlled. Larry Demarse played an active role in meeting with architects and engineers. His experience as an engineer and in the construction of Bristol Mountain was invaluable to the planning process, enabling me to continue to perform my duties with ARA. The ski area was not producing any significant cash flow. There were limited funds for expansion.

Every town in Ontario County had some form of zoning in 1968. As early as 1964, when Bristol Mountain was completed, I attended a Town Board meeting and urged the Town to develop a zoning ordinance. Unwisely, the Seneca Point Group, in the Town of South Bristol, opposed it. They wanted to build or modify their lakeside homes anytime they pleased, without any red tape.

In August of 1968, James Johnson, our architect, Larry Demarse and I presented an "initial" plan to the South Bristol Town Board calling for 200 condominiums on the edge of the Cliffside. About 70 persons from South Bristol attended including vocal members of Seneca Point, under the guise of Canandaigua Lake Area Association Inc. They expressed their intense disapproval and concerns about the plans. Intense pressure was put on the town fathers to create a zoning ordnance, one that would block our plans.

There was a great amount of publicity, letters to the editor and appeals to town, county and state authorities and politicians. The scrapbooks of news articles and letters to the editor for the next three years are over two feet tall. They reflect the attempts of the Seneca Point Group to prevent the master planning or the financing of Bristol Harbour Village. A petition of 5,300 signatures was sent to Governor Rockefeller "requesting that he and all other public officials responsible for health and the purity of our water deny permission for construction of Bristol Harbour Village near Seneca Point on Canandaigua Lake."

Urged by the misinformation of Seneca Point group leaders, I personally received over a hundred letters in opposition. Some letters suggested that my children would forever be hated if my plans were successful. Other letters, including one unauthorized letter, on Kodak letterhead, suggested that my plans could affect the business that ARA was doing with Kodak.

Joe Wilson, founder, Chairman and CEO of Xerox

In early September of 1968, in the midst of this intense opposition, I received a phone call from Joe Wilson, founder, Chairman and CEO of Xerox Corporation. It was in 1963 when Mr. Wilson spoke to me about the two IBM executives he recruited because of the ski brochure his wife brought home from the Chatterbox Club. Joe said, "Fred, a group of influential people have asked me to get involved in attempts to block your planned lake development. I believe it is only fair for me to hear your side of the story before I make a decision. Would I be able to meet with you, your architect and engineer to review your plans?" (Mr. Wilson had built a vacation home on a large piece of land overlooking Canandaigua Lake not far from Seneca Point).

We met at the office of Jim Johnson our architect. Paul Russell, our sanitary engineer joined us for this meeting. They both did a masterful job of explaining the plans to Mr. Wilson, an objective listener. He was impressed with the environmental sensitivity in which the plans were developed and the team of professionals involved. He wanted to know more about overall benefits to the community and the business and financial plans for Bristol Mountain and Bristol Harbour. I discussed the contributions Bristol Mountain had made to the Naples, NY community. Naples was wine country, excelling in both the growing of grapes and the production of wine. In the winter, Bristol provided many jobs for young and old in Naples and the surrounding community. I spoke of the plan to transfer snowmaking crews in the winter to golf maintenance crews in the spring, summer and fall. The same would apply to food service personnel who would move from the ski area food service facility to the clubhouse restaurant for four-season employment. I spoke of the economies involved when one management team focused on both a ski area and a resort, providing year round steady employment. I predicted that Bristol Harbour would be primarily a community of adults seeking a maintenance-free second home. There would be little or no impact on the Naples School District so school taxes on homes at Bristol Harbour would enhance the quality of education for the Naples School District. He was aware of public offerings that were being made during that time with little substance. He felt that our public offering for the sale of shares in our combined ski-lake plan, was sound and had merit since it would minimize high interest costs that could endanger the plan.

I knew of Mr. Wilson's interest in people, who sincerely believed in service to their community. He said and believed that recreation was an essential industry that served the needs of people. I also knew of his reputation for hands on management and walking around his company, remembering the names of his employees as well as those he worked with in the community. If there was someone he did not recognize, he would introduce himself, seeking the name of the other party. He was a gentleman, a man of compassion and sensitive to the needs of the total community. He was also a brilliant leader and motivator.

Joe Wilson did not know that I had such a high respect for his brilliance, character, humility, courage and achievements that I would have dropped the plans for Bristol Harbour Village if he asked me to. I was aware that both Kodak and IBM had turned down Howard Carlson, the inventor of Xerography. Joe Wilson had the vision to see its potential and the "Fortitude" to risk his entire business and fortune on the idea. And even more, he was a religious man. He did "Counsel" with me. He did search for "Knowledge and Understanding". He did it as a "pious" man. He had the objective "Wisdom" to know that the planning was sensitive to the environment. The seven gifts of the Holy Spirit were simply inherent in Joe Wilson's nature.

I knew that if Joe Wilson asked me to drop the plans for Bristol Harbour, he would have also advised me how to minimize my losses and exit the plan graciously. I had great admiration for Robert Kennedy that I wrote of earlier, but no one, not even Bobby Kennedy, earned my respect more than Joe Wilson. I loved that man for his impeccable integrity, his goodness and his genuine concern for his fellow man, which extended down to the janitors in his company and the disadvantaged of the world. With the expansion of Xerox throughout the world in his business plan, this man was, nevertheless, taking time to listen to the plan for Bristol Harbour and Bristol Mountain before he signed a petition against it. That is greatness; that is class; unequalled by any man I ever knew. When the meeting was concluded, Mr. Wilson said, "Fred, I do not intend to sign the petition against your project. This does not mean that you can say that I endorse your plan. However, I do wish you and your people good luck and success in this endeavor".

Shortly thereafter, a major leader of the "group", a vice president of the Canandaigua Lake Association, made it her full time personal goal to block the various government approval requirements. She even organized a group of people to solicit protests in public parks in Rochester, 35 miles from Canandaigua. The misinformation passed out implied that Bristol Harbour Village was the lake's biggest polluter, when in fact a shovel had not as yet been turned in the ground. Albany is the capital of New York State and a six-hour drive from Canandaigua. She made several trips to Albany and to local political officials in an aggressive attempt to block state approval of the plans for both the sewer treatment plant and the marina.

Throughout this period, I kept thinking. This is the United States of America. I served in WWII to protect the democratic process. I am not planning anything illegal. I am cooperating with every NY State agency that the law requires. In spite of the fact that there was no town zoning, these other NY agencies will not permit me to go forward if the plans will harm the environment or the lake. I want to do it right. I value the input of the community. I am sensitive to their concerns. I will make changes that make sense. If the plans disturb our neighbors, they would also disturb the people to whom we would be trying to sell. For all these reasons, I thought, I will commit every last dollar and every ounce of my energy to prevail.

A Shocking Meeting

After the South Bristol Town presentation of plans, I spoke to the Seneca Point Group leader and the vice president of the Canandaigua Lake Association. I asked if I could bring my architect to a meeting with her "group" to address their major concerns. She approved of the meeting and suggested that it be held in her home in Pittsford, NY. I thought this would help me to "Understand" their concerns and help them to "Understand" the controls that we would put into place to make Bristol Harbour Village a good and peaceful neighbor. This attempt to "Counsel" and search for "Knowledge" could alleviate many of their concerns. At this meeting, I explained that the Condo plan had to be approved by the Attorney General of NY State. There would be rules and regulations governing the quality of usage such as noise control, exterior maintenance of the buildings, balconies free of hanging towels or wet clothing, etc. I tried to reason that no one would buy into the project if there were no legal controls for the orderly usage of each living unit. These controls would minimize any disturbance to condominium occupants as well as the "four" Seneca Point lakeside homes adjacent to the planned development. The Seneca Point Group knew that other homes were far removed from the project and could not see the condominium from their properties.

Our architect explained the "initial plan". We made it clear that we would address their concerns and make adjustments wherever we could. Good questions were asked. One rendering showed a multi-story building rising from the beach, 100 feet, to the top of the cliff. It also showed other buildings on the cliff itself. Inside the beach building, an elevator was planned to take residents to their units or residents from other buildings down to the beach area. A member of the group asked, "That is such a small beach area. Shouldn't that area be left as a beach only? Isn't that best for your long term plans?"

Indeed, in our planning process, we had failed to consider the negative impact this beach building would have on neighbors as well as future residents of BHV. Preserving the one-half mile of cliff without a single building fronting it was the most significant and helpful input gathered from this meeting. Anyone standing on the Bristol Harbour Village beach in the future could enjoy the natural wonder of the 2600 feet of the cliff water frontage with minimal views of condominium buildings.

After a brief deliberation with my architect, our response was, "Yes, you are right." The architect put an X through the beach building on the drawing and I said, "It's gone. What else?" Questions regarding the size, quality and estimated sales price of the units were asked? It was to be a high quality product that would attract affluent buyers.

Others asked, "Can you take those five story buildings and nestle them into the trees so that they are somewhat concealed?" We stated that was in the plan. Another good question was asked, "Have you been to Bermuda and looked at all of those pink buildings? Can you match the exterior of the buildings as close as you can to the color of the exposed cliff?" I thought we were making great progress. They were providing input important to future residents as well as our neighbors. The answer was "yes."

Then the tide turned. Another question was, "Fred, you are noted for your community good work and a good neighbor. Many of us have been your friends. Can't you pick another spot on the other side of the lake and do your development there?" Several others at the meeting who suggested alternate sites supported this question. No one voiced objection to this question. My answer was the truth, "No, for marketing reasons, we want to be within fifteen minutes of Bristol Mountain and this is the only land available on the west side of the lake that has lake access."

This question reminded me of my community service in Rochester, NY when important community leaders would support certain housing projects as long as they were not in their back yards. If I write another book, it will be called NIMBY (not in my back yard).

No one seemed to care about the potential convenience of an adjacent golf course, clubhouse and restaurant in the area, nor the sensitivity given to the careful environmental planning, nor the controls that would be put into place. They simply did not want Bristol Harbour Village to become a reality. They wanted the 2600 feet of lake frontage to be vacant as if it were their own private frontage. Even though they previously opposed zoning, even though they did not own the land, they treated the land as if it were their private preserve and we were going to despoil it. The 27-acre, 2600 feet of cliff property had been for sale for four years. All they would have had to do was to chip in to buy it as a private preserve and they would have control of its usage.

It became obvious that the group was not there to listen to reason. They hid under the banner of protecting the lake from our development - yet no one found fault with the suggestion of moving the project to the "other side of the lake." They simply wanted us to go away. If we did not go away, they would use pollution of the lake, overly crowded boating conditions and depreciation of property values as their banner. This would unite the entire lake community with fear and misinformation. Politicians and governmental agencies would get involved. This could have a negative impact on governmental approvals. Funds obtained from the entire lake community could be used to litigate to the fullest extent.

Contrary to the fact that the lake belonged to the people of New York State, they were opposed to sharing it. This included some opposition to the state-operated marinas on the north and south of the lake as well as our planned development.

Data they promulgated regarding pollution of the lake was based on sheer unwillingness to accept scientific fact. Data that Bristol Harbour would destroy the values of the property would prove to be inaccurate. Data that the marina would overcrowd the use of the water ignored the aerial evidence that showed there was ample room for additional boats.

(The living history of Bristol Harbour Village in the year 2000 would serve to prove that the seeds of fear and panic that they spread throughout the lake and in the Rochester community in these earlier years regarding noise, safety, lake pollution and unreasonable boat density were totally unjustified. An award winning golf course and restaurant in their back yard significantly enhanced their enjoyment and contributed to a great increase in their property values. The project made significant tax contributions to the Naples School District with less than a dozen additional children going to the school. Jobs were created and $30 million was added to the tax base with little demand for town and county services. On all counts the opposition was proven wrong.)

In their public attempts to discredit the plan, there was the pretense of protecting the lake "for all people" but in this particular meeting in Pittsford, New York, it was clearly shown that the motive was to protect what they perceived to be "their portion of the lake."

At this 1968 meeting, a shocking question was asked by someone, without objection by anyone present. "What will happen to future sales if the FIGHT organization wants to buy the first building of 14 units?" The FIGHT organization was a group of African Americans and others, who among other causes, wanted to eliminate the prejudice that existed in buying homes in white neighborhoods. I answered that I did not believe the FIGHT organization would be interested in buying 14 expensive condominium units in a resort environment.

Another question, "Well, Fred, of course you know the people who will be buying your condominiums?" I replied, "People who can afford to buy them". "No Fred", came back the reply, "you know, it's the people who are buying condominiums in Florida". I was still naïve. I did not understand. Finally, "Fred, with your Lebanese heritage, you should know what we are talking about?" Still, no one at this meeting raised a voice in protest of the question. (Unlike New York State that had few condominium projects during this period, Condominiums were very popular in Florida. It was true that the Jewish people valued this maintenance-free lifestyle in Florida and were large buyers of condominium units.) I raised my voice in righteous anger and said, "Oh, now I know what you are talking about and I do have an answer for that question. We will sell the first building to the Blacks, the second building to the Jews, the third building to the Irish, the fourth building to the Germans, the fifth building to the Italians, the sixth building to the Lebanese Arabs, etc., and we will change the name of "Bristol Harbour Village" to "United Nations Village". And, of course, we will fly both the American flag and the flag of the other country above each of those buildings."

Then I continued without pausing, "Look you all know that I had my start in the coffee vending business. All of my machines were taught to automatically accept the nickels of all customers regardless of their race, creed or color so as to conform with the law of the land, and the law of the land is no different in regard to real estate sales. There shall be no discrimination in the sale of real estate. Are there any more questions?" One prominent voice of the Rochester community said, "Fred, I want to be disassociated from the questions that have just been asked." There were three or four others who asked to be disassociated from these questions. I asked to be excused from the meeting and the architect and I left.

When the meeting had concluded, I reflected on my childhood and my hatred for any form of discrimination. I was proud that I had the gift of Fortitude to speak out as I did at this meeting. This meeting fueled my determination to make Bristol Harbour Village a reality even if it took my family and me to the doorstep of personal bankruptcy. There would be one exception. I would not put a mortgage on my mother's home. If losing the battle was God's will for me, I knew that with my experience and determination, I could rejoin ARA or find employment anywhere in these United States. However, I knew that my responses to the "group" would only serve to fuel their determination to fight me every step of the way.

On May 6, 1969 The Canandaigua Lake Area Association, led by the "group leaders" who met with us at the Pittsford home, asked if I would consent to a public meeting with my sanitary engineer to answer questions about the Health Departments approval of our $250,000 sewerage treatment plant. Over a hundred people attended. The engineer made a very professional slide show presentation showing what the plant would look like and how the three stages of treatment would result in water cleaner than the lake water itself. He also explained the Department of Health's intensive review and approval of the plans. In the question and answer period, someone asked, "Mr. Sarkis, would you allow your children to swim at the mouth of the creek when the so called treated water is coming into the lake?" I replied, "Yes, based on the professional input you've heard today and the approval of the State Department of Health, I would." His response, "Mr. Sarkis, you would do anything to make a buck even if meant letting your children swim in raw sewage". The meeting failed to convince many of those in attendance. They did not want to listen to the facts. They just wanted me to go away. The hostility of certain uncontrolled members of the audience caused great concern to my brother Joe and Larry Demarse who were in the audience. They actually feared for my safety. Gathering the support of two others, they escorted me out of the meeting and to my car to prevent me from being harmed.

This unruly meeting is best described in a letter to the editor in the Daily Messenger:

June 16, 1969.

"To the Editor:

Considering the multitude of letters to the editor relative to the Bristol Harbour Village project and Fred Sarkis, I trust one more letter will not be a burden to you.

With one or two exceptions, most of the letters have come from those people who have not taken the time and effort to obtain the facts about modern sewage disposal systems recently developed through scientific research and engineering.

At the meeting held on May 6, 1969 at the Trenholm East by the Canandaigua Lake Association, Paul Russell, a sanitary engineer for Mr. Sarkis, tried in vain to present the facts about the new systems that will be used at the Bristol Harbour development.

Unfortunately, this meeting took on the atmosphere of an inquisition directed at Mr. Russell and Mr. Sarkis rather than a meeting to properly hear the facts. I was at this meeting and felt that the chairman should have stopped the discussion until some in attendance stopped acting like hoodlums at a barroom brawl.

I feel confident that the New York State Department of Health, which has approved of Mr. Sarkis' plans for sewage treatment, is in a better position to judge this project than many of the laymen who own property on Canandaigua Lake.

Eventually the State may insist on an inspection of all septic and sewage disposal systems along the lake and request that they meet modern standards along similar plans proposed by Bristol Harbour Village.

I think the real objection to Bristol Harbour Village, by some who own property in the vicinity, is based upon their desire to keep this entire area as a private preserve for their own enjoyment.

In years past the residents of the area had an opportunity to establish zoning. Apparently, for their own reasons, they were not interested. Now that a new development is underway, they suddenly have taken steps to establish zoning regulations.

As a footnote regarding the land purchased by Bristol Mountain Enterprises, all of this property was for sale over a period of years at a much lower price than Bristol Mountain Enterprises paid for it. Many of the residents now opposed to this project were aware of the fact that this land was for sale but did not choose to purchase it.

Herbert M. Ellinwood, West Lake Road, Canandaigua, N.Y."

[Note: Mr. Ellinwood was the broker who sold this property to me on behalf of Bristol Mountain Enterprises, Inc. He was not a close friend. I did not ask him to write the letter. Any member of the "group" who resented this letter would never retain Mr. Ellinwood as their Broker. He jeopardized his business interests as a broker with all lake residents. Mr. Ellinwood passed away many years ago. I am saddened that I never took the time to write him a letter thanking him for his gift of Fortitude.]

The controversy and extensive publicity over the sewerage treatment plant was a wake up call for all sources of pollution on Canandaigua Lake. We received our approvals because the treated water that would be discharged into the lake from Seneca Point Creek would be purer than the lake water itself. In addition, the Department of Environmental Conservation required periodic samples and inspections to insure proper treatment. (In 30 years of operation, this plant has passed every inspection. It has never been cited for pollution).

In June of 1969, I wrote a letter to the editor titled "Easy Pure Waters Test". The idea was taken from the Citizens Committee to save Cayuga Lake in NY State. Packets of a fluorescent dye called Pylam would be distributed free to each of more than 2,300 cottages and residences along both shores of Cayuga Lake. The test consisted of flushing the harmless dye through septic systems. If the system does not meet compliance standards, the dye will appear in the water or on the surface of the ground. A few weeks after this letter was published, the Canandaigua Lake Association in cooperation with the Canandaigua Chamber of Commerce offered the Dye Packs free of charge to about 2,000 cottages and homes on Canandaigua Lake. The Daily Messenger confirmed that this action was a result of my letter.

A few years later, thanks to the Daily Messenger, to Dr. Joe Guattery (President of the Canandaigua Chamber of Commerce and the reawakened Canandaigua Lake Pure Waters Association) and to objective political leaders, a public sewer system was installed along the lake in heavy residential areas. The result was the elimination of many inadequate septic systems that were causing serious lake pollution. I thought to myself, many of those who opposed our plans for a state-approved pollution control system were ironically polluters themselves. I recalled what Jesus said when he was defending Mary Magdalene – "Let he who is without sin cast the first stone."

Ironically, in their highly publicized opposition to our plans, the "group" created the media storm that caused objective sources to focus on major sources of real pollution – the inadequate septic systems of many lakeside residences.

A Summary of Attempts to stop Bristol Harbour Village In spite of Governmental Approvals

We thought we were home free when we received the Health Departments approval for the Sewage Treatment Plant. However, actual headlines thereafter read:

- *June 18, 1969 – "Canandaigua Lake Association Fight Sewage Plant Plan." The Canandaigua Lake Association retained a lawyer-conservationist who found fault with the plans.*

- *June 20, 1969 – "Petition Asks Project Denial." "A petition reportedly bearing 5,300 signatures has been sent to Governor Rockefeller requesting that he and 'all other public officials responsible for health and purity of our water,' deny permission for construction of Bristol Harbour Village near Seneca Point on Canandaigua Lake." This release was sent to the Daily Messenger by the same lady of the "group", as vice president of Canandaigua Lake Association.*
- *July 25, 1969 – "Controversial Sewer Plant OK'd. Bids are due August 5, 1969."*
- *September 30, 1969 – "Seneca Point Suit is Filed" – An immediate neighbor takes us to court with the argument that our beach frontage was an illegal landfill.*
- *October 18, 1969 – "Bristol Dropping Stock Offering. However, first building of 14 units is under construction."*
- *October 24, 1969 –"Injunction Sought to Block Bristol Harbour Project." An attempt to prevent the discharge of water for the sewerage treatment plant that had not yet been constructed.*
- *March 6, 1970 – "Lake Mooring Hearing Delayed." Opponents found a technical error in the application for a 128-slip marina.*
- *April 17, 1970 – "Bristol Harbour Condominium of 14 units 35% complete."*
- *April 30, 1970 – "Attorney General gives 56 Unit OK for Bristol Harbour."*
- *May 21, 1970 – "Start of Dock Hearing for 128 slips."*
- *May 26, 1970 – "End of five day dock hearing."*
- *August 6, 1970 – "Sarkis Says Apartment Work Halted – due to tough money market."*
- *October 6, 1970 – "Suit started over Apartments." – Pertaining to the injunction to prevent the docking facility.*

- *October 7, 1970 – "Seneca Point Landfill Alleged in Supreme Court. Brought before the State Supreme Court."*
- *October 16, 1970 – "Suit on Lake Project Opens." Pertaining to the charge of*

an illegal land fill at the beach area.

- *November 13, 1970 – "Bristol Harbour Sewer Loan Try Supported." – Ontario County supported a plan to obtain federal funding to build the treatment plant.*
- *November 15, 1970 – "Dock Plan Opponents Ask Decision Delay" – Another attempt by opponents to delay final approval of the docks.*
- *December 28, 1970 – "Sarkis Project is Resuming." Sarkis announces a loan in excess of $2 million from General Mortgage Investments in Maryland.*
- *December 30, 1970 – "Sarkis Winner in Civil Suit"- Neighbor's lawsuit on regarding landfill of beach area loses.*
- *January 1, 1971 – "Controversial Piers Nearer." The State Department of Environmental Conservation gives "notice of intent" to approve docks subject to clearance by another governmental agency.*
- *April 14, 1971 – "Annulment Sought for Dock Site." The Canandaigua Lake Pure Waters Association instituted action in Supreme Court seeking to annul the permits granted for the docks.*
- *September 29, 1971 – "Condominium at Bristol to be Occupied by November 1." Sarkis announces successful sales effort.*
- *October 31, 1971 – "Suite to bar 100 foot dock lost by Canandaigua Lake Group. Dismissed by the State Supreme Court."*

The Infamous One Week Dock Hearing in May of 1970

As written in a previous chapter, the skeleton of the 1st building (14 units) was under construction in May of 1970. We had ten buyer contracts for this 1st building and about 15 lot sales, all subject to completion of the entire first phase of the development including the marina. We had not as yet obtained any financing.

In the midst of this financial crisis, we had to seek approval of the State of New York to construct a 128-slip marina that would go out 100 feet into the lake.

The presiding officer for the hearing was Mr. Jeremiah R. Dineen, Senior Hydraulic Engineer, New York State Water Resources Commission. During the next five days, he gave everyone an opportunity to speak. He was democratic, fair, objective and firm when questions became repetitious or did not pertain to the application.

His job was to represent the people of the State of NY who own the lake rather than the landowners who live around it. Approval hinged on one simple question. Would the application for a 128 boat slip marina harm "the health, welfare and safety of the people of the State of New York"?

Our major exhibit was a photograph of the entire lake. We retained a surveyor who superimposed the planned boat docks on Canandaigua Lake. Canandaigua Lake is about 17 miles long and one-and-a-half miles wide. Imagine this page to be the entire lake and consider this "*" being placed on the middle-edge of this page as the size of the planned marina on the lake. The 1,179 pages of the dock hearing would give the reader the impression that the docks would extend three-quarters of a mile on the lake rather than 100 feet.

When the first day of the hearing commenced, the courtroom was full of people. I was out numbered about 110 to 3. The opposition included several major law firms in Rochester as well as many citizens from Seneca Point and the surrounding area.

Even a supervisor from the Town of Canandaigua spoke in opposition to the marina, in spite of the zoning approval we had received from the Town of South Bristol for this project.

Any law firm or resident who gave proper and timely notice could cross-examine any witness. This hearing was one of the final attempts to cripple my plans for a village and to bring me closer to bankruptcy — the final nail for the burial of the building one "skeleton" that was being constructed. Without a marina, sales of condominiums or lots would be crippled. Without a marina, financing for the planned Village would be impossible from any out of town source. I would then be forced into business and personal bankruptcy.

We retained experts in engineering, construction and scientists who specialized in studies related to fresh water lakes. We counted every dock and mooring on the lake. We determined that by the addition of 128 slips for one-half mile of frontage, the average number of boats slips and moors per hundred feet for Bristol Harbour was less than the average number of slips and moorings on the lake per hundred feet.

On two of the hottest days in the preceding summer, we took aerial photos of the lake for boat activity. The photos proved that the north shore was very active with boating activity, the south shore was not as active and the middle of the lake where Bristol Harbour Village would be located was very inactive.

To the deep resentment of our opponents, representatives from the State of New York responsible for the evaluation of boating activity on lakes under the jurisdiction of NY State testified that the addition of 128 slips would not endanger the health, welfare and safety of the people of the State of New York. In fact, one state official stated that the marina would serve as a "safe harbor" for boats in the middle of the lake that were caught in a sudden storm.

In spite of the facts, the hearing lasted for five full days. Attorneys for Seneca Point residents and residents who applied in a timely manner, were allowed to cross-examine any witness.

One humorous example of hundreds of questions related to the estimated 250 aluminum support rods that would rest on the lake bottom supporting the 128 docking slips. The attorney involved was trying to make a case for the harmful effect these rods would have on the fish in this 17-mile lake. When he asked the scientist what impact this installation would have on the fish the scientist replied, "the fish will move". It was the only time in the five-day hearing that everyone in the courtroom laughed.

The hearing officer sustained many objections raised by my attorney designed to discredit me. They are too numerous to mention. Suffice to say, the 1,179 pages of the infamous dock hearing would make for interesting reading as a separate book.

Each day was reported in the newspaper. As the hearing reached an end, a major headline stated that a State Official responsible for monitoring the waters of New York State, supported the application for the docks on the basis that the middle of the lake was not crowded even on the hottest of summer days; that all boats at Bristol Harbour, like other marinas, do not go out at the same time; that there would be no adverse impact on safety; that the people who did not have property on the lake and who used the state launching sites at the north and south of the lake, would find refuge in a storm or emergency in the middle of this 17 mile lake where the Bristol Harbour marina would be located. I thought, "God Bless the State of New York for allowing citizens, other than lakefront property owners to have access to Canandaigua, the Gem of the Finger Lakes."

At the break in the last day of the hearing, exhausted from a full week of hearings and the expected legal costs involved, I rushed to the phone to see how my alternate plan for a search for capital outside of Rochester was doing. My contact reminded me of my visit to the officers of the Florida bank who worked with a firm in Cleveland, Ohio. He said, "Your $20,000 good faith deposit is in the safe hands of the lenders in Cleveland who are supplying the $2 million in funds to the Florida bank for a loan to Bristol Harbour with all your assets including the ski area as collateral. You have the letter of intent. The closing should be soon."

The hearing officer heard everyone who had asked in advance to be heard. He called an end to the hearing. The timing of approvals and the litigation that continued in an attempt to overrule the approvals are summarized in the headlines above.

In spite of the combined wealth and influence of those who participated in the many litigations to block Bristol Harbour Village; in spite of the local banks that found us out of favor because of board members and customers who owned lakeside homes on Canandaigua Lake; in spite of all of this united and powerful opposition to break my piggy bank, this former dark skinned, skinny, bow-legged, pigeon-toed, knocked-kneed boy Prisoner of the Truck, who believed and fought for democracy around the world, discovered that the democratic process works if you are persistent enough to make it work. Although it took months and thousands of dollars for professionals and attorneys, we won the right to install 128 slips.

The day after the hearing closed, an opponent to our application called the Editor of the Democrat and Chronicle to complain that the reporter, Marge Van Iseghem, who covered the daily news of this five-day hearing was my cousin and was therefore biased in her reporting. The opponents considered factual reporting as bias. If it were true, I would be proud to call Marge Van Iseghem my cousin.

CHAPTER 23

Hard Work, Creativity and Financial Miracles

At age 44, in the summer of 1970, to protect our "initial plan", I needed the dollars to begin construction. The local banking institutions considered Bristol Harbour Village a public relations hot potato. Under the new South Bristol Town regulations, there was a clause in the zoning that would allow existing plans to remain in effect as long as there was a substantial start in construction. Based on the advise of our attorneys, I had to commit my dwindling personal funds to clear the site for the sewer plant, construct a road to the first building and build the concrete shell of this building on the edge of the cliff, the "skeleton". The skeleton had no roof, no balcony railings and no stairway. We then had an aerial photo taken, with the date of the photo certified. The Town of South Bristol accepted our effort as "substantial commencement" and all of our costly approvals remained intact and legally protected while we searched for funding.

Shortly thereafter, the Wall Street Journal reported that a Cleveland venture capital firm that was giving fraudulent commitment letters to prominent banks throughout the United States swindled hundreds of businessmen throughout the United States. The article stated that businessmen, desperate for financing, were required to submit a sum equal to 1% of the loan application, refundable if a commitment letter was not received. A bank in Florida had issued a commitment letter subject to funding from this Cleveland firm. The Florida bank had relied on falsified financial statements from the Cleveland firm. I was one of the victims. I lost the $20,000 deposit and the loan commitment.

Timing is everything. In October of 1969, the Bristol Mountain Enterprises, Inc. public offering missed the hot market by two months. Commitments received for all of the shares of a $2.5 million offering faded into dust. I was in deep trouble. The cost of engineers, architects, attorneys and the "substantial commencement" effort consumed almost all of my funds.

Here's how I felt. Since 1963, I tried to develop a successful ski area for the community with a limit on the amount of cash I wanted to invest. That failed.

It was supposed to be super ski area for the novice and intermediate skier. That failed.

Among the community leaders and the affluent people who lived on Canandaigua Lake, I went from being a respected successful entrepreneur of food, vending and skiing to a despised real estate developer. The news articles and letters to the editor filled several scrap books that are over two feet high, including letters that I wrote defending the quality of our plans and our commitment to prevent any detrimental effect on the lake environment. Armed with data prepared by our scientific engineers, I tried to make peace with opponents by meeting with them and addressing their concerns in a positive manner. That failed.

Since I was blackballed in the Rochester financial community, I had to seek a lender outside of the area. That failed with the fraudulent lender.

I tried to go public with substantial assets: the ski area, the lake property and the master plan approvals from all the New York State governmental authorities. The timing was bad and that failed.

There was One More Option - Surrender.

A short time after the October 1969 failure of the public offering, I received a call from Wallace Ely, the President of Security Trust Company. Mr. Ely was President of the Chamber of Commerce. I worked under him as Chairman of the Chamber's Membership Campaign. We met in his office. He asked me how everything was going with my Bristol Harbour Village plans. I asked if he was asking me as a banker interested in giving me a loan or for other reasons. He said he was not speaking as a banker. He was speaking as a middleman between the "Seneca Point group" and me. Since the Group did not see any further progress on the "skeleton" of the first building for six months, they assumed that I had run into financial difficulties. Mr. Ely said that they wanted to know if I would consider an offer for the actual cost of the land and the actual master plan approvals. I told him that there were other interested parties but I would think about such an offer. I also said that I spent most of my life making friends and I was not having any fun making enemies. For a full week, I deliberated on the offer. I discussed it with a few key advisors. We considered the following as it related to the Seneca Point's Group offer.

1) The Cliffside frontage was listed for several years before my interest. That was the Group's first chance to buy it for $46,000. It was reasonable to estimate the combined wealth of 50 owners in the Seneca Point Group at $50 million or more. If each owner pitched in only $1,000, they would have controlled this land and waterfront and preserved it as their green belt.
2) When they heard that I was going to purchase the Cliffside frontage, they should have contacted the seller through the broker to offer more than the list price. Again, $1,000 from each would have accomplished this. I would not have tried to outbid them.
3) They should have purchased the 165 acres and single family home on the Cliffside. Instead, they asked the owner not to sell it to me. This would have cost the

Group $3,000 each. This would have made it impossible to install a sewer treatment plant and limit the 24-acre, 2,000-foot parcel to a few homes. This 165-acre parcel and home, with beautiful lake views, could have become a rental property or a Seneca Point Group party house with tennis facilities etc.

4) The Group's proposal, through Mr. Ely, would be their fourth opportunity. Certainly, we reasoned, with most of our master plan approvals in hand, the Seneca Point Group would not risk the chance of having the property fall into the hands of a major developer with ample cash - a Developer not dedicated to the quality that I sought. This was their 4th chance to act. My advisors and I believed that they would not pass up this last opportunity to prevent the development of Bristol Harbour Village. At this stage, my investment in all of the land and professional fees was close to $500,000. I was emotionally and psychologically ready to throw in the towel. This would cost the Group $10,000 each to control the size and scope of the development. For their investment, they would control 2,600 feet of frontage, 292 acres and the master plan approvals. They could have spun off the land on the west of the Seneca Point Road that had no waterfront and preserved the 27-acre, 2600 feet of Cliffside frontage as a greenbelt.

A week later, I set up a meeting with Mr. Ely. I presented the actual cost of the land and the cost of the master plan approvals and litigation. This was my flag of surrender. Mr. Ely said he would present this to the "Group" and get back to me. Two weeks went by. I heard nothing from Mr. Ely. Instead, I received a phone call from my friend, Jack Carey, who was with Connecticut Mutual Life Insurance Company. He said, "Freddie, I was invited to a party on Seneca Point over the weekend. I was shocked. They heard you were out of cash. They were celebrating your pending corporate and personal bankruptcy." Jack and his associate Van

Albanese tried to get Connecticut Mutual Life interested. Conn-Mutual looked at the master plan, the approvals and the economic model and turned it down.

I reflected on the impact of our opponent's strategy. They caused serious delays in the approval processes, damaged our public relations and caused us to spend over $100,000 in legal fees ($1,000,000 in year 2000 dollars). In the end, in spite of winning all of our approvals, my financial planning failed. They had reason to celebrate.

A few months later, after this charade, on a cold winter evening in early December of 1970, after night skiing at Bristol Mountain, I drove to the lake property. I found a ladder to climb up the skeleton to the top balcony of the fourth floor. I sat on this balcony, without railings, huddled with my knees against my chest, with my back up against the concrete wall. No, I was not thinking about suicide. I did not want to return to my Ambassador Drive home office and the piles of investor proposal papers. It was a clear night. The moon was resting on the top of the snow-covered mountain on the other side of the lake. There I sat in the bowel of the skeleton, the equivalent of 14 stories high from the lake water. I looked at the reflection of the moon on the pure waters of Canandaigua Lake. I thought of the guide boat that would take tourists from the north shore down past the west and east side of the lake, highlighting historical homes and pointing out locations of the few dwellings located along the lake. As the guide boat came down the West Side of the lake, I envisioned the guide pointing up to the white concrete skeleton on the edge of the cliff. He was saying over the boat's loudspeaker, "That's the skeleton of the start of a project that was supposed to be a master planned community of condominiums, a hotel, golf course and marina. A guy by the name of Sarkis spent five years and his personal fortune putting the land package together and fighting for approvals. His affluent neighbors, in great numbers, fought him every step of the way. When he finally got the approvals, he ran out of money and went bankrupt. That's why it is called the 'The Skeleton of Sarkis'

Dream'. Now next to the skeleton is Seneca Point. The Seneca Point area is considered the most affluent of lakeside homes on the lake......."

On this winter evening, overlooking the lake, with lakeside homes closed for the winter, shivering from the cold in the belly of the concrete skeleton that I had created, I talked to God. I asked Him to help me to find the funds to finish Phase One. I told Him that material gain was not what I sought. I said that Phase One would prove that my plan would not harm the beauty of Canandaigua Lake nor would it have an adverse impact on my neighbor opponents. God knew that I did not want that summer boat guide to refer to my skeleton as "The Skeleton of Sarkis' Dream".

I calculated the last time I sent a check to the Carmelites Sisters. I determined the cost of eggs per day since my last check plus the cost of a dozen eggs for the next twelve months. Upon my return, I sent them a check for the total with a short note, "Dear Sisters: Here I am, again asking for your prayers. I am on the edge of a financial cliff. I ask you to pray for the success of my mission." The check was dated December 7, 1970, the date of the anniversary of the Japanese attack on Pearl Harbour.

Sitting in the oak paneled study of my Ambassador Drive home, I feared losing, everything. Meanwhile Helen, my patient and dedicated wife tended to our flock of five children. Fired with new enthusiasm gifted by the Lord, I began a strategy to find a Real Estate Investment Trust partner. I made one phone call after another. I found an interested REIT in Maryland.

This time my timing was perfect. They were looking for projects. On December 15, 1970, Colonel Hal Eichen, from General Mortgage Investments flew in to inspect the site and government approvals on December 15. He was familiar with neighborhood oppositions and attempts to stop a well-planned development. They had no ties to the emotions of a community. He was impressed with the property, the master plan, the approvals that he knew were extremely difficult to get and the fact that there was no mortgage on the entire property. He was also impressed with my perseverance throughout the ordeal. On December 28, 1970 we received a commitment for $2 million for Phase One. This would allow us to proceed with the sewer treatment plant, the conversion of the skeleton into our first 14-unit building on the edge of the cliff, and the erection of the gondola and stairway to the beach. We could also begin to prepare sites for six townhomes, two tennis courts, several single-family residences and a recreation area for children.

I phoned and thanked the Carmelites for their prayers. I pondered on the Seven Gifts. I came to the conclusion that the Gifts don't always work when you are dealing with people who hate your mission.

In the spring of 1971, after the ski area closed, Larry Demarse came to the rescue with his construction experience. Larry supervised the construction of Phase One. His idea for a low-cost bridge and gondola was unique and would result in solidly built structures. He finished Phase One in time for the spring marketing season of 1971. We learned that the vertical rise of the gondola, ten stories high, was the highest vertical cable gondola in the world. When one gondola reached the top, the other gondola touched the bottom. Each gondola held four passengers and was self-operated.

We sold the 14 condominium units. One of the first buyers was Jim O'Neill, the vice president of finance for Xerox. Mr. O'Neill told me that he was shocked when a middle-management executive at Xerox, who was an opponent to the development from the beginning, told him he would be foolish to buy at Bristol Harbour. This Xerox executive said that a Kodak engineer, who also resided on Canandaigua Lake, was concerned about the construction of the condominium. The Kodak engineer said that based on his evaluation, within a few years, the 14-unit building would be in danger of falling into the lake.

Larry Demarse reviewed with Mr. O'Neill the qualifications of the engineer who designed the footings for both the condominium building and the steel bridge that supported the gondola. The motive of the Xerox executive was clear. He believed that if Mr. O'Neill, the number 3 executive at Xerox, purchased in this first 14-unit building, it would trigger sales from other prominent executives in the Rochester area. Mr. O'Neill resented this interference and in support of our plans, allowed us to use his name as a reference to any prospective future buyer. Mr. O'Neill had the integrity and sense of fair play inherent in Joe Wilson, his Xerox boss; he saw me as a determined and honest entrepreneur. He did not respect the unfair tactics used by the middle management Xerox executive.

Franz Mittlemayer, the head of our Bristol Mountain Ski School, provided major assistance to the summer marketing effort. However, in spite of a good marketing and sales effort, lot sales did not materialize as expected. We faced another failure. The payback of our $2 million loan was dependent on the cash flow from the sale of lots and the presale before construction of 44 units for buildings 2 and 3. We knew we would have difficulty in making a payment on our loan in June of 1972. Both Bristol Harbour and Bristol Mountain were collateralized to the Real Estate Investment Trust. In spite of these crises, God had answered my prayer. The tourist boat guide could never point to the skeleton on the edge of the cliff. I had my miracles of owning the coffee vending business, of getting Kodak for a customer and the miracle of completing Phase One of Bristol Harbour Village. I wondered how many more miracles I should expect. Is struggling for development money what God wants me to do the rest of my life? I began to feel that my mission was materialistic. I began to think about the less fortunate, the poor, the hungry and thirsty. TV documentaries and pictures of emaciated children in Africa touched my heart. It seemed that the miracle that I should be praying for would be the miracle of getting aid to these people, to these children.

I knew that I created my own Prison, the Prisoner of a Dream that had turned into a nightmare. Nevertheless, I thanked God for the support of my family and children. I found joy and comfort in their love, their morning and evening hugs, the prayers said for me on their knees and their cheerful spirit. I was determined to find an equity partner to pay off the $2 million and provide working capital for the continuation of the project. I had several leads, made many phone calls and sent informational packages without much success.

1972

At age 45, in March of 1972, I received a phone call from Mother Nesser who was involved with ecumenical meetings at the Cenacle. The Cenacle was a retreat house for ladies located on East Avenue about ten minutes from where I lived. In addition to retreats, they held weekly prayer meetings. My sister Betty knew that I was having difficulties again. She did not know to what extent. Mother Nesser wanted me to attend one of the ecumenical meetings. I said, "Mother Nesser, we both went to St. Joseph's school. I do not need to go to prayer meetings. When I get up in the morning, I do what the good Sisters of Notre Dame taught me. I offer my work up as a prayer and believe me, it ends up being one big prayer." Mother Nesser said, "Look, maybe if you take a mini-vacation of two hours from whatever stress you are facing, it will be good for you. At least come to one evening meeting. You are not that far away." I sang with Mother Nesser in our St. Nicholas church choir for years. She was living Saint. I decided to attend a meeting.

I just sat and listened and observed. The group, numbered about 25, was indeed ecumenical – Protestants, Catholics and Jews. It was very informal and relaxed. Anyone could speak. Some shared experiences for which they thanked God. Others talked about loved ones that were having difficulties with their marriage or their health or that were on drugs. Some asked for prayers to assist with these problems. Someone asked to be prayed over. Those in attendance would put their hands on that person who was sitting in a chair and pray for his or her intentions. One enthusiastic young man, who told a story of helping drug addicts in a coffee shop in the inner city, was praying in a strange manner. It was not the "gift of tongues" that Jesus gave his apostles when he appeared to them after His death. It was gibberish. I said nothing and left the meeting.

A week later, my curiosity about the young man's strange language got the best of me. I went again to see what I could learn. A lady talked about her experience that morning. She said her husband had gone off to work and the children were sent off to school. She said their combined income made it difficult to make ends meet. She had to go to work but the sink was plugged. Hand pumping failed. She thought, "We can't afford a plumber, Lord." All of a sudden the water in the sink drained quickly on its own. The group said, "Praise the Lord". That was, as she described, "a miracle."

Again, I said nothing and could not wait to get out of this setting. On the ten-minute drive home, I began to think about this lady's plugged sink. I realized that I had formed two judgments in two meetings in which I said nothing. One judgment was that the young man, who prayed in gibberish, was kind of crazy; the other judgment was that considering an unplugged sink to be a miracle was ridiculous.

Then I began to feel that I had lost my common touch. I was so obsessed with my own "huge crises". I had overlooked the reality that what I thought were "small" problems for others were, in fact, "huge crises" in their lives. I thought of people with financial problems, scraping enough dollars to buy food & clothing. I thought of people trying to pay the rent for fear of eviction, or losing their homes in a mortgage foreclosure. Or having their cars, refrigerators, washing machines repossessed for inability to make their payments. I thought of the financial crises associated with helping a loved one with a drug, alcohol or gambling addiction; or with medical care that they could not afford; or with a marriage that was falling apart. I thought of my childhood and my Prison. In many ways, people were in Prisons without bars; prisons of financial stress, sickness, addiction, divorce or separation. I thought of the sad impact these Prisons had on the inmates and their children.

I thought people's crises were like a high-rise building with many people hanging onto the windowsills for their dear lives — by the tips of their fingers. If they were on the fifth floor or the twentieth floor, the fear of the fall was the same and the consequences of the fall were also the same. The prayers to prevent the fall, regardless of the height, were all equally important in the eyes of God.

These thoughts led me to the third prayer meeting. I felt that I had something to learn. I especially wanted to question the 21-year-old young man who worked with young people who were addicted to drugs and alcohol. A few minutes after the meeting began, I spoke my first words to him. I said, "I have been to two meetings. I have said nothing. At each meeting your prayers sound like a lot of gibberish to me when you pray over someone. The Holy Spirit did not give the gift of gibberish. He gave the gift of a language so that the word of the gospel could be spread throughout the world. If it is gibberish, why can't you just speak in English and share your outpouring of prayer with others?" He simply replied, "Yes, it may sound like gibberish to you, but here's how I feel. When I try to comprehend God and his Greatness, I cannot find the English words to praise him. What I do is a simple outpouring of my soul in praise for Him. What comes out of my mouth is my way of praising the Lord. That's just me." Feeling a bit humbled and less judgmental, I sincerely thanked him for explaining his feelings. I came to realize that I must respect the differences in the way people praise the Lord.

A few minutes later, a lady asked us if we would pray for her boss. Someone said, "Is he sick?" She said, "No, he is a businessman and a good Christian. He needs $3 million dollars to help save his business. He is sending packages about his business to all kinds of lenders and venture capital people. Within six months, if he doesn't find the $3 million he will be out of business. I said to him, you should pray for help. He said that you pray for the poor, the hungry, the thirsty, you do not pray for $3 million dollars. I am asking this group to pray that my boss will totally surrender his crises to the Lord", with her eyes suddenly focused on mine, she continued, "and in that surrender he will find peace. In that peace, he will become less panic stricken, more relaxed, more creative and in that creativity he will find his $3 million."

I was emotionally hit by her words. It was as if the Holy Spirit was sending me a message through her soft and sincere voice. She had described the exact sum that I was seeking and, at this particular point in my life, like her boss, I felt the same way he did about prayer. Yes, I could write a check to the Carmelites asking them to pray for my intentions and I could to talk to God and ask for his help. However, the thought of "totally surrendering" my problem to the Lord and allowing myself to become more creative had never entered my mind, in spite of my spirituality.

I kept my business very confidential. No one knew that I was seeking a $3 million dollar partner, not even my family. Everyone remained where they were seated and said a group prayer for her boss. Then I heard someone say, "Does anyone want to be prayed over." To this day, I cannot explain it. As if I was in a hypnotic stage, I found myself going to that seat in the middle of the room and sitting down. The group surrounded me. Hands were touching my head, shoulders and arms. A voice said, "What is it you want us to pray for?" I could not say $3 million dollars. I found myself saying "Peace of Mind". It was as if every person touching me could feel the struggle I was living with. My eyes were closed. I heard their prayers. Many were in English. Others were in different languages, including the young man who spoke gibberish. Tears flooded my eyes. I felt as if a great burden had been lifted from my shoulders. I left the meeting and got into my car. I felt intoxicated with joy. If someone had been in the back seat, he or she would have concluded that I was drunk. I had this overwhelming sense of peace. I surrendered my crises to the Lord. I thanked Him for granting peace of mind to this tired and weary Prisoner of a Crisises.

I woke up the next morning refreshed. My spirits were high. I felt that the Holy Spirit had sent an Angel who spoke to me through the lady at Cenacle gathering. I spoke of this experience to my wife. She was glad it gave me peace. My kids came into the study that was surrounded by packages to be mailed to financial leads outside of Rochester. They gave me a hug and kiss and went off to school. How precious they were. How blessed I was to have such an understanding and supportive family. Gina had turned 14 and was helping her mom around the house and with her younger brothers. Greg was 11 and enjoyed his new role of replacing the gardener and handling snow shoveling in the winter. Wade was nine, Fritz was seven and Josh was three. I was truly a blessed man. They were all such a great joy and comfort to me.

After they left for school, the phone rang. It was Van Albanese from Connecticut Mutual. He wanted to know why I was tardy in the payment of my life insurance premium. I said, "Van, I can trust you. I just don't have the money." He said, "Fred, only a few months ago, I read the success story of the sale of your first building." I said, "Van, they call that public relations." He said he wanted to help me. I reminded him that we had sent a package to Conn-Mutual a few years ago. He said, "Yes, but there's a new guy at the helm in the real estate investment department." I calmly and creatively said, "OK, but this time around I am going to send him pictures of the completed Phase One, with dramatic lake photographs from the balcony of Building One and a complete description of the master plan approvals. If they want to see the economic model, they will have to sit with me on the balcony of our first 14-unit condominium building for a comprehensive review."

A week later a mortgage broker, an expert in resort properties, was sitting on the balcony of the condominium with me reviewing the economic model. He had already driven around the entire lake, talked with the Chamber of Commerce regarding the history of Bristol Harbour, visited Bristol Mountain, checked my references and interviewed two or three owners in the condominium building. He said, "Fred, I cannot believe what you have accomplished in the approval process. To obtain the master plan approvals for 874 units, a 200-unit hotel, a golf course, and a 124-slip marina and to have the first Homeowners Association Offering Plan ever approved by the Attorney General's Office is a remarkable feat. You have been totally undercapitalized with a great location. What ideas do you have in structuring the deal?"

Within six weeks, we signed papers that made the Connecticut Mutual Life Insurance Company our partner. They valued the project at $1,000,000. I would receive $500,000 in cash that could be used for the ski area. I would leave $500,000 in the joint venture for a 50% ownership and they would make a loan to the joint venture for $6 million dollars. This would be used for the purpose of paying off the REIT, buying more land to equal 454 acres, retaining Robert Trent Jones to build the golf course and commence construction of buildings 2, 3, 4 and 5 for a total of 176 condominium units on the edge of the cliff. Jack Britton, the mortgage broker, who put the deal together said, "Fred, I have been in this business for 25 years. I have never seen a deal go so quickly and smoothly as this one and do you know what Fred, I can't explain it."

I said, "I can explain it, Jack. It was a miracle and let me tell you why." Jack was fascinated with the story of the Cenacle and said, "I believe it was a miracle, too."

I sold my prestigious 6,000-sq. ft. home on Ambassador Drive. We moved to a 1,200-sq. ft. prefabricated vacation home at Bristol Harbour within walking distance of my office. With mixed emotions, we had a garage sale. Moving was not a happy experience for any of us. However, my family took it in good stride and quickly made the adjustment to our new surroundings in the Naples School District and closer proximity to the lake and ski area.

The opponents to the project found some satisfaction in knowing that there would be a prestigious Robert Trent Jones Golf Course and Restaurant in their back yard. The pressure was off; I had an insurance company for a partner. My thanksgiving prayer was simple:

"Thank you Lord for this miracle. I will give it my best effort. If this Joint Venture fails, I will continue to be ever grateful for helping me to bring this dream to reality in a manner that will please Bristol Harbour residents and their neighbors."

Then sings my soul, my Savior God, to thee;
How great thou art! How great thou art!

CHAPTER 24

The Butterfly Symbol

In 1974, in a marketing meeting of this new Joint venture with Connecticut Mutual Life Insurance Company, our advertising agency and our team players, struggled for a full morning over a symbol for Bristol Harbour Village. We spoke of a shield with four parts to it – a golfer, a tennis player, a boater and a swimmer. Since other resorts had similar symbols, we decided to adjourn for lunch and discuss it in the afternoon.

My mother was now living in a town home at Bristol Harbour Village. We sold her home in Rochester. She was now living temporarily in one of the Bristol Harbour town homes, a short walk from my Bristol Harbour office. She was awaiting the completion of her new Bristol Harbour Cliffside condominium that would be connected to the condominium that was planned for my family's needs. When we moved in, she could lock the inside door separating the two units whenever she felt a need for privacy. During the next several years, she loved the visits of her grandchildren. She never locked the door. Our children had free access to visit her whenever they wanted to. Many times when we thought our older children were in bed, they were sitting next to grandma, under her blanket on the sofa, watching TV.

After we adjourned the marketing meeting that day, I went to have lunch with my mother in the town home. Sister Sadie Nesser, the nun who encouraged me to attend the prayer meeting that led to the Connecticut Mutual miracle was visiting my mother. During lunch I mentioned the struggle we had over a symbol for Bristol Harbour. On the wall of the town home, there was a colorful painting of a butterfly. Sister Sadie looked up from her luncheon plate and said, "There's your symbol, the butterfly. Look, it has the color of the sands on your future beach, the color of the greens of your future golf course, the color of blue for the clear blue of Canandaigua Lake's pure waters." I did not think much of the idea and said, "I've got to go back to the meeting with more than that. I don't think the group would buy it."

Then she said, "You know you spoke of a miracle in your new partnership with Connecticut Mutual. Did you know that the butterfly is the symbol of the Resurrection of Jesus? In his tomb, His body was wrapped head to foot in a white cloth, like the cocoon that holds the caterpillar. Then Jesus broke his cocoon and arose from the dead, somewhat similar to the transformation of the caterpillar to a butterfly. Also, when He arose from the dead, he descended upon the 12 disciples and empowered them with the Seven Gifts of the Holy Spirit that you have been devoted to since childhood and that, dear Fred, is why Christianity is almost 2000 years old."

I said, "Sister Sadie, I never knew that the butterfly was a religious symbol. I still can't go to a meeting and relate it to Bristol Harbour Village." Without hesitation she said, "Fred, you are trying to get your future buyers to come out of the city into the country. You want to transform their busy caterpillar lives in the cocoon of the city and bring them out to this beautiful resort so that they can fly around enjoying life as butterflies" My mother said, "Fred, that's your symbol, use it."

That afternoon, the idea that we were trying to bring people from the city to Bristol Harbour Village on Canandaigua Lake to fly around the golf course, beach, lake and marina like butterflies struck home. The group unanimously agreed on the symbol and it was widely used in newspaper advertising, brochures etc.

Our partnership put up a standardized colorful butterfly sign on many properties to guide people to Bristol Harbour. For directions, our advertising would read, "Follow the butterflies to Bristol Harbour Village." When the State of New York officials asked us to remove the butterflies, we successfully argued that the butterfly was an environmental symbol. There were no words on it. No advertising. Just a butterfly on a pole.

Over the many years that followed, one could not enter any of the 176 Cliffside Condominium Units without finding the butterfly – on towels, on wall paper, on pillows, on chinaware, on window drapes, in paintings, in miniature collections, etc. As I write this, on the landscape where Cliffside Drive enters the complex, there is a magnificent variety of colorful flowers that is formed into a huge butterfly, surrounded by green grass and trees. It is created annually by the Bristol Harbour Village Homeowners' Association that has adopted the butterfly as its symbol.

A newspaper reporter picked up on this symbol in the following article:

"Vision Becomes Concrete Reality"

July 26, 1974

Daily Messenger
Edited
By W. C. Dannenbrink

"From cocoon to butterfly ". *The full-fledged metamorphosis is now complete. But the transition from a man's dream to reality now appears assured.*

Bristol Harbour Village, once just a vision to its originator, Frederick W. Sarkis, apparently has overcome a rather tumultuous beginning and with the help of major financial transfusions is becoming a reality.

In July 1968, Sarkis, then a resident of Pittsford announced that he was planning a $12 million, 200-unit condominium development on 145 acres of land which included a 2,600 feet of frontage on Canandaigua Lake. The development was to be located just north of Seneca Point in the Town of South Bristol.

In the ensuing months, Sarkis and his associates were confronted with tremendous opposition. Residents of the area, environmentalists and others protested the planned development.

Hearings were held by state agencies, state legislatures were contacted, and civil action was taken in the courts. Actions like a lengthy hearing before state public health department agencies, what Sarkis once described as a "tough money market," and other factors stretched his resources to the breaking point.

By August 1970, work on the first of a planned 10 condominium buildings stopped because of the fiscal squeeze. Two months later it was announced that arrangements had been made with a Maryland mortgage investment firm and work was ready to begin again.

The following January 1971, the State Department of Environmental Conservation announced that it would approve a 120-boat dock to be placed at the foot of a 120-foot cliff below the condominiums. (The decision was fought by Canandaigua Lake Pure Waters, Ltd., a lake area environmental group, but the courts ruled against the group in November 1971.)

By January 1972, Bristol Harbour was growing – at the site and on the drawing boards. It was planned to be an 867-unit development on 424 acres. Fourteen of the new constructed condominiums had been sold. Total cost of the development was estimated at $35 million.

In May of 1972, the development got a major boost from Connecticut Mutual Insurance Company. It joined the venture and, in Sarkis' words "insured proper financing.' Connecticut Mutual is a limited partner and owns 55 percent of the stock. It *has committed $12 million to the first phase of development of what is now described as a $60 million development. An estimated $750,000 is being spent on water and sewage treatment facilities.*

By September 1972, plans were pretty much what they are today: 874 units on 440 acres; an 18 hole golf course, riding and hiking trails and tennis courts.

There are still objections to the development from some who fear it will lead to environmental or other problems. But the butterfly (that's the symbol the developers have adopted for the complex) is emerging from the cocoon. What was once an idea has moved from drawings on paper, to models, to the real thing."

CHAPTER 25

Age 46 to 55-
Losing to Bobby Riggs
Losing Bristol Harbour Village
Losing Bristol Mountain Ski Area

Losing to Bobby Riggs

In 1972, at age 46, I left ARA when Connecticut Mutual became our partner to participate in the execution of the plan for Bristol Harbour.

In that same year, I had my first prostate surgery. Six weeks later, I received permission from my Doctor to play a challenge match against Bobby Riggs who had a tennis exhibition in Rochester. My sister Ann arranged the bet. If I lost, Riggs would get $500. If I won, I would get $50. It received good publicity in the local media. It was an 8 game pro set. I was able to get to 3-4 with Bobby. When we changed sides, he whispered to me and said, "Didn't your sister Ann tell you that I am helping you with the promotion of your resort and you are not supposed to win?" Riggs did not know about my addiction to the "principle" of the issue. That was not my understanding. He was psyching me out. I even imagined a national news headline, "Country Boy Beats Riggs." In tennis, like in business, you should keep your cool. I didn't. I changed my game, played more aggressively and made more errors. On his match point, he gave me a trick serve that had so much spin on it that I missed it by a foot. The audience loved the entertainment.

We then proceeded to my Condominium where Riggs bet our Canadian Broker $100 on the flipping of a deck of cards into a hat from a sitting position on the couch. One by one, the broker flipped them at the hat. He got 48 out of 52. Riggs took the deck and, as if he were a machine gun, the 52 cards flew in rapid succession into the hat and he grabbed the $100.

Riggs told us stories of his betting matches. He would bet an opponent that he could beat him while carrying an almost full bucket of water in his left hand throughout the match. He would even carry it while serving, throwing the ball up with the same hand holding the racquet. If a drop of water spilled, the point went to his opponent. The bets were never less than $100 and he won 90% of them.

He would also place bets with obstacles on his side of the court. Two folding chairs would be placed on a court. Whenever he hit the ball, he would return to a third chair where he sat down after he returned the ball. Then he would leap up each time the opponent hit the ball to either return it or prevent it from hitting one of the two chairs. If it hit the chair, it became the opponent's point. The bets were never less than $100 and he won 90% of them. Riggs was indeed a great sportsman and entertainer.

Losing Bristol Harbour Village

At age 48, in 1974, Bristol Harbour models were ready. There were four new condominium buildings constructed totaling 162 units. We were ready for our grand opening in the summer of 1974 with new decorated models. We ran an outstanding 16-page advertisement supplement in the Democrat & Chronicle. It introduced the project, the amenities and our team of professionals. The butterfly logo was prominent. It was then that the energy crises reached its peak. Gasoline had gone up 400%. People cut back on driving to vacation spots or to resorts. Resorts all over the US felt the impact. This included Bristol Harbour Village.

I could not blame the gasoline shortage on my neighboring opponents. They may have had influence and power in the local area but I doubt if they had any influence over the energy crises. I am sure that if the primary leader of the opponents could have traveled to the oil nations to cause the energy shortage, in order to cause my next failure, she would have. And it was a dramatic failure for me.

The concept of a partnership is when two parties put in what they call "equity capital". In this case, we left $500,000 in equity in the partnership, which in effect, were my personal dollars loaned to Bristol Mountain Enterprises, Inc. Connecticut Mutual put in $500,000. The partnership was called Bristol Venture. Connecticut Mutual then lends money to Bristol Venture, the partnership. The loans were now in excess of $12 million. If you don't sell condominiums fast enough, you don't get the dollars needed to make payments on the loan. As our timing was good in finding Connecticut Mutual, our timing was bad when we hit the energy crises.

So the grown-up Prisoner of the Truck was in deep trouble. In a partnership, each partner gets his share of the profits or losses. If there are losses, they can be deducted from the partner's earnings. If your earnings are huge, as in the case of Connecticut Mutual, then you deduct these earnings from your huge profits. If your income is small, as it was in my case, you cannot immediately deduct these losses.

Therefore, Connecticut Mutual, toward the end of 1974 reasoned, with a shotgun to my head, that they should take over our interest and 100% of the losses. This would give them complete control. In exchange for my cooperation in this clean surrender of my part ownership without the involvement of attorneys, they would release their lien on Bristol Mountain, whose unpredictable earnings were of little interest to a major insurance company.

I was happy to salvage the Ski Area even though the profits were marginal and the cash-generating potential was poor. Because his income potential at the Bristol Mountain was limited, Larry Demarse, after ten years of dedicated service, joined a company that sold "airless" snowmaking systems to ski areas. Ironically, the two General Motors engineers who wooed a willing financial partner into the ski business, went on to become the world's leading suppliers of "air" and "airless" snow making systems in the world.

A new ski area management team was assisted by the $500,000 Connecticut Mutual returned to Bristol Mountain in 1972 when the Bristol Harbour Village partnership was formed, as well as a $1 million loan from the Farmer's Home Administration obtained by the new management for expansion purposes. This new team, headed by Joe Kohler, supervised ski area improvements and significantly increased the development of school and college programs for night skiing from 1972 to 1980.

Prior to the energy crises, in my prayers, I kind of made a deal with God. I said that if it was necessary to take material gain away from me, I could accept that. Material gain was not the primary issue for me. I wanted to overcome the forces that tried to take away my freedom to build my dream, the freedom that GI's fought for in WWII. My battle with the "opponents" was a competitive one. There was a principle at stake.

I believed that I had fought fairly and within my rights. I believed that they fought unfairly, using every attempt to financially cripple me so that the project could not go forward. Whenever I attempted to share information with them, they would take that information and find a way to use it against me. When I offered surrender terms, they preferred to watch me agonize with pending bankruptcy. They assumed that since bankers from the Rochester community banned me, no one would give us a loan. It is common for an out-of-state lender to call local banks seeking information about a loan applicant. Therefore, my "opponents" believed that a bad referral would kill an out-of-town deal. There are times in a person's life when you fight for principle with total disregard for personal cost. I had my spiritual partner. He knew that I put a higher value on principle than I did on money. With the knowledge of His presence in my life, I did not let the battle affect my health, enthusiasm, strength or energy. Getting Bristol Harbour properly financed and built was my victory. Losing my percentage of ownership was not the end of the world. As my father once said, "You can lose your business, but never your education", and indeed at 48, my education in the world of business and community service was highly marketable. I did not lose that.

When a real estate project fails with a major insurance company, their management turns to outside consultants to determine what to do about the problem. They cannot go to the founder of the project who got them into the financial failure. It always looks better to employ a consultant. In this case, with many condominiums completed on the outside and ready for finishing on the inside, a marketing consultant makes the most sense. That way, if heads like mine have to roll, they can tell the Connecticut Mutual Board that the marketing consultant said, "The founder's head has to roll." This shifts the burden of termination from their shoulders and places it heavily on the shoulders of the marketing consultant.

In spite of my financial loss, I wanted to stay and work for Connecticut Mutual. I did not want to be terminated by the marketing consultant they retained. His name was Chic Lewis. He was a well-respected marketing consultant to many businesses in the Rochester area. Chic asked me to prepare a marketing and sales strategy to sell the remaining condominium inventory of about 100 units within the next two years. He was impressed. Much to the surprise of the Connecticut Mutual, he recommended that I remain along with Bernice (Bernie) Caprini, who had joined Bristol Harbour when Connecticut Mutual became a partner.

Within two years, Bernie and I sold the remaining inventory knowing full well that we were, in fact, working our way out of a job. The pay was not that great but the achievement was. We sold the inventory within the 24 months.

In 1976, we were no longer needed. Connecticut Mutual hired another consultant to determine their next course of housing construction. You do not listen to the founder or the team that had their finger on the pulse of the project in marketing and sales. You don't choose the team that knew every potential source of new buyers. You don't choose the team who knew what the market was saying about new housing products. No, if you are a major insurance company, you again hire a consultant from out-of-town and if you are from out-of-town, that makes you an expert. If things go bad the first time around, you blame it on the founder. If they go bad the second time around, you blame the consultant. That way, no one in the insurance company has to accept the blame.

The insurance company was now burdened with very high fees to the consultant and the new team hired by the consultant. With this change the overhead became significantly higher than under my administration. After the inventory was sold, our hope to remain as key management persons with Connecticut Mutual, based on our performance, did not materialize. Instead, the new Connecticut Mutual team began to develop a new "patio" product of 30 homes to be built alongside the golf course. The consultant believed that this was the product of the future. The plan called for immediate construction and quick sales so that they could move on to another section of the golf course.

I called Bill Fishman, the co-founder and CEO of ARA who had asked me to return if my investment plans did not work out. When I left ARA, he advised me to return before age 50 if things did not work out. I had just turned 50. It was only four years since my departure from ARA. Bill greeted me warmly. He took me into an office and introduced me to the man in charge of the Business & Industry division where I had years of successful experience. I was ready to move to any area of the country and work hard to regain the credibility I had in the past.

It was a confusing meeting. When Mr. Fishman left, I spoke briefly with the head of this division. He excused himself for an interruption. He had me speak to another official while I waited. The head of this division came back, treating me as if I were an interruption in his day, then said they would research their management needs and phone me within ten days. I had completely forgotten the selling lessons learned in the strawberry story. I thought my track record would speak for itself. I returned home but never received a phone call from ARA. I assumed Mr. Fishman was aware of the facts. I came to the conclusion that they advised Mr. Fishman that I was "overqualified" for any openings they may have had.

I was back to square one. I had very little in my bank account. I had to find a way to support my family and my mother and hang onto our condominium homes and the Ski Area. Gina 18, Greg 16, Wade, 14 were all earning summer money in various jobs at Bristol Mountain and at Bristol Harbour. My wife and kids knew Dad was in trouble and they were supportive in every possible way. They dreaded Christmas if Bristol Mountain was not open or if it was raining on Christmas Eve or Christmas Day. They knew their Dad was just going through the motions of a Merry Christmas. They also joined Dad in prayers every Sunday at St. Januarius Church in Naples, NY where he was active in teaching confirmation classes and in the parish counsel. Throughout this period, my wife and mother's faith in me never diminished. They knew that my faith had been tested and that I remained strong in the conviction that God watches over us.

I had to develop a plan where I could stay close to the family and work on the success of the ski area. I was disappointed that ARA did not give me the courtesy of a response. However, I was somewhat relieved that I did not have to move the kids out of the Naples School District where they had become so attached. Their academic and sports achievements and their relationships with students and teachers were outstanding. They were New York State ribbon-winning ski racers and becoming excellent golfers.

I read that the Rochester Chamber of Commerce was looking for an Executive Director. I felt that at 50 years of age, I was well qualified for the job. I had served on the Board of Trustees. I had been honored for my service to both the Junior and Senior Chambers of Commerce. They knew of my results in membership campaigns and in fundraisers such as the United Way. They knew of my success in providing food and vending services. They knew that I had managed a mini-city that included sewer, water and recreational services. I did not get the job.

Bernie, with her real estate broker's license in hand, and I discussed a business plan. Bernie could choose to remain with Connecticut Mutual or with me on a joint business plan. She bought a house and garage on Seneca Point Road, a short distance from the entrance to Bristol Harbour Village. We formed a resale, rental and property management company on that property and agreed to pay rent for the use of our new home office. We put a big sign in front, "Resales & Rentals Bristol Harbour Village." The homeowners that we sold units to originally, now turned to Bernie and her daughter Ann for assistance with their resale and rental needs.

The annual contract for the management of the properties at Bristol Harbour Village was held by Connecticut Mutual. Bernie and I knew the homeowners and the homeowner-elected leaders. There were four separate contracts for what were called the Association, Condo I, Condo II and Condo III. Our bid was the same as Connecticut Mutual on a cost plus basis. In spite of our small status, we won all four contracts to start on January 1, 1977.

Two weeks prior to the start of this contract, I had a supra pubic prostatectomy. My first prostate operation failed. This was radical surgery. The Doctor said the operation was bloodier than heart surgery. In the recovery room, I was bleeding internally. Fortunately, it was caught on time. I was wheeled back into the operating room in time to stop the bleeding.

During recovery, around the Christmas Season, I interviewed Daryl Braun and Charlie Fischer, two talented and loyal maintenance men, who agreed to leave the insurance company to work for us. In my weakened condition, I recall the chills that ran through my body from both the operation and the mental impact of losing my part ownership in the Bristol Harbour Village project.

This grown-up Prisoner of the Truck, who became a millionaire at the age of 34, who built a ten-state operation with 4000 employees, was now 50 and struggling to support his mother and family of six in whatever way he could. Yet, in this loss, I did not feel panic. I recalled the peace and calmness that I felt after the miracle of the "prayer meeting" four years earlier. Whatever God's plans were for me, I would remain calm and continue to put forth my best effort in providing for the needs of my mother and family in the spirit of "Fortitude".

I earned about $10,000 from Bristol Mountain, about $15,000 from Sarkis Maintenance Service, Inc., the management company. It was not enough. I had to find other sources of income. My brother Joe, the super strawberry salesman, who did not need to be taught how to sell, was unhappy with his new boss at ARA. His boss had crude human relations skills. Joe spoke to me about it. My non-competitive agreement had expired with ARA. Joe had never signed one. Since my work at the ski area and my venture with Bernie were part time, I had the benefit of time to put my creative juices in other directions. I told Joe to quit ARA. They had been unfair to both of us. In early 1977, Joe and I decided to use our past connections to get five-year agreements for vending or food service. I would find the financing on the strength of these contracts. Central Trust, our ski area lender, became our lender. Joe Shuhda, my sister Betty's husband from Brooklyn, provided seed capital of $75,000 for a percentage of the company. This would get us through the first year. Unlike our competition, we were not burdened with high investments in obsolete vending equipment. We could start anew, offering the latest models of high tech machines. We named our company Sarkis Management Services, Inc.

In addition to our strong contacts with the Human Resource Managers in the greater Rochester area, we had contacts with men and women who were tried, tested and had proven track records in vending and food service operations. We could pick the cream of the crop. I assisted in the development of a strategy and a proposal to win the coffee vending service for Kodak's 40,000 employees. Our proposal was most unique. One of Kodak's advertising gadgets was a king size version of a roll of Kodak film with a handle on it to carry items. Don Sarkis, our Supervisor of Vending Maintenance, obtained this enlarged container. We inserted our written proposal into this round Kodak cartridge. In order to read it, it had to be pulled out slowly like any roll of paper. The proposal was as unique as the package. It put the client in the driver's seat on a cost plus basis and made our company subject to periodic Kodak audits of our costs and metered reports of sales. I suggested that we have our proposal "blessed" by a priest at Our Lady of Victory Church, not far from St. Joseph's Church were I had served as an altar boy. Sadly, a fire had destroyed St Joseph's Church. All that remained was the tower and the shell that held it up.

We won a five-year contract. ARA lost the account. Mr. Fishman, the CEO of ARA called to ask me why I chose to become a competitor rather than work for ARA. I told him about my experience with the two executives to whom I was referred. He said I should have called him. He asked what caused Joe to leave ARA. I told him about Joe's mistreatment. Again, as he was about to hang up, in sincere disappointment, he said that we should have never taken our friendship with him for granted. He said that if we had called him, he would have insured that Joe was treated right and that I would have been given a major responsibility in the company. I replied that since I never heard from him inquiring about my progress with his people, I had no choice but to assume that he had to go along with his chain of command and their lack of interest in me.

In the business world, I had the same degree of high respect for Mr. William (Bill) Fishman as I did for Bob Kennedy, Joe Wilson of Xerox, Richard P. Miller, Sr., executive director of the United Way organization and his son Richard P. Miller, Jr. It was Richard P. Miller. Jr. who wrote a letter to the editor in defense of Bristol Harbour's plans. He did this in spite of his friendship with many of those who were in opposition.

Mr. Fishman was the man who made me feel that my merger with ARA was the right decision. Bill was the man who handed me the top Area award at the national ARA meetings. Bill enjoyed my mother's company as well as her irresistible Lebanese dinners and would always ask about her. Bill Fishman was not only brilliant, he was caring. During the time I was working for ARA, my brother Jim, who was 30 years old, was struggling with his priesthood. Mr. Fishman, sensitive to my overwhelming concern for my brother's problems, asked if he could talk to him. Mr. Fishman believed that, as a member of the Jewish faith, Jim would not feel threatened by his involvement. Jim respected Mr. Fishman. He also believed that a man of the Jewish faith was capable of giving objective advice. After a lengthy meeting, Bill Fishman advised Jim that he should seek counseling at Menninger's, an internationally famous center in Topeka, Kansas, noted for treating those who are seriously confused, including Catholic priests. Bill offered his Lear Jet to fly Jim to Kansas. Jim refused. He returned to Boston where he was working as a garden caretaker.

Jim's pattern of confusion continued. I made a deal with him. We would accept Mr. Fishman's offer. The pilot would pick Jim up in Boston, pick me up in Rochester and fly to Topeka and wait for the Director of Admissions to interview each of us. I proposed a condition. One of us needed help. One of us would stay for the treatment program. We would let the Director of Admissions make this determination. The pilot would fly only one of us back to our homes. Jim agreed and we packed accordingly. My wife, I believe with the intent of humor, and her keen awareness of the intense pursuit of my dreams, suggested that it might be me that would stay for treatment.

After the interview, the Director determined that Jim should stay. Jim refused. Outside of the Director's office, Jim and I sat out on the grass in the hot Topeka sun. Jim asked why I was crying. I told him the story of the conversation I had with our father a few months before he died. I said that I did everything in my power to honor the authority vested in me to be a father to my brothers and sisters. Menninger's offered him the professional assistance needed in his transition from a priest to a professional career, marriage and children. I had also taken the precaution to pick up his medical insurance that the Catholic Diocese had dropped. And his refusal to seek treatment was devastating to me causing me to feel that I was failing as a surrogate father.

Jim changed his mind and stayed. Surrounded by the best of counseling and care, Jim moved from the treatment program into a work program; learned how to live with a non-Catholic volunteer family; learned how to cope with dating relationships, etc. He met a young lady who had her degree in Library Science. A year later, my mother and I attended his Kansas wedding and we were both joyful that he found the stability and happiness he was searching for.

I made a mistake in not calling Bill Fishman. I do know that my respect for Mr. Fishman was so high that if I had had the opportunity to work for him, after my major setbacks, I would have returned to ARA. However, the die was cast. Joe and I were excited about our fast growth. Our capture of some of ARA's business in the Rochester market was insignificant to ARA, but it was a great morale booster for us.

This new venture into food and vending services, combined with my other income kept my head above water. I was able to provide for my family's and my mother's needs.

That same year, 1977, Ralph Globus, my ARA boss who had retired, phoned me. He was involved with a coin-operated blood pressure business and he wanted me to take on the territory of Western NY. The units were successful in shopping malls. I told Ralph that I had nothing to invest. He said he would provide the capital and we'd share in the profits 50-50 after the machines were paid for. It was a simple business. I installed the machines myself and collected the cash. The units took in $500 a month on average. However, at the end of 12 months, people knew what their blood pressure was, and repeat usage diminished to a point where it was unprofitable. Ralph advised me to ship the machines to another partner he had in Pennsylvania. I lost my time. Ralph salvaged his investment. However, in later years, my experience with this product had a profound effect on what turned out to be the greatest business achievement in which I ever participated.

Losing Bristol Mountain Ski Area

In 1980, interest rates leaped to 20%. Our interest totaled $365,000 a year for Bristol Mountain. When the ski area was closed, each morning while shaving, I would think of the $1,000-a-day in interest payments. I would jokingly tell friends that fortunately, I did not shave with a straight razor. My ski area management team had attended a ski area convention. A speaker gave a talk on "How to Deal with Your Banker in this Period of High Interest Rates." We had borrowed $100,000 in a working capital loan. It was the spring of 1980 and Central Trust wanted this unsecured loan paid back. Our ski management team sought the advice of a bankruptcy attorney. They all supported a plan of action saying that if we were forced into bankruptcy, it was best to do it when we had the most cash on hand at the end of the ski season.

My ski management team knew that I was a classmate of the President of Central Trust. He was Angelo Costanza, the eighth grade classmate of mine, who turned down the YMCA membership and the scholarship to St. Joseph's Commercial, for which I was eternally grateful. Ange was a graduate of Aquinas, Rochester's well known Catholic High School. He was an intelligence officer in the armed forces and upon return earned a degree in law that led him to becoming President of Central Trust.

Aware of my friendship with Ange Costanza, the team made me promise that I would speak firmly about the crises we were facing and seek some form of relief from the bank, especially since $1 million of the $2 million loan was guaranteed by the Farmers Home Administration, as arranged by our ski area. Our ski area president had been successful in obtaining this FHA guarantee for a major expansion program. The team believed my leverage for obtaining relief was the $100,000 unsecured working capital loan that had not as yet been paid back.

I promised the management of the ski area that I would remain firm. If it worked for other ski areas I would try it. I met with Ange and explained that our ski area could not survive at 20% interest rates (on a $2 million loan the interest costs alone were close to $400,000 a year). I felt that with 50% of the loan guaranteed by the government, we should be entitled to a smaller interest rate. Ange said, before we talk about anything, I want you to pay that $100,000 in working capital that we loaned you and then we'll talk. I said that I would pay it if he would give me an idea of what he could do for us in a reduction of the interest charged. He was angry. He again demanded that we pay the $100,000. I was getting nervous about our strategy and said I would pay the $100,000 if he would just share with me what it was he could or could not do in terms of a reduction in our rate of interest. I became even more concerned as he expressed stronger anger. He said I must have been getting some bad legal advice from that Syracuse attorney. I took a deep breath and tried once more. I calmly said that I was trying to be reasonable; that based on his banking experience with government guaranteed loans, at least, for friendship sake, give me an idea of what effort he could try to make on our behalf. I said that I realized he had executive loan committees and nothing he said would be binding on him or the bank. I said if he would just give me a hint of possibilities, I would have the $100,000 working capital check written immediately.

He pounded on his desk. He said that if I didn't pay the $100,000, he would throw the book at me; he would have his law firm start foreclosure proceedings and would personally do everything in his power to wipe me out. He said that my reputation would be ruined in the community and no one would ever want to do business with me again. He said he wanted me to remove the Sarkis Management Services Inc., account from his bank. He didn't want our business.

I returned his anger with anger. I said that all he had to do was outline a possible program for assistance and I would have the check written. I couldn't understand his unwillingness to show some concern for our plight and suggest a few things that might be done in the future. I resented his threats to wipe me out and if it was a battle he wanted to engage in, I could handle it. After all, I told him, I won the battle of Seneca Point. I could win the battle with him.

In May of 1981, at age 55, I surrendered the ski area to Ange Costanza and his bank, in an out of court settlement that returned 50 cents on a dollar to unsecured creditors. I was one of the unsecured creditors and I was fortunate to get a return of $150,000. My entire loss on the ski area was in excess of a million. My wish to give something back to the community was fulfilled for the community, but was a failure for me.

In this meeting with Ange, where did I fail? In spite of the advice that I received from my ski management team, as President Truman once said, the "buck stopped at my desk". I lost the ski area because I compromised my principles. Webster's definition of principle: "a) a truth that is the foundation for other truths. b) A fundamental belief, *religious principles."* I compromised the Holy Spirit's Seven Gifts. I did "counsel" with Ange. I had "knowledge" of his feelings on the matter. I failed to "understand" his position.

My "fortitude" in a determination to win a battle was not based on "wisdom". My "piety" and "love of the Lord" was replaced with anger. Fighting opponents for my legal right to build my dream of Bristol Harbour Village was not the same as fighting with Angelo Costanza on an issue of principle.

We had verbally promised to pay Central Trust $100,000 in a working capital loan when we had the cash. In the winter and spring of 1980-81, we had the cash. We should have written the check for $100,000 when due and then sought Ange's advice on our crisis. He could have very well proposed a plan that he executed after the Chapter 11 proceedings. That plan was simple. He would have his bank invest $1 million into needed improvements in the ski area if the Farmers Home Administration would accept a loss of their $1 million. The function of the FHA was to create jobs and this would insure existing as well as new jobs. For FHA to take a loss on loans was not uncommon, if there was an on-going benefit to the community.

A few years after I lost the ski area, I phoned Ange Costanza and apologized to him for compromising my integrity. If there were any wounds between us, they were immediately healed.

For several years, I could not drive down Route 64 to the site of the ski area. The memories were too vivid: my struggle to make it a better place to ski; the many successes of the programs for the blind and for the schools and colleges; the fighting spirit of the management and employees as they coped with the weather patterns and the number of days for skiing that affected their income; the sense of excitement of kids rushing out of school buses in a winter escape from books and learning. All these memories contributed to a great sense of pride in my involvement.

This was a difficult financial and mental loss to overcome. I felt like the Cuban fisherman in Hemingway's Book, the "Old Man and the Sea." All his life he dreamed about the "big fish" that he would catch. He spent years in this mission without success. In his old age, in his small rowboat, he finally hooked the "big fish" the length of his boat. It was so big it dragged him out to sea. The struggle lasted for three days and nights. His hands were raw from attempts to pull it in. Finally, he was able to bring the exhausted "big fish" beside his small boat. He set his oars and headed for home. He anticipated the excitement of his fellow fisherman. His dream was accomplished. A shark attacked. He fought it off with his oars and a hand knife. Another shark was successful in getting a chunk out of the big fish. The battle with sharks seemed endless. Tired and completely exhausted, he arrived at the fishing docks as a worried group of family and friends awaited his return. The only thing left of his "big fish" was the head floating about the surface and slightly below the surface of the water, the skeleton of this once magnificent "big fish".

I identified with the Old Man and the Sea. Every year, for 17 years, the ski area would embark on a 90-day mission to catch the "big one". Every year, the sharks of warm weather, rain, capital improvements, wrong decisions, competition and high interest rates would take their toll. In terms of the cash flow, the season would end with a "skeleton" cash flow. It was a struggle. In each of these seventeen years, new provisions had to be obtained and the journey would begin again. However, there was one major difference between the two struggles. The Mountain was not a skeleton. For seventeen years of expansion and improvements, it continued to provide a service to skiers of all ages. In common between the two, no matter how difficult the task, the Old Man of the Sea and the Old Man of the Mountain, courageously embarked annually on their journey determined to catch the "big one". It was a difficult loss.

In the year 2000, Bristol Mountain, under the ownership and leadership of Dan Fuller, who has invested heavily in major improvements and expanded services, enjoys a great reputation for its successful service to the skiing public. For me, in this year 2001, at age 75, it is now like looking back at a child who has grown up, is on its own and doing very well.

CHAPTER 26

Age 56 to 64 Turning Failure into Success

In 1971, I was on the verge of business and personal bankruptcy. In 1974, I lost my investment in Bristol Harbour Village. In 1981, I surrendered Bristol Mountain Ski Area to a bank. From 1964 to 1991, a period of 27 years, I became a Prisoner of my own struggle to raise my family and keep my head above water.

During this period I thought about the words of Sister Ludolpha, the principal of St. Joseph's Commercial School, who said, "There are times in life when you will be faced with great adversities. In spite of your best effort, there will be hardship, obstacles, failure and disappointment to overcome. It may take years to understand God's plan for you. Trust in God. Never give up. Keep on trying."

Recovery One - Bristol Harbour Village

In 1980, at age 54, the year before I lost the ski area, Connecticut Mutual (CM) threw in the towel at Bristol Harbour Village. It had taken them three years to sell the 30 patio homes. It was the wrong product. Every department, overstaffed, was losing money. I estimated their operating losses to be over $500,000 a year in 1979. CM had a sale pending with a Rochester builder. Prior to closing, the builder made several major errors. He sent other businessmen to look at the golf course, marina, sewer and water plants. His plan was to buy the project and immediately spin off these amenities. This would leave him with the undeveloped land at no cost.

The Board of Directors of the Bristol Harbour Village Association Inc., under the capable leadership of Don Wolcott and Don Greenhouse, President and Past President were opposed to this spin-off plan. The Homeowner's Association wrote to CM recommending that the project be sold to experienced management people, who lived within Bristol Harbour and who cared about all residents. They recommended me for my general management experience, Bernice Caprini for her sales and public relations results and Otto Layer for his knowledge of land development and construction.

CM accepted these recommendations and agreed on a price of $500,000 for the undeveloped land, utilities, golf course facilities & marina.

I formed a limited partnership. With Bernie's assistance, we raised $555,000 from a maximum of 35 investors – mostly all within five miles of the project. A General Partnership was formed. I became the President of the General Partnership. Bernie and I moved our headquarters back to the project's offices. We borrowed $500,000 from Canandaigua National Bank for start up costs. We put on our ultra-conservative hat, limited any construction programs to a small group of town homes that sold quickly. We eliminated the high salaries and ran a tight ship. I accepted a small management fee, one that allowed me to continue to participate in other business ventures without a conflict of interest. Bernie earned her income on the commissions generated from resales and rentals. In one year, we eliminated the $500,000 in losses experienced by CM and turned it into a small profit. This was primarily accomplished by the savings in salaries and wages related to the CM consultant and the high-cost management team that had replaced us in 1976.

From 1980 to 1990, all operations involving golf, marina, sewer and water were stabilized. The golf course and marina were generating profits. Sewer and water profits were minimal with rates controlled by government authorities. Bernie and her daughter, Ann Caprini, through their company, Bristol Hills Realty, developed an outstanding rental and resale program for families that helped to increase resale values. Sue Ryan assisted them in both rentals and resales.

For market reasons, developments of new housing were kept at a minimum. With part of my income from the Bristol Harbour partnership, part from Sarkis Management Services (food & vending company) and part from Sarkis Maintenance Services (services to the residents of Bristol Harbour), I was just able to support my family. The hours were long but I was only three minutes away from my Bristol Harbour Condominium home where I could be with my family.

A sense of humor is essential for coping with hard times. One evening, during this difficult period in my life, when my five children were about six to sixteen, I arrived late for dinner. It had been a rough day. I quickly sat in my regular dining stool. I looked at Wade and said, "Fritz, pass the salt". Wade said, "I'm not Fritz, I'm Wade", as he passed the salt. I began to eat and said, "Greg, pass the bread". Greg said, "Dad, I'm not Greg, I'm Fritz", as he passed the bread. I threw down my fork in anger and said, "Look you guys, I've had a tough day. It seems that my entire day has been one of mistakes. Every phone call, every meeting, every thing I typed went wrong all day long. I know who you are. I came home to escape problems and you have to remind me of my simple mistakes." I stormed out of the kitchen and went to my bedroom.

I washed my face to cool down. Knowing that I most likely disturbed the entire family's dinner, I returned within three minutes. Feeling sad about my outburst, I avoided any eye contact. My eyes were cast down at my dinner plate. There was a total silence. The only noise I heard was the use of utensils on the china plates. After a minute or two, I finally looked up. I burst into laughter when I noticed that my five children all had name tags on their shirts – and they roared with laughter with me.

The Department of Environmental Conservation and the State Department of Health were pleased with their periodic inspections of our sewer and water facilities. In addition, the reformed Canandaigua Lake Pure Waters, Inc. conducted objective scientific tests at the mouth of all tributaries on the lake. The Bristol Harbour Sewer Treatment plant was never cited for pollution. The drinking water was of superior quality. The marina never became a threat to the *health, welfare and safety of the people of the State of New York.*

Many of the former opponents to the Bristol Harbour plan became happy members of the Robert Trent Jones Golf Course, judged the finest and one of the most challenging in Western New York. Their property values were enhanced by the golf course and restaurant within minutes of their lakeside homes.

Two key professionals, Dan Fuller and Tom German, who worked with me at Bristol Mountain, were able to purchase the Ski Area from Central Trust. They continued to upgrade the ski area each year of operation and to win new and happy skiing customers.

Bristol Harbour was then close to 250 residential units. Our residents and the Seneca Point neighbors established friendships through golf and tennis events. Any sign or form of prejudice no longer existed. The governing boards of the various condominiums and the master association effectively enforced the conditions of the offering plans approved by the attorney general. Through contracts with Sarkis Maintenance Services, these volunteer boards spent many hours helping to maintain the properties for quiet enjoyment and in good condition and appearance. Dan Martin and

Nancy Caprini professionally managed community service operations and administration. Dale Stoker and Elaine Zukatis later succeeded them with great efficiency. A uniformed community relation's officer in the summer months helped to minimize disturbances to the Bristol Harbour residents. Bristol Harbour became a successful single-family community and a respected neighbor in the Seneca Point community.

I was invited again to participate in the Seneca Point tournaments. The animosity disappeared. I welcomed the opportunity to be friends again and was grateful for the new peaceful relationships and the end of combat.

I was active in the community. I received the following citation from the Ontario County Industrial Development Agency:

In Tribute to Fred W. Sarkis
Chairman of Ontario County Industrial Development Agency
1984-1985
10 Projects, $40,200,000 value, 1,057 Jobs
We thank you for your Service and Dedication

Plans for Retirement

By 1988, I was an eight-year member of the national American Resort Development

Association, consisting of resorts that sold both whole and fractional ownership interests in resort properties throughout the United States. At the 1988 meeting, this Association announced an executive-loan plan. For $1,000 plus travel costs, a member could pick a prominent resort executive to act as a consultant for a day. The $1,000 would go to the Association.

Our partnership, which planned to operate for ten years, was now eight years old. I was going to be 64 in 1990 and was planning my retirement. I chose Ed McMullen as our loan executive. Ed was an executive vice president for Marriott's vacation ownership program (timesharing). Ed was an entrepreneur who built a timeshare project in Hilton Head. It was noted for its quality, good service and integrity of operations. Marriott bought out Ed's interest and hired him to head this new division. When I met Ed, he was responsible for this successful and fast growing division of the Marriott Corporation. At that time, the timeshare industry was getting mixed reviews. There were many unscrupulous, under-financed, get rich-quick developers who gave the industry a poor image.

Ed McMullen visited and marveled at what he saw at Bristol Harbour. He advised that in order to sell the project, we needed to retain an expert in market research. He recommended Ragatz Associates out of Eugene, Oregon. Richard Ragatz was one of the nation's most respected authorities on resort properties. This research would enable us to build a five-year economic model reflecting future growth and earnings. He recommended that this information be incorporated into a professional package with aerial and other photographs of our beautiful location. My son Wade, a graduate of the Hotel School at Cornell, provided major assistance in the development of the economic model. Wade had extensive experience in training employees of major hotels in the operation of sophisticated computer systems and in concert with Ragatz used his computer skills to develop the economic model.

I followed Mr. McMullen's recommendations. I was ready to find a financially responsible buyer for the project. At the 1989 American Resort Developers Association conference in San Diego, I wore a big button on my lapel that read, "Take the 60 second test". If anyone attending the conference asked me what that was all about, I gave them a sheet with ten questions. The test took just 60 seconds requiring yes or no answers. If all of the questions were yes, I had a prospective buyer with the essential financial requirements to purchase and continue the development. After the end of one of the 60-second tests, a gentleman by the name of Larry LaGue said he wanted to review our research, economic model and financial statements. After his review and phone calls, he approached me the next day and said that he had buyers from Boston with the financial capability of buying the project and moving it forward.

I reviewed the financial statement of one of the future partners of the buying group. He had a significant net worth. His partner had an impressive resume in the development of properties. In 1990, our partnership sold the project for $4.8 million, almost ten times what we paid for it in 1980. Our introduction of the new owners and their plans to the Bristol Harbour Village Association, Inc. and its members were well received. We owed a great deal to the Association and we wanted them to be as happy with the turn over to new owners as we were. My partners and I were well rewarded for our ten-year investment.

Immediately, after the sale, the residents of Bristol Harbour Village honored me with the following plaque. In most instances, Developer's fear to live at the project that they build nor are they ever honored with appreciation plaques. This weathered plaque is placed on a huge rock adjacent to the twelve-foot flowered butterfly at the entrance to Bristol Harbour's Cliffside Drive.

In recognition of Fred Sarkis
Who first envisioned this community
and whose persistence made it happen.
Bristol Harbour Village Association
1990

Recovery Two – Sale of Sarkis Management Services, Inc.

In 1986, after nine years of growing the business, Sarkis Management Services, Inc. (the food & vending company) was sold to the Rochester Coca Cola Bottling Company through Harvey

Anderson, its president. In nine years, Joe and I, as founders, achieved a remarkable return on a zero investment. I recovered most of the loss I experienced in the ski business. Harvey valued the professional team we built in the management of food service operations. He was expanding his company's operations for a sale. A few years later, Harvey and members of his family sold their company to another major Coca Cola Bottler out of Chicago and moved to Florida. Harvey, an honorable and worthy competitor, retired, moved to Florida and started a successful banking business.

(When I retired in 1996, Harvey wooed Helen and me to the Racquet Club of El Conquistador in Bradenton, Florida, where we bought a bayside condominium home and discovered a new family of tennis friendships, many who belonged to the Tennis Club of Rochester when we lived on Ambassador Drive, prior to my financial crises.)

Recovery Three – A Business Venture with Three Sons

In 1987, Jack Manning, retired in Florida, the former Director of Marketing for Kwik Kafe and a life long friend, suggested that I consider re-entering the automated blood pressure measurement business. The marketing concept had changed. Instead of coin-operation, the machines were leased directly to pharmacies that provided the service free to their customers. Western NY was open as a territory.

My two sons Greg and Fritz were interested. Greg was an entrepreneur, painting houses and winning major ski races in the Northeastern United States. Fritz had just graduated with a degree in marketing from St. John's Fisher College. We obtained an exclusive dealership for Vita-Stat. Vita-Stat was a division of SpaceLabs, a major supplier of medical monitoring devices for intensive care units in hospitals.

The company was named CHESS, Inc. (Computerized Health Education and Screening Service). Patrons of pharmacies were able to monitor their blood pressure accurately, keep track of their readings and review them with their Doctors if they had concerns.

My father died of a heart attack related to untreated hypertension. We would now be in the business of the early detection and treatment of hypertension with the potential to spare an individual and family the devastation of a heart attack or stroke. The unit would be plugged into the customer's power source; the temperature was 70 degrees year round; it was not dependent on the weather; the rental checks came in monthly; there was no product to spoil; it was a high quality product with measurement on the upper arm as recommended by the American Heart Association and the technology and accuracy met all government standards including the Federal Drug Administration.

Within five years, Greg and Fritz were successful in penetrating 80% of the potential Western NY pharmacies, the highest in the United States. This led to a dealer agreement that awarded CHESS all of Canada on an exclusive basis. When my son Josh graduated from Middlebury College, he joined the company to assist in the marketing and servicing of the product in Canada.

As the year 2000 draws to a close, they own, manage, operate, lease and service over 3,500 units in pharmacies and businesses in Western NY and Canada, giving 38 million free blood pressure measurements a year. They are financially self-sufficient. They have developed a Canadian and Western NY network that provides an excellent service to their pharmacy and business customers. They each own a 1/3rd of the business. They give their father a royalty payment and consider him their coach.

With a perfect blend of skills and a unique harmonious working relationship, they became the largest and most successful Vita-Stat distributor in the world.

The Blessings that came from my 27-year Struggle

During this period of time, I had the full support and patience of my wife, Helen and five children. If God's plan for me involved the raising of unspoiled children, who worked together to assist me financially and to save money for their college education, it was truly a blessing, born of my adversity.

Their mother provided for their needs in every possible way. She drove them to ski races throughout Western and Central NY. Gina, Greg, Wade and Fritz became junior champions. Greg became a national ski champion in his age group in 1999. He has won the New York State title in his age group for nine consecutive years. In 2001, he strives for his 10th consecutive New York State championship – and still manages to help run a business and raise a family. Wade and Fritz are past Bristol Harbour Golf Club Champions. In 1998 Western and Central NY ski races, it was not uncommon for Greg, Wade and Fritz to be in the top five. All of our grandchildren, who are old enough to ski, spend their winter weekends and holidays at Bristol Mountain. Leigh Frances Cushing, my grand daughter, at age 11, made the top six in the Eastern Nationals, held in Gunstock, New Hampshire 1998 and in 1999 she made the New York State team and went to the Eastern Junior Olympics at Sunday River in Maine. Her goal is to become a member of the US Olympic ski team – and her grand parents believe she will.

During the hard times, when my children were youngsters, they shagged balls on the golf course. In their teens, in the summer, they worked at the ski area, mowed and irrigated the grass on the golf course, checked bags for golfers, handled public relations in the pro shop, beach and marina and waited on tables at the restaurant. In a computerized speed typing test, my daughter Gina tied me as she assisted in the Bristol Harbour offices with administrative needs before attending Cornell University. They all learned the importance of a sense of humor, good study habits, enthusiasm, hard work and pleasing people with good service. Three of our five children were class presidents at Naples High School, in Naples, NY.

These youthful experiences prepared them for the real world and in this year 2000, they are all successful entrepreneurs - the three sons in the health monitoring business, a daughter Gina and her husband Grant Cushing, who own and manage a business called Brownfield Restoration Group, a national environmental consulting firm that specializes in the restoration of environmentally distressed properties and my son Wade, owner and head of Sarkis Financial Group, who has won national awards for his performance as a Certified Financial Planner. Among his many clients, he manages the portfolio of his mom, dad, brothers and sister.

Four of my children have solid marriages. Josh, as yet has not taken the step. We have eleven grandchildren, all within 40 minutes of our Bristol Harbour Condominium. Helen and I have 11 active grandchildren all less than 12 years of age, with twin grand daughters who will be a year old on December 30, 2000.

Sister Ludolpha, God rest her soul, was right. Indeed, my 27-year adversities were a blessing in disguise.

After the Sale of Bristol Harbour Village

After 1990, refinancing failures lead to a change of ownership of the Bristol Harbour development. In 1998, the new owners, who are successful Rochester-based entrepreneurs, added a $3 million dollar lodge with a most spectacular view of Canandaigua Lake. Further expansion is planned for 2001.

When I lost the Ski Area in 1981, Dale Stoker, a graduate of the Rochester Institute of Technology, Hotel School, chose to leave Bristol Mountain to work as the Resident Manager for Sarkis Maintenance Services, responsible for all maintenance and accounting services to the residents. After my partnership purchased the Bristol Harbour Development from Connecticut Mutual in 1980, Dale became the General Manager of all operations, including sewer, water, marina, restaurant and golf. To this date, under the current ownership, Dale continues to operate as the General Manager. His ability, loyalty and integrity to all those whom he serves have always been beyond reproach. He and the project owners continue the dream for Bristol Harbour Village into the new Millennium.

For the past ten years, Dan Conroy, Resident Manager, and Tammy Benzinger continue to provide a dedicated and complete maintenance service to the residents of Bristol Harbour Village. For 20 years, Mark Knickerbocker has earned praise as the golf course superintendent.

Bristol Mountain, under the professional ownership and management of Dan Fuller, who served as vice president of marketing when I was involved, completed an expansion program in 1999 and 2000. In terms of attendance, skier satisfaction and employee moral, year 2000 was the best year in the ski area's history. Each year, Dan Fuller's skillful planning, major improvements, good skiing conditions and respected leadership continue to capture a greater percentage of the regional ski market. The ski area is financially stable and Dan continues the dream at the turn of the century.

Larry Demarse and Ron Ratnik (co-founding GM engineers of Bristol Mountain) went on to become the world's leading suppliers of snow making systems - Larry with an airless system and Ron with a compressed air system.

Joe Kohler, who was a past, loyal and dedicated President of Bristol Mountain and Larry Demarse formed a company called Ski-View, a company that would put high quality advertisements on ski towers. Joe and Larry took the idea, paid me a substantial finder's fee, and with unique entrepreneur skills, turned it into a profitable venture that they sold a few years later for significant gains. Today, this company now installs 5,000 signs at 160 ski resorts throughout the United States. Advertisers use Ski View to reach an estimated 54 million skiers and snow-boarders annually.

My former food service partner John O'Donnell, who left Rochester 40 years ago, is retired in Coos Bay, Oregon and to this day, as an adopted brother, communicates with me on a weekly basis while he recovers from two total knee replacements.

The Three Jewels of the Town of South Bristol

John Brahm III, a leader in Ontario County's tourism industry, was born in South Bristol. His family farmed grapes and raspberries. John is currently an entrepreneur with a successful award winning wine operation and store for visitors and tourists. To quote, John in year 2000, "There are now three jewels in the Town of South Bristol - Canandaigua Lake, Bristol Harbour and Bristol Mountain." When combined, the ski area and lake resort represent a town-assessed value of over $35 million and combined employment in high peak seasons of close to 500 with no increased pressure on the Naples School District. The 35-year impact on the development of residential and hotel properties related to the ski area and golf course is immeasurable.

John Brahm II, a life long dairy, grape and raspberry farmer was the South Bristol Town Supervisor from 1972 to 1981. As supervisor, he objectively oversaw the development of Bristol Harbour. He died on June 25, 2000. I salute his fair treatment in the development of the Bristol Harbour Village in his nine years of service to the Town.

My Most Cherished Award

It was presented to me at the annual meeting of the Canandaigua Lake Pure Waters, LTD in 1994. This Lake Association could trace its roots back to 1970, when it was formed to prevent Bristol Harbour Village from becoming a reality. The main thrust of the 1970 organization was to block my Village plans by spreading fears of lake pollution and over crowding of boating on the lake. Scientific facts and studies presented in many months of meetings and hearings to ease concerns, only served to intensify the opposition. Previous Chapters clearly reflect the extent of this hostility.

A few years after its formation in 1970, leaders became more rational and objective about all sources of lake pollution. Today, Canandaigua Lake Pure Waters LTD, with an elected volunteer Board, continues to watch over the lake and its tributaries for all sources of water pollution in cooperation with the Canandaigua

Lake Watershed Task Force. These two organizations, working hand-in-hand have achieved results that serve as models for other communities interested in protecting the purity of their waters.

The plaque reads:

Canandaigua Lake Pure Waters, Ltd.

Friend of the Lake Award

In appreciation of his efforts to promote development designed to conserve Canandaigua Lake and in gratitude for service to CLPW, including a decade as a CLPW Director, a term as President and years as Membership Committee Chairman,

Fred Sarkis

is recognized as the
1994 Canandaigua Lake Pure Waters
Friend of the Lake.

May we all bring to the lake his boundless enthusiasm, energy and optimism.

The volunteer organization that was originally formed to block the development of Bristol Harbour became an organization that objectively acts on any and all sources of water pollution from any source in the Canandaigua Lake watershed. To this date, Canandaigua Lake remains one of the purest fresh water lakes in the world. In light of the history of intense and hostile opposition to the development of Bristol Harbour Village thirty years ago, this was one of the most significant honors of my lifetime.

CHAPTER 27

My Brother Kenny and my Baby Brother Lee

In 1987, it was my brother Ken, 16 years younger than I, who took his New York City brother Lee into his Palm Springs, California home to care for him in the last difficult months of Lee's long-suffering life. Lee was my baby brother, 19 year's younger than I. When my father died in 1950 at the age of 56, Lee was only five years old. Ken was eight years old. Throughout their lives, they remained loving brothers, friends and confidants.

On June 3, 1987, at age 42, Lee was one of the early victims of AIDS. A talented artist, he composed a legacy of music. He was an example of physical, moral and intellectual courage in the face of the devastation caused by AIDS related illnesses. Our family never judged Lee for his lifestyle choice. Instead, he was, without compromise, deeply loved by his mother, brother, sisters, nieces, nephews and friends for the goodness of his heart, mind and soul.

Two weeks before his death, my daughter Gina and I visited him again in Palm Springs. His body was emaciated. When I arrived, he said, "Fred, as my older brother-father, all I remember about you is your worry and care for mom and your brothers and sisters. During your visit, I want you to make a promise to me. I want you to act like a twelve-year old boy. I do not want to see one bit of sadness - do you hear me? Instead, I want you to entertain me, to make me laugh and tell me jokes and I will then order everyone around my bed to bring me the ingredients to make you a salad with the best dressing you ever had in your life."

In the California sunshine, by Lee's room facing a swimming pool, I stood under the lemon tree in my bathing suit and swayed my hips to the tune of the song "Lemon Tree". The words were, "Lemon tree, very pretty, and the lemon's flower is sweet, but the fruit of the lemon is impossible to eat." For thirty minutes, as I gazed at and stroked the lemons on the tree, I repeated the words and melody with variable movements of my arms, legs, body and hips that made Lee laugh heartily.

In that bed, with death at his side and Jesus in his heart, Lee ordered Ken and his friends to bring him the fresh vegetables and ingredients for a salad dressing. I kept my promise – I kept making him laugh. He kept his promise - it was the best salad I have ever had in my life.

Kenny and Gina assisted Lee to the swimming pool. Lee was uttering child-like sounds of joy and relief as they lowered him into the pool to give comfort to the sores that covered his entire body. I concealed my tears and sadness as I watched from a window inside Kenny's home. When they returned, I watched with deep emotion as my Gina gently massaged his body with a lotion without any fear of touching him. Gina had studied AIDS and knew what could be done to relieve a patient without fear of catching the disease.

To this day, when I read of the spread of AIDS throughout the world, I feel a deep compassion for the brothers and sisters in my spiritual family throughout the world, who are Prisoners of a Spreading Epidemic of pain and sorrow with no chance of escape. My brother Lee died a Prisoner of AIDS.

CHAPTER 28

Age 74 A Shocking Discovery- My Father's Addiction Revealed

Any adult may smother memories of an abused childhood. For over 60 years, I may have smothered the memory of my seven-year childhood prison. In sharing the first draft of the "Prisoner of the Truck" with my family in the summer of 1998, I made a shocking discovery that made it difficult for me to finish the book. It was my warden-father's secret addiction.

In November 1998, I had written most of the chapters of "Prisoner of the Truck". I returned to Rochester from our second home in Bradenton, Florida. My cousin Dr. Richard Sarkis, then Chief of Staff of Sarasota Memorial Hospital, accompanied me on this trip. In Rochester, my brother Joe, who was 67, had suffered complications from a quadruple by-pass operation on his heart. Six weeks later he was about to undergo a second operation to remove a tumor inside the heart. The chances for a tumor inside the heart were 1 in 500,000. It was not discovered prior to his first operation. This small mushroom shaped tumor inside the heart could break lose and cause his immediate death. My cousin Richard and I wanted to be there to offer support to Joe during this life-threatening second operation. At 67, Richard and Joe were both four years younger than I was. I have always been very close to Joe and to my cousin Richard. We never allowed a disagreement to affect our deep love and respect for one another.

The family, including Dr. Sarkis waited anxiously in the lobby. The second operation was a success. A day after his surgery, I went to visit Joe. Only immediate relatives were allowed. The door to his room was closed. I quietly entered. I was the only family member there.

Joe was being fed intravenously. The oxygen inserts were in his nose. He looked as if he had been hit by a truck. His face was puffed up but he had good color in his cheeks. In spite of his post-operative pain, the Doctors had assured the family that he would recover.

I touched his arm. He opened his eyes. We talked about his recovery. He was grateful that Dr. Sarkis had talked to his heart specialists prior to the second operation. It helped to give Joe confidence in recovering.

Joe broke the silence, "I liked the first chapters of your book." That was just like Joe. Always concerned about me, and what I was doing. As I sat beside him, holding his swollen hand, I thought how fast time had flown. Here it is 1998. I found the "key" to my freedom from the truck in 1940, over 48 years ago. Joe, who was four years younger, also worked on my father's truck. He started when he was ten years old. During the strawberry season, Joe was the brother who outsold me four to one before I changed my attitude with coaching by my warden. For years I assumed that Joe's childhood experiences on the Prison Truck were the same as mine and he was just as glad to be "free" of the truck as I was. Surprisingly, we had never talked about it before.

With his eyes, semi-closed and breathing heavily, Joe squeezed my hand and said, "Until I read the first chapters of your book, I didn't know how much you hated your work with Pa. We are different I guess. I never considered it a Prison. When I worked with him, he was not feeling well and was cutting back on his hours of work. You worked six days a week. I only had to work

Tuesdays, Thursdays and Saturdays while our brother Jim worked on Mondays, Wednesdays and Fridays. Maybe that made a big difference."

As he grimaced with a chest pain, he said, "I read where you hated, most of all, those four hours on winter Saturday nights when you were locked in the back of the truck while he was at Hedges Bar & Grill."

In the 48 years since our father's death, we had never talked about Hedges Bar & Grill. Joe, somewhat drugged by medication to relieve the pain, seemed to be falling asleep. His eyes were closed when he said, "Why didn't you go into Hedge's with him?" I said, "He wouldn't let me. I think he was trying to protect me from seeing what he thought was bad behavior in the bar."

I did not know whether Joe grimaced from the pain of his operation or from some kind of pity for me. Joe said, "After the first few Saturday nights, I just told Pa that I was going in Hedges with him. Pa said, 'No, you stay in the truck." Joe took a deep breath of oxygen and said, "I said, Pa, there was no way I would stay in the back of that cold truck. Pa said no again. I just ignored him and stubbornly walked behind him into the bar as I did every Saturday thereafter. He never struck us. What could he do? He had to accept my boldness."

My first thought was, "Just like Joe. No one could ever make Joe a prisoner. No one could force Joe to do something that he didn't want to do. He had more guts than I did. He was never the shy and timid boy that I was."

I remained quiet for several minutes. I continued to hold his hand as I thought about the tremendous mental and physical pain that he suffered with two major operations within six weeks — both with his knowledge that our Father had died of a heart attack. His doctors had already confirmed that if they had conducted a more comprehensive test, they would have discovered the small "mushroom like tumor" sooner and could have taken care of it in the first operation.

Believing that he was still awake, I innocently said, "You read the draft of my book. You know what Pa told me — that he was trying to sell fruits & vegetables to the bar customers at Hedges because they would not last until Monday. Why did it take him so long?"

Joe, still drowsy from his pain medication, replied, "Fred, after all these years, I cannot believe that you are so naïve. He wasn't selling fruits & vegetables. He was shooting dice. While he gambled, I played the pinball machines. Often, when he was losing, he would say, 'Here Bah (Joe), you shoot for me.' At the public market restaurant, I played the pinball machine while he played a coin operated gambling device." Having said that, Joe fell into a deep sleep. The nurse came in to check on him and asked me to leave.

As I walked past the nurse's station and down the hallway of the hospital, I went into an empty waiting room. I was in shock. The little boy in my 72-year old body came alive. My previous chapters credited my warden-father for the lessons I learned on the truck and the motivation he gave me to become a good salesman, to excel, to escape the Prison of the Truck. I served in the US Navy, writing to him in gratitude for the lessons learned. I had this image of a warden-father who worked long hours to support his family.

Yes, my Mother feared his temper. Yes, as a Father, he was strict with his daughters. Yes, he physically abused my Mother on two occasions that I was aware of. However, as the previous chapters revealed, I shared my Mother's compassion for his struggle to support his family in those depression years.

When I asked my Father about customers at Hedges Bar & Grill, he said, "I must get rid of the left over fruits and vegetables before they spoil. That is why I spend four hours on Saturday night's in the Hedges Bar." I believed and trusted him. He lied and betrayed me. I was a weakling for not following him into the bar as Joe did. I felt anger — and it was hurtful and the hurt was deep. In the quiet of that empty hospital waiting room, I broke down and cried — uncontrollably I cried.

I walked around the different levels of the hospital parking lot in a daze looking for the car that I had rented, forgetting what it looked like. I was staying with my son Fritz and his wife Kelley and their one-year old son Frederick William III. After fifteen minutes of walking in circles, I found my car. Within 15 minutes, I drove toward Fritz's home on Landing Road.

Instead of turning right on Landing Road toward my son Fritz and his family, I turned left around the corner of East Avenue into the parking lot of the Friendly Home, the nursing home where my mother died eight months earlier at age 95. It was about 10:00 PM. In the chill of a November wind, I stood outside of the window of the room where she died. I thought of her difficult life with my father. As a child, I recalled the many arguments between my mother and father, spoken in Arabic. His voice was angry. Her voice was gentle. I reflected on his unpredictable moods when we arrived home. He could be either cheerful or depressed. I put the pieces together. He would be cheerful when he won and he would be depressed when he lost. I thought of my mother's need for money to pay for groceries. I wondered if the physical and mental abuse she lived with related to his gambling and her questioning of it. I reflected on her defense of his behavior when I was a boy, when I witnessed my mother being dragged across the kitchen floor by her hair. Was my father's uncontrolled anger related to his gambling losses as well as questions she may have asked about the need for household money?

In late 1949, my father warned me that he would die of a heart attack within a few months. He made me promise to take care of my mother, brothers and sisters. He died instantly two and a half months later. He was sitting in a chair in the back room of Hershey's Smoke Shop on East Avenue with either a deck of cards or dice in his hands. He was gambling.

He wasn't having coffee in the morning at the Public Market restaurant. He was gambling.

He wasn't selling fruits and vegetables to bar patrons for four hours on Saturday nights. He was gambling.

When I escaped the truck at age 15 to find a job that paid three times the minimum wage, saving every penny for three years to buy my mother a home, like the home she lost in the depression, he was gambling.

In previous chapters, I wrote that his truck broke down one evening when I was 12 years old. I saw him empty his purse dollar by dollar in a crap game in the repair garage. Almost in tears, he lectured me on the evils of gambling – "If you win, you take the food out of the mouth of the loser's family, if you lose, he takes the food from the mouth of your family." He deceived me. I believed that his gambling in this garage was a one-time event. As I thought about all of this, on this cold 1998 November evening, outside of the room where my mother died, I again cried uncontrollably and asking out loud, "Pa, how could you do this to mother and me? How could you?"

I left the Friendly Home. The light was on as I drove into the backyard of Fritz's driveway about 11:00 PM. Kelley and little Freddy were asleep. Fritz, as always, gave me a hug and I went to the guestroom. I said nothing to Fritz. I was exhausted. My emotions were drained. I fell sound asleep.

The next day I visited my sister Ann and her husband Bill who lived on Hurstbourne Road in Rochester. Ann was my Mother's caretaker for the last 15 years of her life and Bill was always there for both Ann and my Mother. After dinner with Ann and Bill, I tried to tell her about my conversation with Joe. Again, I could not talk about it without breaking down.

That second evening before bed, I tried to maintain my composure as I told Fritz & Kelley of my new discovery. Again, I could not control my feelings. Kelley left her chair to hold me as I attempted to tell them how deeply I was hurt; how I had almost finished my book; how difficult it would be to finish knowing that my father was not the man I thought he was.

Kelley referred to gambling as a disease, like alcohol and drugs. Fritz & Kelley said that it would take time for me to heal; that I must get over my hurt, my anger and my devastation and find a way to finish Prisoner of the Truck.

Early the next morning, I met Richard (Dr. Sarkis) at the airport for our return trip to Florida. I told him what I had learned from Joe. Richard was not surprised. He said that many of the relatives knew that my father was a gambler. Richard, like Kelley the previous evening, tried to explain his experience with all forms of addictions. He said it would take time for me to understand the problem of gambling addiction, to forget my hurt and in my heart to forgive my deceased father. At 67, Dr. Sarkis was a survivor of a by-pass operation that developed into hepatitis, and also prostate cancer, colon cancer and surgery related to severe spinal problems. He and his wife Lynne had two children, who bravely overcame problems with drug addiction. He was a walking miracle, by his own diagnosis. So I listened carefully to every word Richard said about "gambling addiction" and resolved to do my best to make peace with my feelings.

The next day, in Florida, while checking my e-mail, I found this message from my son Fritz:

November 18, 1998
Dad,

I will pass your thank you along to Kelley. She felt badly that she did not see you in the morning before you left. I guess we didn't realize your flight left so early.

Anyhow, you are always welcome to stay at our house. You must be the easiest houseguest on earth. Cheerios, bananas, milk, coffee, Ovalteen and a bed. No problem - we have all of that stuff every day. Next time bring Grandma with you.

It was wonderful to see you. I'm sorry we didn't get to visit more; and I'm very sorry about Uncle Richard's condition. It must be very difficult for him and his loved ones, including you.

I have thought a lot about you and your father, my grandfather. I believe there is nothing wrong with the way you feel right now. Being locked in the truck was definitely a form of child abuse. The memories that haunt you are real, and you cannot blame yourself for the way you feel about those cold nights in the truck.

The abuse you endured, however, was dealt out by a man with an addiction. Gambling is a proven addiction. People put their addictions before the ones they love. To overcome addictions, usually professional intervention is required; your father did not have the opportunity to get help. I'm sure your father wanted desperately to be a good father and provider. His illness got in the way. You, being the oldest son, and Siti (Grandma in Arabic) being his wife, were exposed more than anyone else to his weaknesses.

Your Father loved you very much. Why else would he have lectured you about getting an education? He wanted you to have a better life than he had. Why did he come to you when he knew he was dying? Because he knew you could take care of the family. He trusted and loved you as much as he trusted and loved anyone or anything. I'm sure he is up in heaven, very proud of the way you took control and became a provider for the last 50 plus years.

So, in my opinion, it is ok to feel the way you feel about those years on the truck. But you must understand you father was human and, unfortunately, had an addiction that effected the way he treated the ones he loved. It is good to talk about it, and eventually, you will forgive your father. Always remember that he loved you, your brothers and sisters and Siti very much.

Please give our love to Mom and tell her we miss her.

Love,
Fritz

This was my e-mail reply to Fritz:

November 19, 1998
Fritz, my son:

It was such a joy to hug and hold Frederick William III. I am so glad that I shared my pain with you and Kelley: By sharing, I keep learning. I would have never experienced Kelley's reaction as she quickly moved over to the couch I was sitting on, to hold me. I would have never realized what an impact it had on you and the words of wisdom, echoed by Kelley and shared by you in your last e-mail. I had no idea that Kelley's father experienced similar pain with his father.

As I told you, I do not dwell on this daily. It is only when I talk or write about it with family or friends that I break down and cry. For example, Cousin Richard on the airline from Florida to Rochester this week said, "Didn't he pat you on the head or give you a hug during those long winter evening hours when he came to the truck to get fruits & vegetables?" This only stirred the memory of those nights into a new awareness — my Father was so overwhelmed with his gambling losses that he did not know I was even in the truck, or, yet alone, show me a shred of concern or affection. Not one word. Not one hug. Not one pat on the head.

Your message was uniquely sensitive. It helps free me of guilt for the anger that I have been building toward him; it reminds me that a gambling addiction can cause humans to "put their addiction before the ones they love."

Yet, I am still having difficulty understanding, regardless of his gambling addiction, how he could not see me huddled in the bitter cold in the back of that truck next to a kerosene lamp and not notice me – as if I were an ear of corn. He had made his son a prisoner of his addiction. On winter Saturday nights, at Hedges Bar & Grill, there were times, in those four hours, when he didn't open the back of the locked truck. Were those the days he won? When he did open the truck about once every hour without a word or a touch, were those the days that he lost his entire day's receipts? After losing his cash, was he paying off gambling debts with leftover fruits and vegetables? Did the addiction blind him to my existence? His only notice at the end of these cold, lonely nights while I remained in the back near the kerosene lamp was when we arrived home, and he unlocked the back of the truck . Without an exchange of words, we entered the kitchen while your grandmother heated our dinner.

I did not whine to my mother. I was aware that she had her hands full of her children as well as his behavior. That is really the answer to your question as to "Why didn't she get involved?" or "Why didn't she tell my father's brothers - Charlie and George or Uncle Deeb, the eldest Sarkis." In those days, they all got involved with the happiness of each other's children, but I did not complain to anyone because I thought my father was working hard to support his family. I did not know he was gambling. I felt compassion for his long hours and hard work.

I am touched that you want me to think about forgiving him. How do you forgive a 39-year-old intelligent Christian father, a leader in his church, who forced me to be on a truck for 100 hours a week, when I was really not needed at all? How do you forgive a father who locked me in the back of that truck for four hours on winter nights while he gambled? How do you forgive a father who never offered me a hot breakfast in the morning or a hot dinner in the evening because he did not want his son to see him gambling? How do you forgive a father when an addiction blinds him to the needs and loneliness of a son locked for four hours in the back of the winter prison? My God, I was a small boy of eight when it started and it lasted for seven years. How do you forgive all of this? How do you?

In the summer, I peeked through the window of Hedges. I saw him with the round leather container in his hand throwing dice. I saw him carry out the pinball machine from the public market restaurant. I saw him playing cards on Sundays with the men of the parish. In my childlike and sheltered simplicity, I thought all of this was his form of recreation. In the bar, I thought it was a way of making a friend before you make a sale.

With his lies and deceit, he took cruel advantage of my innocent and trusting nature. Indeed, what he did was a form of child abuse. Sometimes I think I would have rather suffered a mild beating for a half-hour every day and had the rest of the day free. Can you believe that when your 72-year-old father allows himself to think and write these words, he becomes that little boy all over again and he breaks down and cries?

Indeed, the strawberry selling lesson and his five-minute lecture on education motivated me to study to escape the Truck Prison. I doubt that I would have achieved what I did had it not been for those two brief lessons of strawberries and empty baskets. I did study in the cold, like Abe Lincoln, under the lights of that kerosene lamp to earn my freedom. Using the gifts of the Holy Spirit, I did take my suffering experience and use it to help mold my character.

I know there is, and continues to be, much good that comes from my boyhood prison. This I celebrate. I will need more time to "celebrate" my forgiveness, if that time should ever come.

I am very proud of our entire family and I want all of them to know it. For this reason, I have shared your correspondence and my reply with all of them. I know you are all loving parents. I hope my experience will make all of you even "more" loving in your relationship with family, relatives and friends.

Your loving Dad

In 1999, after the discovery of my father's addiction, I put my book aside. I was confused. Should I go back to all the chapters that I had written and rewrite them with this new discovery? I simply did not know how to end the book so I put the unfinished book aside.

After my e-mail to Fritz, Kelley and my family, I did not dwell on my discovery of my father's addiction. Instead, I focused on Senior Tennis Tournaments in the 70-75 age bracket. My goal was to go from 17 to the top ten in Florida. I had fun playing competitive tennis, but something was missing in my drive and determination. I did not achieve my tennis goal. Also, in Florida, there were many other tennis and social events with newly formed friendships for both Helen and me. Only if I spoke of my shocking discovery with friends, who were awaiting the completion of my book, did I become emotional.

In the spring of 1999, Rick Born, a former priest and now a married math teacher at the Palmetto High School, in Palmetto Florida asked me about the book he heard I was writing. Rick was a member of the El Conquistador Tennis Club where Helen and I play tennis in our Bradenton Condominium home. We spend our winters in Florida and our summers at Bristol Harbour Village on Canandaigua Lake, New York, a resort that I founded.

I told Rick the draft of the book was called Prisoner of the Truck. It was to be a motivational book — a book that might help kids to take whatever "Prison" they are confronted with and turn it into a study center. It only took five minutes to tell the Strawberry Story and the Five-Minute Talk with my father. Rick asked if I would tell these stories to his class and turn the stories into a motivational talk.

I enthusiastically accepted. I was introduced as the man who was writing a book called "Prisoner of the Truck". The talk was well received by the students. This led to an introduction to Herb

Tschappat, Principal of Palmetto High School. The student population is about a one-third African-American, one-third Hispanic and one-third white.

On April 28, 29 and 30, in morning and afternoon classes, I gave twelve highly emotional motivational talks to 1,200 high school students in classrooms and in the cafeteria. In my business career, I was a speaker on many occasions. I know when an audience is truly listening. These kids were listening. Some of them identified with the skinny, knock-kneed, pigeon-toed, bow-legged, and black kid who had a very low-self esteem. They loved the selling lessons of the strawberry story and the five-minute conversation with my father that motivated me to study to escape my prison, to become number one in my graduating class and to achieve a remarkable success in business. My whole purpose was to motivate them to be the best they can be. I believe I succeeded with many of the kids. I never spoke of my father's addiction in any of these talks. I felt this would be a distraction to my message.

I received many compliments from teachers and students. There were many requests to let them know when "The Prisoner of the Truck" would be available in bookstores. I did not explain the delay caused by the discovery of my father's addiction.

A month after my talks at Palmetto, I returned to Rochester. I received a call from Jim Roman, a fellow member of the Tennis Club of Rochester. He heard of my talks in Palmetto. He asked if I would speak to about 40 men (active in mission work outside of Rochester) at the Church of the Transfiguration in Pittsford, NY, a suburb of Rochester.

On June 15, 1999, I was asked to sit on a tall stool in the chapel to speak to the group. I gave a similar talk that I gave the students – poor self image, strawberry story, five-minute talk with my warden that changed my attitude and study habits, achievements in school, naval service and business.

During the question and answer period, someone asked if I had finished the book. I told the story of visiting my brother Joe and my discovery of my father's addiction. I said I was having difficulty trying to finish the book because I kept thinking about that little boy locked in the back of the truck. I said that the book did not portray my father as a man with a gambling addiction and the recent discovery of his addiction confused my writing.

Again, as was the pattern when I spoke of the pain of my discovery, I lost control of my feelings. I could not find my voice. Tears flooded my eyes and were running down my cheek. I held up my hand to prevent anyone from coming forward to comfort me. I was embarrassed. In that chapel, for the first time since my discovery, I found myself saying in a hurt and angry voice, "He stole my childhood. He stole my childhood". My talk ended on that note.

I was surrounded by many of the men in attendance. They praised my talk. Some of them spoke of various addictions in their own families. They said that in time I would heal and forgive my father and would pray for that intent.

At this meeting, keenly aware of my emotional struggle with this new discovery of my father's addiction, the Deacon Mike Piehler tactfully asked if I knew Dennis Boike, a psychologist and experienced counselor in Canandaigua. He suggested that I speak to Dr. Boike about my book and my new discovery of my deceased father's gambling addiction.

At 73 years of age, I made my first ever appointment with a Counselor. On July 27, 1999, I met Dr. Boike in his office. He allowed me to tell my story from boyhood to the discovery of my father's addiction. Again, when I spoke of the loneliness in the back of that truck during those bitter-cold winter Saturdays, I lost control of my feelings. I had difficulty finding my voice. I could not speak without crying.

Dr. Boike said treatment programs for drug, alcohol and gambling addictions did not exist in the years I was a prisoner of the truck. He said that my father had an illness and there was no treatment for that illness in those days. He said that of all the addictions, gambling is the most difficult illness to cure. Yes, the addiction is so serious that when my father opened the back of the truck and did not see me, it is part of the illness.

I asked Dr. Boike why a man with a gambling addiction would not give his kid five cents to take a fifteen-minute trolley home. Would an alcoholic or a drug addict lock their kid up in a truck or car for four hours while they gave in their addiction? He said that in my case, I was a "cover" for my mother. Our time ran out and we scheduled another appointment.

I never thought of the "Prisoner of the Truck" as being a cover for his father. This made matters worse. Addiction or not, how could any human being be that cruel? I was anxious to talk about this in our second appointment.

On August 19, 1999, I met again with Dr. Boike. Dr. Boike said something similar to what Fritz had written to me a few months earlier.

"The abuse you endured was dealt out by a man with an addiction. Gambling is a proven addiction. People put their addictions before the ones they love. To overcome addictions, usually professional intervention is required; your father did not have the opportunity to get help. I'm sure your father wanted desperately to be a good father and provider. His illness got in the way."

Regarding my book, Dr. Boike suggested that I do not change what I had written prior to my discovery of my father's addiction. He recommended that I deal with the discovery of my father's addiction in a final chapter. The following events made it possible for me to write a final chapter.

On August 20, 1999, the night after I spoke to Dr. Boike, I was standing on the balcony of my condominium at Bristol Harbour Village on Canandaigua Lake looking at the lake and clear sky. I recalled a night in 1949, 50 years past, when I searched the same sky for a shooting star for an answer to a prayer. That was the night that my father told me that he had a few months to live.

The remembrance of that night, so many years ago, again triggered my emotions. With tears in my eyes, I looked up at the sky and said aloud, "OK, Pa, show me a shooting star within the next five minutes and I will accept that as your apology for the hurt and anger that I know feel. You stole my childhood. They say you were suffering from an illness, an addiction for gambling. I want to see your shooting star. If I do, I will see your words trailing behind it, 'I'm sorry Fred for the pain and hurt I caused you and your mother.' "

There was no shooting star. I went to bed praying that I would find a way to forgive, to finish my book.

The very next day, on August 21, 1999, on my brother Joe's birthday, I went to the mailbox. I picked up a large brown envelope. It was from Palmetto High School, in Palmetto, Florida. In the envelope there were 122 letters from students and six letters from teachers, with an apology for a delay in mailing. I read each letter as if it were a precious gem. As I finished reading these letters on the balcony of our condominium, overlooking beautiful Canandaigua Lake, *I was healed.* The contents of the envelope spoke for my father. The message from my father was clear:

"Fred, you did not see a shooting star last night. Instead, you have the large brown envelope from Palmetto High School. The letters in that envelope are my responses to you. The lessons you learned on the Truck made you a good father, a successful business man, a builder of a ski mountain and resort village and a 27-year survivor of new prisons of your own making. You received high honors for your community service. I died before seeing your wife, Helen and my grandchildren, Gina, Greg, Wade, Fritz & Josh. Your family is blessed with happy marriages and you have eleven grandchildren that are twelve and under. All of your children are successful entrepreneurs and you are comfortably retired.

You would not be able to share the story of the Prisoner of the Truck, if there were no truck or no warden. There would be no children to motivate, no motivational book to write or talks to give. My addiction caused me as much suffering as it did you and your mother. Forgive me, my son, as your mother has. Go on with your good work and treat all letters you receive from children, both now and in the future, as hugs from me."

I, Frederick W. Sarkis, the former Prisoner of the Truck, "celebrate" my forgiveness, my healing, my closure and my love of my father.

Epilogue

Hugs — Made Possible by my Father

I spoke to about 1,200 students at Palmetto High School in Palmetto, Florida on April 28, 29 and 30 of 1999, giving as many as four talks a day. In this autobiography, I referred to the brown envelope with 119 letters from Palmetto High school that ironically arrived on August 21, 1999, the day after I asked my deceased father to show me a shooting star as a sign of saying "I'm sorry if my addiction hurt you."

This Epilogue contains excerpts from many articles, and letters I have received since my epiphany and redirection, Here are a few of the letters received from Palmetto High School:

Rick Born, PHS Math Teacher – (Rick is my tennis-playing friend. He was the first to ask me to speak to his class. That talk led to more talks to the entire school and many talks thereafter.) *"Fred, you did a fantastic job. Not many people would agree to deliver the talk so many times."*

Lisa P. Jones, PHS English Teacher – *"I walked away feeling warm and encouraged. Many of my students (all freshman) have written letters to express their appreciation. I was happy to see through their responses that you have made an impression. I hope you will be encouraged to continue telling your story to others, especially after reading their comments. They really were listening and obviously learned something. I think these letters will let you see that you do make a difference."*

Jan Ayola, PMS Teacher – *"After hearing your talk, I shall never again look at a strawberry in the same way. Students talked about you and your story, so know that what you shared was heard. You tackled a difficult task – talking to a group of teenagers – quite beautifully. We discussed your message in my class. Thank you for your words of encouragement and inspiration."*

Student – *"I really appreciate your coming to Palmetto to tell us about your life. I really respect you because your life sounded exciting. And my life is exciting but football gets boring."*

Student – *"I thoroughly enjoyed the motivational speech that you gave our class and I know what it's like to have failures and triumphs to learn from. I've heard that one of life's greatest teachers is experience and you have certainly been taught. I have learned that following your heart with an open mind, might be a rougher road, but it's the only one I care to travel."*

Student – *"I'm sorry you had to live that kind of life. I live somewhat similarly. I got abused a lot by my step-dad who would beat me up a lot. It was very scary. I hated living like that. I really enjoyed your coming to our school. I think it touched some of us. It did me."*

Student – *"I will carry that lesson with me for the rest of my life. I learned that you have to work hard in your life to achieve your goals. Since I will be going to college your speech will be well-used."*

Student – *"My favorite part about your speech was when you told us about how you were trying to sell strawberries, but your dad said you had the wrong attitude about it."*

Student – *"In listening to your speech today, I realize that in order for me to accomplish everything that I want in my life, I must think positive."*

Student – *"I think it really touched some of our hearts. I like the stories you told us about strawberries. It showed me how not to settle for less. It also showed me if you make a mistake in life, there always is a second chance."*

Student – *"Like you, I have grown up roughly and now I am going on to make something of my life. Thank you for your motivation and your time."*

Student – *"Your message gave a clear picture of what education can do for you. The story of your childhood and determination to be the best you could be was an inspiration to me. I only hope that my education will bring me the happiness that yours has brought to you."*

Student – *"Your visit has encouraged me to continue to work hard, have patience, and be determined."*

Student – *"Your motivational message spoke to me in a special way. I believe we all have "trucks" to get off of in life. Your positive outlook on life has made me think more positive and less on the negative."*

Student – *"Everything you said hit home. I lost my father and mother at a young age. To hear you talk about your experiences made me feel better about my situation. If there was anyone in the world to come and tell us about their life, I'm glad it was you."*

Student – *"The speech meant something to me because since I was 6 or 7, I've always had to go to work with my dad. It was really hard doing that while my friends played. But since I'm not the only one, I feel better."*

In early September of 2000, I was standing in a one and a half hour long funeral line paying my respects to a friend at the Kennedy Funeral Home in Canandaigua. Chief Police Patrick McCarthy was standing behind me with his wife Patty, whom I had never met. We chatted and when Chief McCarthy learned of my Florida talks and my work on Prisoner of the Truck, he invited me to talk to the special kids in their Phoenix Program. I spoke to this group. Chief McCarthy has allowed me to include his letter in my book.

CANANDAIGUA POLICE DEPARTMENT
21 ONTARIO STREET
CANANDAIGUA, NEW YORK 14424
(716)396-5035 Phone
(716)396-5034 Fax
Dial 911 for All Emergencies

Patrick W. McCarthy
Chief of Police

September 14, 2000

Mr. Fred Sarkis
Cliffside Drive
Bristol Harbour
Canandaigua, NY 14424

Fred
Dear Mr. Sarkis:

This letter is forwarded to you to express our sincere gratitude for the generous donation of your time and talent on the occasion of your motivational and, I might add, inspirational presentation to the 70 participants of the Phoenix Program's summer session here in Canandaigua. Your audience of young listeners can best be described as "completely absorbed" as you expertly wove a tapestry of a life and how that life evolved from a burdensome beginning into a model success story. Your emphasis upon the virtues of enthusiasm, positive thinking and a strong and resilient faith will long be carried in the memory of your listeners, I am sure. In a word, your presentation was the perfect concluding message to our summer program youngsters as they prepare to resume their studies this fall.

Again, Fred, thank you and please call upon us at any time to aid you in spreading a most important and motivating message.

Sincerely,

Patrick W. McCarthy
Chief of Police

PWMcC:cb

This talk to the kids in the Canandaigua Phoenix Program led to several articles that follow including "Our Towns" front-page news article with color photographs as shown in this book.

September 23, 2000
Courtesy of Rochester Democrat & Chronicle
By Staff Writer – Michele Locastro Rivoli

"Motivational Millionaire"

byline: Real estate developer, Fred Sarkis now helps children build their lives with inspiring talks.

Fred Sarkis knows what it's like to struggle – and he knows what it's like to survive.

The self-made millionaire has endured everything from 100-hour work weeks as a child during the Great Depression to cancer and bankruptcy.

And at 74, the coffee vendor-turned developer of Bristol Mountain Ski Resort and Bristol Harbour Golf Course, marina and condominiums, has a new goal.

Sarkis wants to reach 100,000 children with a message.

"I want them to know they have it within themselves to overcome whatever adversities or obstacles life may send their way," he said. "And I want them to know that, regardless of the circumstances they find themselves in, they have the power to achieve any goal they set."

He's getting his message out in a variety of ways. Sarkis is now offering his services free as a motivational speaker. He talks to children dressed as a clown and to teens in regular street clothes. Regardless of the presentation, the message is the same.

He talks about a positive self-image, taking responsibility for their actions, setting realistic goals and following through one step at a time.

James Brown, 18, of Palmyra, heard Sarkis speak at Palmyra-Macedon High School earlier this month, and was impressed with what he heard.

"He's a captivating speaker," said Brown. "I don't think I took my eyes off him once when he was speaking, and I was in awe of what he said for four or five hours after he was done."

Brown said he walked away from the talk with a lot to think about.

"He really emphasized responsibility and that the world doesn't want to give you anything," Brown said, "I have to take what I have in myself, show the world who I am, and that I can go out and do anything."

Sarkis also speaks to adults about the importance of becoming mentors.

And he has just completed an autobiography about his childhood, titled Prisoner of the Truck. He hopes to have a publisher lined up soon.

"I do not know how successful the book will be," he said. But I do know that, if successful, any royalties will be set up in a trust fund for the benefit of children."

[The reporter wrote of hard times, success and failure as outlined in the book.]

And he recently made a presentation to 70 children ages 7 to 16 in Canandaigua's Phoenix Program.

The program provides children ages 7 to 16 with activities between the end of the school day and when their parents get home, and during summer vacations, said Canandaigua Police Chief Patrick McCarthy.

"Fred's presentation had the kids talking," McCarthy said, "And that's always a good thing. It obviously made an impact on them."

Despite the adversities, Sarkis will tell you he's thankful and grateful for the life he's led.

But he'll also tell you that there still a lot to be done. In his mission to reach 100,000 children, he says he's spoken to about 2,000 so far.

"What's really important to me is helping kids," he said. "And if I can make a difference in even one of their lives, it's worth it. Money can't buy that kind of success or satisfaction."

September 27, 2000
The Naples Record/The Honeoye Herald
By Mike Fowler.

"His Mission is to Motivate"

Fred Sarkis is a man on a mission. At the age of 74, the man built Bristol Mountain and Bristol Harbour has found new meaning in his life and he wants to spread the word to young and old alike.

Actually, Sarkis has two messages – one for senior citizens and one for children – and he takes different approaches to get his message across.

In the past year he's spoken to more than 1,000 senior citizens in retirement communities in Florida and New Jersey, and 1,000 kids in various schools.

"I'm on a mission to get seniors to become mentors to kids because they have so much to give, so much experience," Sarkis said recently during an interview at his Bristol Harbour home. "I give the seniors a message about getting involved. I'm 74 and I'm not sitting around bored."

There's a child in everyone of us," he continued. "Never let the child in you die. Too many seniors get too wrapped up with their aches and pains, and you can forget all that if you get involved."

Sarkis draws heavily on an unhappy childhood for inspiration and motivation. His autobiography titled Prisoner of the Truck details his early years working on his father's fruit truck.

"I hated it. I hated life," Sarkis said. "And to make matters worse (from 8 to 14) I spent winter Saturdays locked inside that truck for four hours while my father was in the bar playing dice."

Sarkis got off the truck at age 15. He graduated from St. Joseph's Commercial School and got a job as a speed typist. It wasn't long before he saved enough money to buy his mother a house. By the time he was 34 Sarkis had started up and then sold his business Kwik Kafe for $2 million.

But life wasn't all smooth sailing after making his first million.

"I went from poor to rich to poor to almost bankrupt," he said. "Failure is part of the game of life. You have to be willing to accept failure. I spent 25 years in my own self-imposed prison trying to make two ideas work – one a mountain, one a village. What a struggle."

Accepting failure and then turning it around are both part of Sarkis' message. "You do that with a spiritual partner," he said. "I never could have done it alone. My faith sustained me."

A conversation with Sarkis is filled with words such as fortitude, courage, and faith.

"My favorite word is 'enthusiasm'", he said. "That's what I try to instill in the kids. I tell them to have the courage of their convictions and the fortitude to put self-discipline to work. Take your life into your own hands and make something of yourself."

Sarkis says his goal is 100,000 people. "If I have an impact on one in 10 kids, then I'm a happy guy," he said, "and based on all the letters I've gotten, I think I'm having a significant impact."

And he's having fun.

"I'm really having a wonderful time," he said. "I've never had as much fun as I'm having right now. This is the kind of work that makes an old man feel good."

The Impact of these September News Articles

I was flooded with phone calls. Before I returned to Florida, I only had two weeks in October that were free for talks. In these two weeks, I gave 18 talks to about 1600 students, church and Boy Scout groups. After these talks, I received close to 400 letters from teachers and kids. A few abridged letters are as follows:

Dear Mr. Sarkis,

The bible states 'Man judges a person by his outer appearance; I judge a man by his heart.' You certainly have a big heart. May God bless you always.

P.S. Your talk was great!!! Adam G. Schwartz, Teacher, Canandaigua Elementary School."

Student – *"Some of the things I learned today is that if you are selling cookies never say, "You don't want to buy cookies, do you?" That is because they probably won't buy them because of your attitude. One more thing I learned is that you should be all you can be and don't be who you are not. I think that you should go to more classes because you are really great and you can teach kids many things."*

Student – *"I learned a lot about what you had said. It helped me with my problems with my mom and dad. My dad does not live with me anymore, he lives with Grandma."*

Student – *"Your stories really touched me. I pray that you reach your goal of speaking to 100,000 kids. Those kids need to hear your words."*

St. Lawrence School

...A Great Place to Grow

1000 North Greece Road Rochester, NY 14626 Phone: 225-3870 Fax: 225-1336

Oct. 24, 2000

To the Principals of other Catholic Schools,

There are many stories about people that are learned best by reading them from a book. There are a few special stories, however, that must be experienced first hand from the heart and wisdom of the one, whose journey can touch so many other lives. Such a story, such a life, is present in Mr. Fred Sarkis.

We first learned about Mr. Sarkis from an article in the local Rochester paper. It mentioned his willingness to bring a message of hope, self-esteem, and determination to school aged children. Though he has spoken to business groups like those at Xerox, his real ministry is to reach children. We immediately called him to schedule two free assemblies.

Mr. Sarkis spoke and performed for our K-5th grade students and also our 6-8th grade students. Each assembly lasted about 45 minutes. During that time, all eyes, all ears, all hearts were on Mr. Sarkis. While relating true stories of his youth, his rise to wealth, his failures and his successes, Mr. Sarkis insured that each one knew this was not about how to make millions. It was a story of how to find the strength through the presence of Christ to fully become what God has called you to.

I strongly recommend Mr. Fred Sarkis as an inspirational speaker. Feel free to contact me at Jholl1647@aol.com, or area code 716 at the phone or fax number above. His ministry is to share, in age appropriate language, clowning, and stories, his journey with Christ from rags to riches. The kind of riches you cannot put in the bank, they are riches that you put in your heart.

Sincerely,

Joseph P. Holleran

Joseph P. Holleran
Principal

THE CATHOLIC SCHOOLS OF MONROE COUNTY

Student – *"Your talk meant a lot to me. I liked your life story. When you were down in life, you turned failure into success. I learned that if life is filled with obstacles, overcome them and never give up. Right now I am experiencing stress and your talk made me realize that I needed an attitude change. My life changed after your talk when I walked out of room 3B."*

Student – *"I liked how you overcame your obstacles. For four years my mom and dad have been trying to get a divorce. One time we had all of our stuff packed ready to move to Virginia. The next day my dad didn't sign some papers and we had to unpack everything. Another thing that happened was my family had to go bankrupt and we almost lost our house. Right now, I'm not seeing my dad and I don't really want to because he's hurt me, not physically, but he's hurt my feelings in so many ways. Your talk encouraged me to overcome my problems and when I get older I want to go to college and become a meteorologist."*

Student – *Your talk meant a lot to me because I can relate to it. Right now my life sucks! We just built a new house. Our insurance company screwed us over (sorry about the language). And we don't have the weekly payments so my parents feel bad not being able to give us everything we want. I feel so bad that I want to kill myself to help them so they don't have to spend money on me. But now, thanks to you, I don't feel that way anymore. You helped me to realize that I have a chance in making my life better. Thank you sooooo much!!!!!!"*

Student – *Your talk really moved me. What you said meant so much to me. See, my family is struggling financially, and it's hard living, but after your talk, things looked better. It's because I now look at the situation differently. Before I thought, 'We're gonna fail, we'll lose our house and go hungry', but now I see the light in the end of the tunnel. Things will get better, just like you said. I learned from your talk that life goes on.*

Your clown act was cute. From what you said and reading in between the lines, it had a serious message. The 1st chair was the present. The 2nd chair the future. The rope in between the two chairs was needed to get to the future. The net was like a safety net; sometimes we fall into it, most times we don't. The umbrella was like security, a false security or worldly security. We need to keep our eyes on the eternal goal, and use God as our safety and security. Anyway, thank you very much for talking to us."

Prisoner of the Truck Foundation, Inc.

Any royalty payments from the sale of this book will go to the Foundation.

The mission of this not-for-profit Foundation is to provide resources to various community organizations, including gathering places for youths and young adults, prisons and other community organizations. The company will use the resources of speeches, books and videos to demonstrate how good character traits, ethical behavior and business practices can be used to inspire, motivate and empower individuals to turn any adversity or failure into a successful and positive life event.

yespa.org and **prisonerofthetruck.com** will take the reader to the same Prisoner of the Truck Foundation website.

This noncommercial professional website offers the following to parents, grandparents, teachers, students and others who seek to better their lives:

* A free digest of this book called "Yes Pa", easy reading for ages 10 to 100.
* A free built-in parent-teacher-student study guide.
* Free links to character education websites.
* A guest book with entries from children and adults.
* Availability of Fred's talk in video or CD/DVD format as part of a total character education program.

The Foundation will accept contributions for it's mission. The Foundation will also seek character education grants from State and Federal Government Agencies in pursuit of it's Mission.

A special thanks to Sharon Smith who is currently assisting the Foundation as a volunteer Executive Director.

Please visit:

www.yespa.org

About the Author

For 4 years, from age 8 to 12, Fred worked up to 100 hours a week on his father's vegetable truck. At age 12, two 5-minute conversations with his Pa taught Fred that a positive Attitude, Courage, Enthusiasm and Determination would affect his life's direction.

He finished business school at age 16, tops in his class. At age 17, he bought his mother and eight brothers and sisters a six-bedroom home. He became an entrepreneur at age 24 and a multi-millionaire at 34. He built a ski resort, golf course and condominium community.

And then he faced failure. Fred applied the same lessons he learned at age 12 to turn adversity and failure into success. His genuine and heartfelt stories inspire others.

Visit YesPa.org for information about the Character Education Mission of the Prisoner of the Truck Foundation.

LaVergne, TN USA
07 January 2011
211411LV00001B/120/A

9 781410 724922